SPOTLIGHT on MUSIC ™

30079500

Authors

Judy Bond

René Boyer

Margaret Campbelle-Holman

Emily Crocker

Marilyn C. Davidson

Robert de Frece

Virginia Ebinger

Mary Goetze

Betsy M. Henderson

John Jacobson

Michael Jothen

Chris Judah-Lauder

Carol King

Vincent P. Lawrence

Ellen McCullough-Brabson

Janet McMillion

Nancy L. T. Miller

Ivy Rawlins

Susan Snyder

Gilberto D. Soto

Kodály Contributing Consultant

Sr. Lorna Zemke

HAL•LEONARD®

Mc Graw Hill Macmillan McGraw-Hill

i

ACKNOWLEDGMENTS

Creative Direction and Delivery: The Quarasan Group, Inc.

From the Top-On National Radio! selections are adapted from the nationally distributed public radio program, *From the Top.* CEOs/Executive Producers: Jennifer Hurley-Wales and Gerald Slavet. Authors: Ann Gregg and Joanne Robinson. © 2001, 2002, 2003 From the Top, Inc.

The Broadway Junior® logo and MTI® logo are trademarks of Music Theatre International. All rights reserved.

Grateful acknowledgment is given to the following authors, composers, and publishers. Every effort has been made to trace the ownership of all copyrighted material and to secure the necessary permissions to reprint these selections. In the case of some selections for which acknowledgment is not given, extensive research has failed to locate the copyright holders.

Songs and Speech Pieces

A Zing-a Za, Brazilian folk song. Arranged by Mary Goetze. Copyright © 1986 Boosey & Hawkes. Reprinted by Permission.

Aeyaya balano sakkad (Come, Children), Words by Smt. Chandra Bhat. English Words by John Higgins. Music by M.B. Srinivasan. Copyright © 2000 by MUSIC EXPRESS LLC. International Copyright Secured. All Rights Reserved.

Allá en el Rancho Grande (My Ranch), English Lyric by Bartley Costello. Spanish Lyric and Music by Silvano R. Ramos. Copyright © 1935 by Edward B. Marks Music Company. Copyright Renewed. International Copyright Secured. All Rights Reserved. Used by Permission.

Aquaqua, from Aquaqua del a Omar. Israeli Children's Singing Game. Collected by Rita Klinger. Copyright © 1980 by RITA KLINGER. International Copyright Secured. All Rights Reserved.

¡Ay Jalisco, no te rajes!, Words by Ernesto M. Cortazar Hernandez. Music by Manuel Esperon Gonzalez. Copyright © 1941 by Promotora Hispano Americana De Musica, S.A. Copyright Renewed. All Rights Administered by Peer International Corporation. International Copyright Secured. All Rights Reserved.

Backwater Blues, by Bessie Smith. © 1927, 1974 (Renewed) FRANK MUSIC CORP. All Rights Reserved.

Ballad of the Underground Railroad, The, Words and Music by René Boyer-Alexander. Copyright © 2001 by HAL LEONARD CORPORATION. International Copyright Secured. All Rights Reserved.

Beauty and the Beast, from Walt Disney's BEAUTY AND THE BEAST. Lyrics by Howard Ashman. Music by Alan Menken. © 1991 Walt Disney Music Company and Wonderland Music Company, Inc. All Rights Reserved. Used by Permission.

Big Big World, by Bill Harley. © 1996 Round River Music/Bill Harley. All Rights Reserved. Used by Permission. www.billharley.com

Big Yellow Taxi, Words and Music by Joni Mitchell. © 1970 (Renewed) SIQUOMB PUBLISHING CORP. All Rights Reserved. Used by Permission.

Change Is Good, Words and Music by Ed Kaecher, Jim Tullio and Rick Danko. Copyright © 2000 TOOLS MUSIC. All Rights Controlled and Administered by SONGS OF UNIVERSAL, INC. International Copyright Secured. All Rights Reserved.

Change the World, Words and Music by Wayne Kirkpatrick, Gordon Kennedy and Tommy Sims. Copyright © 1996 by Careers-BMG Music Publishing, Magic Beans Music, BMG Songs, Universal - PolyGram International Publishing, Inc. and Universal Music Corp. International Copyright Secured. All Rights Reserved.

Cidade Maravilhosa (Wonderful City), Words and Music by Andre Filho. Arranged by Elizabeth Souza. Copyright © 2002 by MUSIC EXPRESS LLC. International Copyright Secured. All Rights Reserved.

Circle of Friends, Words and Music by Roger Emerson. Copyright © 1999 by HAL LEONARD CORPORATION. International Copyright Secured. All Rights Reserved.

City Blues, American Folk Song. Arranged by Jerry Silverman. Copyright © 1983 by Saw Mill Music Co. International Copyright Secured. All Rights Reserved.

Cuando salí de Cuba (I Went Away from Cuba), Words and Music by Luis Aguile. © 1967 (Renewed 1995) EMI APRIL MUSIC INC. All Rights Reserved. International Copyright Secured. Used by Permission.

Dance for Piccolo, Oboe, Bassoon and Side Drum, by Richard Gill. Copyright © by RICHARD GILL. International Copyright Secured. All Rights Reserved.

Dance for the Nations (Round and Round We Go), Words and Music by John Krumm. Copyright © by JOHN KRUMM. International Copyright Secured. All Rights Reserved.

Deta, Deta (The Moon), Japanese Children's Song collected and transcribed by Kathy Sorensen. © 1991 Kathy B. Sorensen. All Rights Reserved.

Ēinīni, (Little Birds Sleep), Gaelic Folk Song. Arranged by Cyndee Giebler. Copyright © by PLYMOUTH MUSIC CO., INC. International Copyright Secured. All Rights Reserved.

El jarabe (Mexican Hat Dance), Mexican Folk Music. Adapted by José-Luis Orozco. Copyright © 1997 by José-Luis Orozco/Arcoiris Records, P.O. Box 461900, Los Angeles, CA 90046 International Copyright Secured. All Rights Reserved.

Estrella brillante (Shining Star), Mexican Carol. Arranged by Nancy Grundahl. Copyright © 2003 by HAL LEONARD CORPORATION. International Copyright Secured. All Rights Reserved.

Every Day I Have the Blues, Words and Music by Peter Chapman. Copyright © 1952 (Renewed) by Arc Music Corporation (BMI), Fort Knox Music Inc. and Trio Music Company, Inc. International Copyright Secured. All Rights Reserved. Used by Permission.

Everybody Rejoice, from THE WIZ. Words and Music by Luther Vandross. Copyright © 1975 (Renewed 2003). © 1975 TWENTIETH CENTURY MUSIC CORPORATION. © Renewed 2003 EMI ROBBINS CATALOG INC. All Rights Controlled by EMI ROBBINS CATALOG INC. (Publishing) and WARNER BROS. PUBLICATIONS U.S. INC. (Print). All Rights Reserved. Used by Permission.

Feel Good, Words and Music by L. Craig Tyson and Leonard Scott. Arranged by Barbara Baker and David J. Elliott. Copyright © by Boosey & Hawkes Co., Inc.. International Copyright Secured. All Rights Reserved.

continued on page 457

A

The McGraw·Hill Companies

 Macmillan/McGraw-Hill

Published by Macmillan/McGraw-Hill, of McGraw-Hill Education, a division of The McGraw-Hill Companies, Inc., Two Penn Plaza, New York, New York 10121.

ISBN: 978-0-02-296702-4
MHID: 0-02-296702-8
3 4 5 6 7 8 9 DOR 16 15 14 13 12 11 10

Printed in the United States of America

CONTRIBUTORS

Consultants

Brian Burnett,
Movement

Stephen Gabriel,
Technology

Magali Iglesias,
English Language Learners

Roberta Newcomer,
Special Learners/Assessment

Frank Rodríguez,
English Language Learners

Jacque Schrader,
Movement

Kathy B. Sorensen,
International Phonetic
Alphabet

Patti Windes-Bridges,
Listening Maps

Linda Worsley,
Listening/Singable
English Translations

Sr. Lorna Zemke,
Kodály Contributing
Consultant

Recordings

Executive Producer: John Higgins

Senior Music Editor/Producer: Emily Crocker

Senior Recording Producer: Mark Brymer

Recording Producers: Steve Millikan, Andy Waterman

Associate Recording Producers: Alan Billingsley, Darrell Bledsoe, Stacy Carson, Rosanna Eckert, John Egan, Chad Evans, Darlene Koldenhoven, Chris Koszuta, Don Markese, Matthew McGregor, Steve Potts, Edwin Schupman, Michael Spresser, Frank Stegall, David Vartanian, Mike Wilson, Ted Wilson

Project/Mastering Engineer: Mark Aspinall; Post-Production Engineer: Don Sternecker

Selected recordings by Buryl Red, Executive Producer; Michael Rafter, Senior Recording Producer; Bryan Louiselle and Buddy Skipper, Recording Producers; Lori Casteel and Mick Rossi, Associate Recording Producers; Jonathan Duckett, Supervising Engineer

Contributing Writers

Allison Abucewicz, Sharon Berndt, Rhona Brink, Ann Burbridge, Debbie Helm Daniel, Katherine Domingo, Kari Gilbertson, Janet Graham, Hilree Hamilton, Linda Harley, Judy Henneberger, Carol Huffman, Bernie Hynson, Jr., Sheila A. Kerley, Elizabeth Kipperman, Ellen Mendelsohn, Cristi Cary Miller, Leigh Ann Mock, Patricia O'Rourke, Barbara Resch, Soojin Kim Ritterling, Isabel Romero, Carl B. Schmidt, Debra Shearer, Ellen Mundy Shuler, Rebecca Treadway, Carol Wheeler, Sheila Woodward

Multicultural Consultants

William Anderson, Chet-Yeng Loong, Edwin Schupman, Kathy B. Sorensen, Gilberto D. Soto, Judith Cook Tucker, Dennis Waring

In the Spotlight Consultant

Willa Dunleavy

Multicultural Advisors

Brad Ahawanrathe Bonaparte (Mohawk), Emmanuel Akakpo (Ewe), Earlene Albano (Hawaiian), Luana Au (Maori), Bryan Ayakawa (Japanese), Ruby Beeston (Mandarin), Latif Bolat (Turkish), Estella Christensen (Spanish), Oussama Davis (Arabic), Mia Delguardo (Minahasa), Nolutho Ndengane Diko (Xhosa), Angela Fields (Hopi, Chemehuevi), Gary Fields (Lakota, Cree), Gilad Harel (Hebrew), Josephine Hetarihon (Bahasa Indonesian, Minahasa, and Maluko dialect), Judy Hirt-Manheimer (Hebrew), Rose Jakub (Navajo), Elizabeth Jarema (Fijian), Rita Jensen (Swedish), Malou Jewett (Visayan), Alejandro Jimenez (Hispanic), Chris Jones (Hungarian), Wendy Jyang Shamo (Mandarin), Amir Kalay (Hebrew), Michael Katsan (Greek), Silvi Madarajan (Tamil), Georgia Magpie (Comanche), Nona Mardi (Malay), Aida Mattingly (Tagalog), Mike Kanathohare McDonald (Mohawk), Vasana de Mel (Sinhala), Marion Miller (Czech), Etsuko Miskin (Japanese), Mogens Mogenson (Danish), Kenny Tahawisoren Perkins (Mohawk), Pradeep Nayyar (Punjabi, Hindi), Renu Nayyar (Punjabi), Mfanego Ngwenya (Zulu), Wil Numkena (Hopi), Samuel Owuru (Akan), Nina Padukone (Konkani), Hung Yong Park (Korean), James Parker (Finnish), Jose Pereira (Konkani), Berrit Price (Norwegian), John Rainer (Taos Pueblo, Creek), Lillian Rainer (Taos Pueblo, Creek, Apache), Arnold Richardson (Haliwa-Saponi), Ken Runnacles (German), Trudy Shenk (German), Ron Singer (Navajo), Ernest Siva (Cahuilla, Serrano [Maringa']), Bonnie Slade (Swedish), Cristina Sorrentino (Portuguese), Diane Thram (Xhosa), Elena Todorov (Bulgarian), Zlatina Todorov (Russian), Tom Toronto (Lao, Thai), Rebecca Wilberg (French, Italian), Sheila Woodward (Zulu), Keith Yackeyonny (Comanche)

iii

Contents

Spotlight on Music Reading.........241

In the Spotlight

There is a light that shines in America,
from the Statue of Liberty to the Golden Gate Bridge,
from Denali to Old San Juan.
It is the light of hope!
It is the light of freedom!
It is the light of all that have come before us
and all that will follow in our footsteps.
We step into that light with a song in our hearts.

Step into the Spotlight

Spotlight CD
Track 1

Words and Music by John Jacobson,
Emily Crocker, and John Higgins

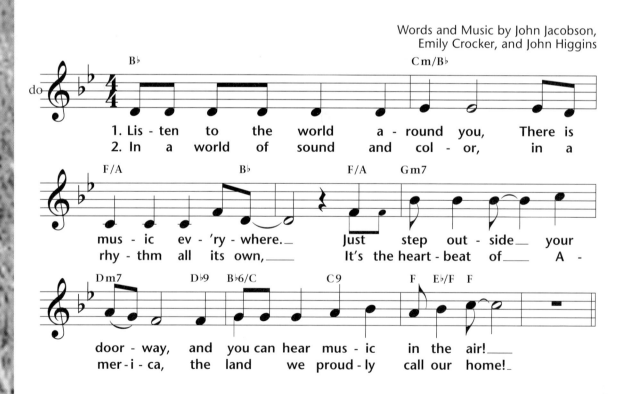

1. Lis - ten to the world a - round you, There is
2. In a world of sound and col - or, in a

mus - ic ev - 'ry - where.___ Just step out - side___ your
rhy - thm all its own,___ It's the heart - beat of___ A -

door - way, and you can hear mus - ic in the air!___
mer - i - ca, the land we proud - ly call our home!_

A

In the Spotlight

We sing the songs of America.
In New York City, a chorus dancer steps
into the spotlight to become a star.
In Nashville, country artists stride onto the stage
and bask in the historic glow of the Grand Ole Opry!
In Hollywood, they are singing the songs of the movies.
In Detroit, New Orleans, Memphis, Chicago,
and all across the nation,
the lights are shining on
Motown, blues, jazz, hip-hop, rap, reggae, and more.
And beneath a star-filled prairie sky,
the light of the moon frames the cowboy.
With moon as his spotlight,
we hear the songs of the open range.

In the Spotlight

The songs of America are songs about everything and anything.
When something makes us happy, we sing a song about it.
When something makes us sad, we sing then, too.
When Americans have something to say, often the very
best way to say it is with a song.

Big Yellow Taxi

**Spotlight CD
Track 7**

Words and Music by Joni Mitchell

1. They paved pa - ra - dise   and put up a park - ing lot,___
2. They took all the trees   and put 'em in a tree mu - seum

with a pink ho - tel,___   a
and they charged the peo - ple   a

bou - tique   and a swing - in' hot   spot.___ }
dol - lar and a half just to   see   'em.___

Don't it al - ways seem___ to go   that you

don't know what you got_____ till it's gone. They

paved pa-ra-dise and put up a park - ing lot.

Don't it al - ways seem_____ to go that you

don't know what you got_____ till it's gone. They

paved pa-ra-dise and put up a park - ing lot.

They

paved pa-ra-dise and put up a park - ing lot.

es! There is a light that shines in America.
That light is reflected in the songs we sing,
alone or together.

"You're a Grand Old Flag ... "
"This land is your land, this land is my land ... "
"America! America! God shed His grace on thee ... "

We sing these songs with love and pride.
Then it is the light of America that shines on me!

Patriotic Medley

**Spotlight CD
Track 10**

Words by George M. Cohan,
Woody Guthrie, and Katharine Lee Bates

You're a Grand Old Flag

You're a Grand Old Flag, you're a high flyin' flag.
And forever in peace may you wave.
You're the emblem of the land I love,
The home of the free and the brave.
Ev'ry heart beats true for the red, white, and blue,
Where there's never a boast or brag.
But should auld acquaintance be forgot,
Keep your eye on the grand old flag.

This Land Is Your Land

This land is your land, this land is my land
From California to the New York Island.
From the redwood forest to the Gulf Stream waters,
This land was made for you and me.
As I was walking that ribbon of highway,
I saw above me that endless skyway.
I saw below me that golden valley.
This land was made for you and me.

America, the Beautiful

America! America! God shed His grace on thee.
And crown thy good with brotherhood,
From sea to shining sea!

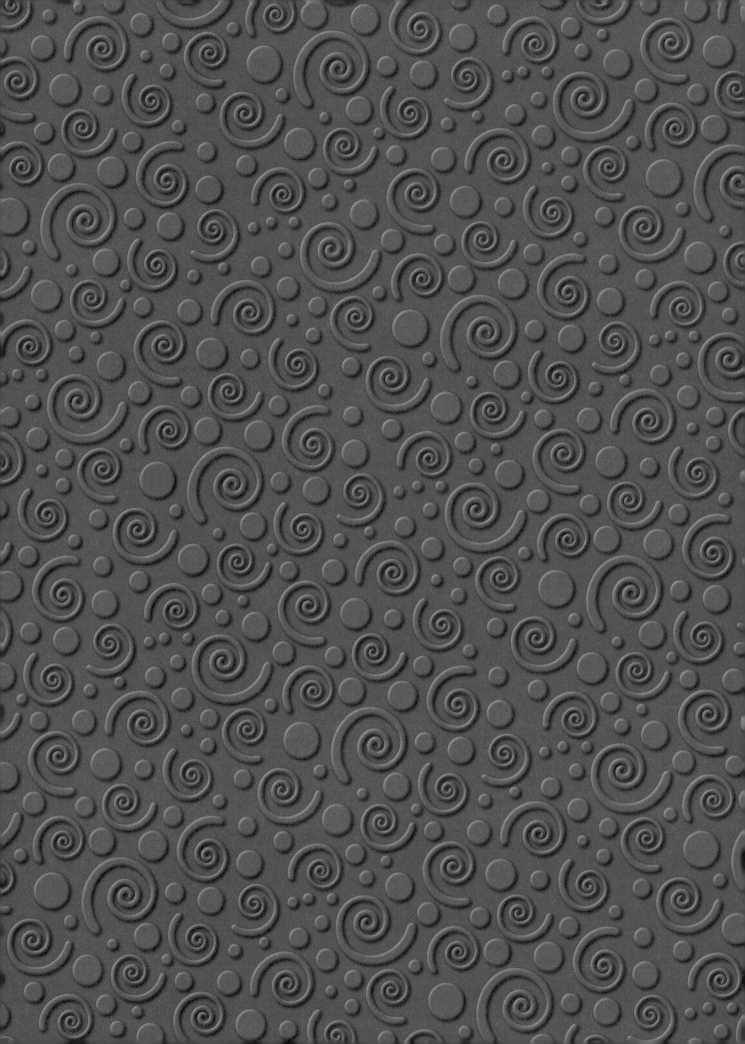

Spotlight on
Concepts

Spotlight on **Concepts**

Spotlight on Concepts

Americans Sing!

American music comes from people of many different backgrounds and cultures. In Unit 1 you will sing and play many kinds of music representing the rich musical heritage of the United States.

What kinds of music do you hear in your neighborhood?

Coming Attractions

Perform styles from spirituals to bluegrass.

Play Latin American rhythms.

Move to a famous swing song.

Sing "God Bless America" with expression and energy, thinking of the meaning of the words.

CD 1:1

Words and Music by
Irving Berlin

LISTENING CD 1:4

God Bless America
by Irving Berlin

Kate Smith introduced "God Bless America" during her radio broadcast in 1938. She was a popular singer at that time. The song was an immediate sensation. Many singers have recorded the song since then.

Listen to Daniel Rodriguez sing "God Bless America."

▲ Daniel Rodriguez, a singer, police officer, and 9/11 survivor, sang "God Bless America" at the 2002 Winter Olympics in Salt Lake City, Utah.

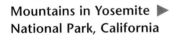

◀ Maine lighthouse by Atlantic Ocean

Mountains in Yosemite ▶ National Park, California

▼ On the prairie in Nebraska

Space Needle ▶ Seattle, Washington

Sing Together in Rhythm

CONCEPT
RHYTHM

SKILLS
LISTEN, SING, PLAY

LINKS
READING, LANGUAGE ARTS

Singing draws people together and can help express feelings. You can express your feelings about the United States through songs like "Sing, America Sing!"

Listen to "Sing, America Sing!" and feel the beat.

SING, AMERICA SING!

CD 1:5

Words and Music by
Emily Crocker and John Jacobson

Singing and dancing at a Fourth of July celebration in Lanham, Maryland

Refrain

Sing! Sing! A-mer-i-ca, sing! Lift up your voice_ and sing out_ strong.

Sing to-geth-er and stand_ up tall. Lift up your voice_ and

sing. (A-mer-i-ca, sing,) A-mer-i-cans all!

Recognizing Rhythms

The silent pulse in most music is the **beat**. Music is usually built on a steady beat. You can feel the beat inside yourself or move to the beat as you listen to music.

Combinations of long and short sounds and silences is **rhythm**. You can hear catchy rhythmic combinations in popular music from jazz to hip-hop.

Look at these symbols. They show the note values used in many rhythms.

Sounds	Silences
o **whole note**, 4 beats	▬ **whole rest**, 4 beats
♩ **half note**, 2 beats	▬ **half rest**, 2 beats
♩ **quarter note**, 1 beat	𝄽 **quarter rest**, 1 beat
♪ **eighth note**, $\frac{1}{2}$ beat	𝄾 **eighth rest**, $\frac{1}{2}$ beat

In $\frac{4}{4}$ **meter**, a measure has four beats and the quarter note lasts for one beat.

Explain the meter signature in "Sing, America Sing!"

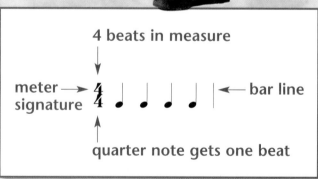

4 beats in measure

meter → $\frac{4}{4}$ ♩ ♩ ♩ ♩ | ← bar line
signature

quarter note gets one beat

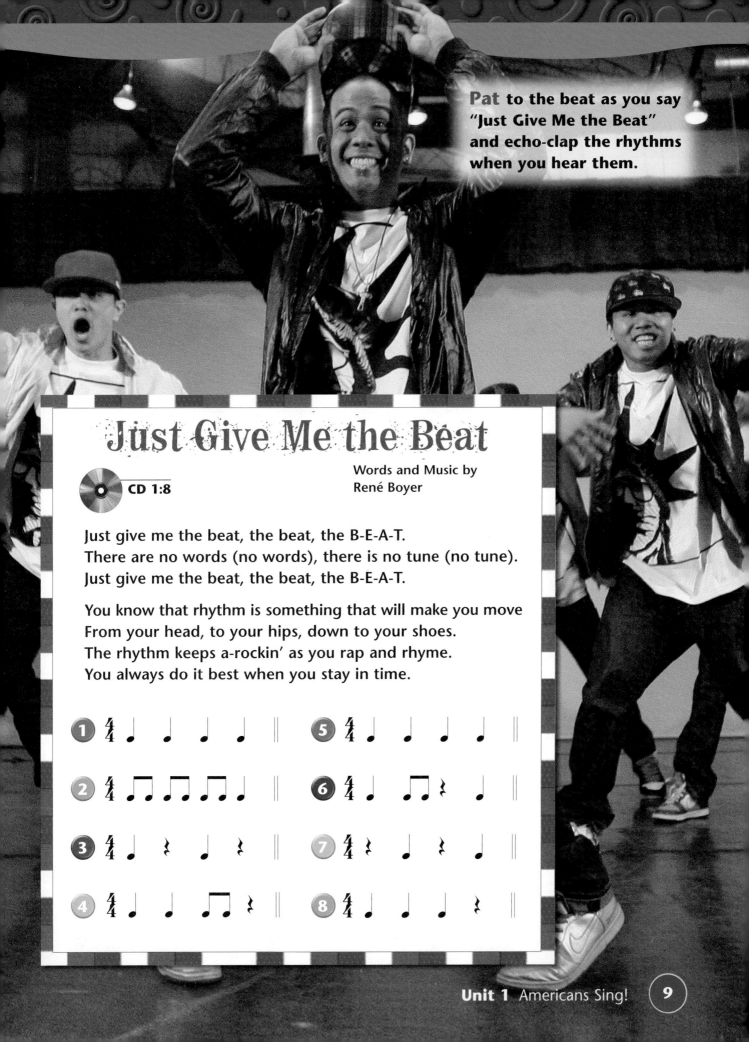

Pat to the beat as you say "Just Give Me the Beat" and echo-clap the rhythms when you hear them.

Just Give Me the Beat

Words and Music by
René Boyer

CD 1:8

Just give me the beat, the beat, the B-E-A-T.
There are no words (no words), there is no tune (no tune).
Just give me the beat, the beat, the B-E-A-T.

You know that rhythm is something that will make you move
From your head, to your hips, down to your shoes.
The rhythm keeps a-rockin' as you rap and rhyme.
You always do it best when you stay in time.

CONCEPT
MELODY

SKILLS
DESCRIBE,
SING, PLAY

LINKS
HISTORY,
FINE ART

Listen to "In That Great Git'n Up Mornin'" and tell what you notice about the singing.

Listen for the pitches as you sing the melody of "In That Great Git'n Up Mornin'."

In That Great Git'n Up Mornin'

CD 1:11

Traditional Spiritual

Refrain

In that great git-'n up morn-in', fare thee well, fare thee well.

In that great git-'n up morn-in', fare thee well, fare thee well!

Verse

You may talk a-bout the trou-ble all a-round you, fare thee well, fare thee well!

You may talk a-bout the trou-ble all a-round you, fare thee well, fare thee well.

"In That Great Git'n Up Mornin'" is an old African American spiritual. A **spiritual** is a song with a religious message on the surface. The words also might have a hidden meaning. Certain words were code words for enslaved African Americans trying to reach freedom.

"In That Great Git'n Up Mornin'" expresses the wish to get along well on the "great getting up morning," which was Judgment Day, and get to Heaven. *Judgment Day* was a code word for time of escape, and *Heaven* was a code word for a better life in the North.

Art Gallery

Fugitives Arriving at Levi Coffin's Indiana Farm

This art is a detail of a painting created by Charles Webber (1825–1911) in about 1893. It shows African Americans who had been enslaved reaching a place of safety on the Underground Railroad.

Pentatonic Power!

Most melodies are based on an ordered series of pitches called a scale. The five pitches *do re mi so la* form a **pentatonic scale**. "In That Great Git'n Up Mornin'" uses the pitches of the pentatonic scale, including both *do* and high *do.* In this song, the pitch letter names of *do re mi so la do'* are C D E G A C'.

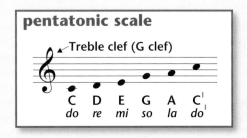

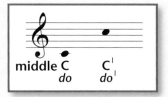

Name each pitch in the refrain of "In That Great Git'n Up Mornin'."

The home tone, or strongest pitch of a scale, is the **tonal center**. The pitch *do* (C) is the tonal center of "In That Great Git'n Up Mornin'." That pitch occurs in both its low position and its octave-higher position. An interval made up of a pitch and the next pitch that uses the same pitch letter name is an **octave**.

Identify the tonal center of "In That Great Git'n Up Mornin'" in its high and low positions by raising your hand when you hear it.

Many pentatonic melodies like "In That Great Git'n Up Mornin'" can be accompanied by playing or singing only the pitch of the tonal center. The bass xylophone part uses the two pitches of an octave. The other parts use other pitches of the C-pentatonic scale.

Written music that has all the parts arranged one on top of the other is a **score**.

Read these parts using pitch syllables or letter names. Then play or sing them with "In That Great Git'n Up Mornin'."

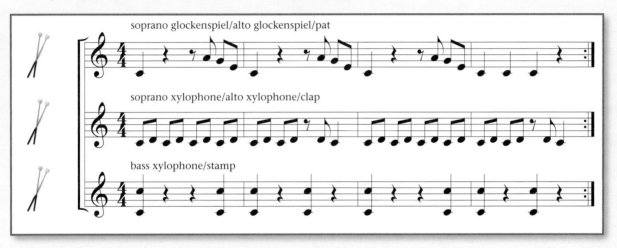

Sing or play these patterns that use pitches from the C-pentatonic scale.

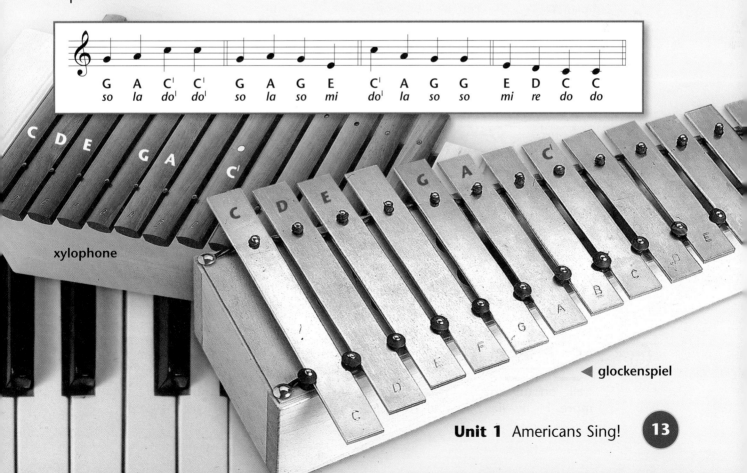

G	A	Cᴵ	Cᴵ	G	A	G	E	Cᴵ	A	G	G	E	D	C	C
so	*la*	*do'*	*do'*	*so*	*la*	*so*	*mi*	*do'*	*la*	*so*	*so*	*mi*	*re*	*do*	*do*

xylophone

◀ glockenspiel

LESSON

3

CONCEPT
RHYTHM

SKILLS
SING, READ,
PLAY

LINKS
CULTURES,
DANCE

Latin Rhythms

People have come to the United States from Spain, Central and South America, and other Spanish-speaking areas. Some of the latest American hit tunes come from Hispanic musicians.

Sing "Reach" and listen to the rhythms. What rests do you find in the song?

REACH

CD 1:16

Words and Music by
Gloria Estefan and Diane Warren

Meet the Musician

Gloria Estefan (b. 1957) and Diane Warren (b. 1956) are the composers of "Reach." Cuban-born Estefan performed the song at the 1996 Summer Olympics, in Atlanta. The song uses rhythms that show her Latin roots. Estefan has also written music with her husband, Emilio Estefan Jr., and together they performed in Latin pop group Miami Sound Machine.

Gloria Estefan performing at the 1996 Summer Olympics

Refrain

if I could reach high-er, just for one mo-ment touch the sky, from that one mo-ment in my life, I'm gon-na be strong-er, know that I've tried my ver-y best, I'd put my spir-it to the test, if I could reach. reach.

Rhythms for a Cumbia

The cumbia, a kind of popular music and dance, came from the Atlantic coast of Colombia. The cumbia developed from three South American musical traditions: Hispanic, African, and indigenous peoples.

Traditionally, the cumbia is performed at night. The woman wears a long, flowing skirt. She holds a candle and dances with shuffling steps. The man is dressed in white with a red kerchief around his neck. He moves in a zigzag pattern around the woman.

Listen to "Cumbia del sol" and pat-clap to the beat.

MAP

PANAMA
VENEZUELA
ECUADOR
COLOMBIA
PERU
BRAZIL

Dancing the cumbia at the 2002 International Festival in Modesto, California

Cumbia del sol

Cumbia of the Sun

CD 1:19

Popular Colombian Dance
English words by Emily Crocker

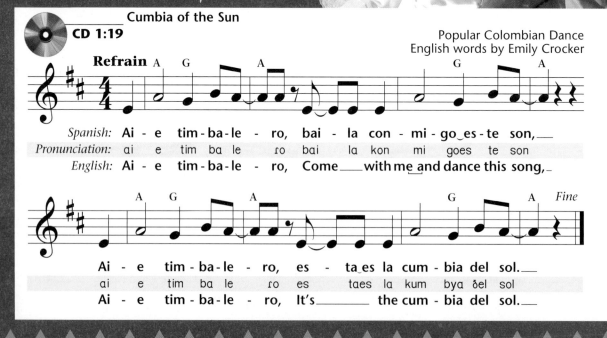

Refrain

Spanish: Ai - e tim-ba-le - ro, bai - la con - mi-go_es-te son,___
Pronunciation: ai e tim ba le ro bai la kon mi goes te son
English: Ai - e tim-ba-le - ro, Come___with me_and dance this song,_

Fine

Ai - e tim-ba-le - ro, es - ta_es la cum-bia del sol.___
ai e tim ba le ro es tɑes la kum bya ðel sol
Ai - e tim-ba-le - ro, It's___ the cum-bia del sol.

The speed of the beat is the **tempo**. A song's tempo might be slow or fast or even change speeds.

Describe the difference in tempo between "Cumbia del sol" and "Reach."

Often rhythms that sound complicated are really layers of simple combinations of notes and rests. A combination of quarter notes, eighth notes, and quarter rests can work together to create a Latin flavor.

Read the rhythm patterns in the score. Then clap or pat one of the patterns with "Cumbia del sol."

Play the rhythm patterns with "Cumbia del sol."

Playalong

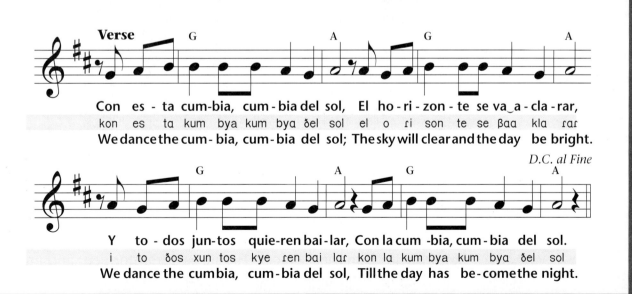

Verse

Con es - ta cum-bia, cum - bia del sol, El ho - ri - zon - te se va_a - cla - rar,
kon es ta kum bya kum bya ðel sol el o ɾi son te se ßaa kla ɾaɾ
We dance the cum- bia, cum - bia del sol; The sky will clear and the day be bright.

D.C. al Fine

Y to - dos jun-tos quie-ren bai-lar, Con la cum -bia, cum - bia del sol.
i to ðos xun tos kye ɾen bai laɾ kon la kum bya kum bya ðel sol
We dance the cumbia, cum-bia del sol, Till the day has be-come the night.

Pentatonic in Two Keys

CONCEPT
MELODY
SKILLS
ANALYZE,
READ, LISTEN
LINKS
HISTORY,
CULTURES

For another
activity with
"Amazing Grace,"
see *Spotlight
on MIDI*.

Have you ever noticed that a certain song was better for your voice than another? If a song is too high or too low for your voice, it is harder to sing. The distance from the lowest to the highest pitch of a song is its **range**.

Identify the lowest and highest pitches in "In That Great Git'n Up Mornin'" to discover the range.

The relationship of a series of pitches to a tonal center is the **key**. The name of a key includes the tonal center (C, F, G) as well as the type of scale (pentatonic, major, minor).

Some keys suit the range of your voice better than others. Everyone's voice is different, so your most comfortable key may not be the same as your neighbor's.

Sing the melody of "In That Great Git'n Up Mornin'" in two keys. Is C pentatonic or G pentatonic better for your voice?

Look at the pitches used in the melody of "Amazing Grace" on the staff at the right. The pitches so_1 and la_1 are below the tonal center. Use this information to identify the tonal center, pitches, key, and range of "Amazing Grace."

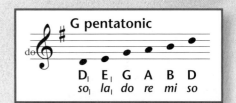

Meet the Musician

John Newton (1725–1807) was an English seaman and later a clergyman and a hymn writer. He made some poor choices in his early days and at one point was captain of a ship used in slave trade. Newton almost lost his life in a storm at sea. This made him realize that he needed to make changes in his life and inspired him to write "Amazing Grace." His life was transformed, and he later became an evangelist and antislavery activist. He wrote the words to many hymns, including "Amazing Grace."

Amazing grace, how sweet the sound. . . . This hymn is known and loved by many people. The pitches of its melody form a pentatonic scale with a range of an octave.

Amazing Grace

CD 1:23

Traditional American Melody
Words by John Newton

1. A - maz - ing__ grace, how sweet the sound
2. 'Twas grace that__ taught my heart to fear,
3. Thru man - y__ dan - gers, toils, and snares,

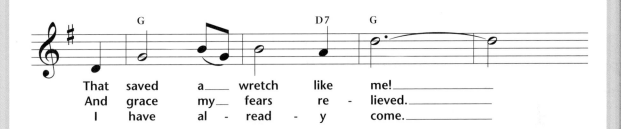

That saved a__ wretch like me!_____
And grace my__ fears re - lieved._____
I have al - read - y come._____

I once__ was__ lost, but now am__ found,
How pre - cious__ did that grace__ ap - pear
'Tis grace__ hath__ brought me safe__ thus__ far,

Was blind, but__ now I see._____
The hour I__ first be - lieved._____
And grace will__ lead me home._____

Pentatonic Practice

Sing the pentatonic melody "Amazing Grace" in other keys.

Sing these pentatonic scales.

C D E G A C'
do re mi so la do'

D, E, G A B D
so, la, do re mi so

Read and sing these melodies using pitch syllables or pitch letter names. Match the key and range of each one to the pentatonic scales above.

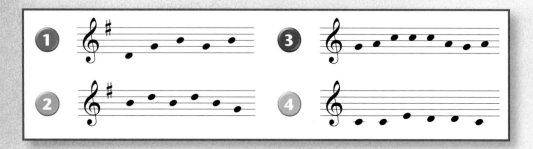

Play these harmony parts with "Amazing Grace" without the recording.

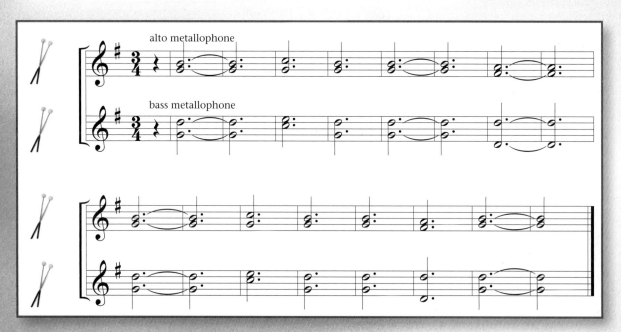

LISTENING

CD 1:26–29

"Amazing Grace" Four Ways

"Amazing Grace" has been performed in a variety of ways.

1. Judy Collins, folk

2. Tramaine Hawkins, contemporary gospel

3. Charlotte Church, classical

4. David Hooten, dixieland

Listen to the different versions of "Amazing Grace" and match the pictures to the music you hear.

THINK!

Which performance of "Amazing Grace" was your favorite? Why?

Bluegrass Sounds

CONCEPT
TONE COLOR

SKILLS
LISTEN,
DESCRIBE

LINKS
READING,
SOCIAL STUDIES

LOG
ON

See **music**
.mmhschool.com
to research
bluegrass music.

Think of a favorite piece of music. How would you describe its style? The special way that people use elements of music, such as pitch, rhythm, form, and tone color is called **style**.

One style of country music is **bluegrass**. It was made popular in the 1940s by Bill Monroe and the Blue Grass Boys. The original bluegrass style was a combination of traditional Appalachian music with the blues. The mandolin, banjo, guitar, fiddle, and bass are used in most bluegrass bands today. Bluegrass performers sing and play their instruments at the same time.

Many people around the United States travel to bluegrass festivals, where everyone is involved in making music. The musicians in a group take turns playing solos. Each player tries to do something different with the song.

Bill Hilly's bluegrass band plays at the Stan Rogers Folk Music Festival, Nova Scotia.

Pictured below are the most common instruments used in bluegrass music.

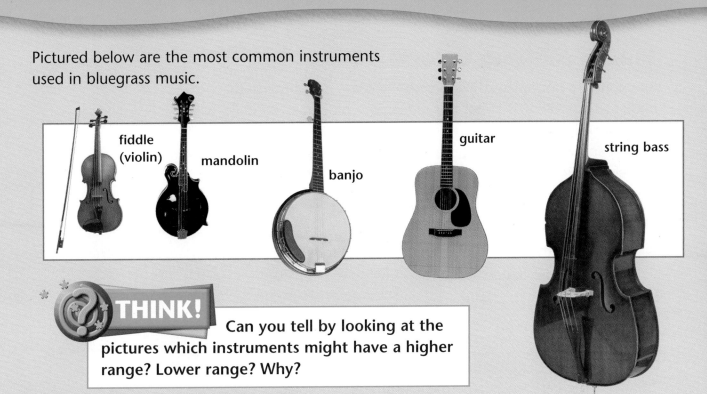

fiddle (violin)

mandolin

banjo

guitar

string bass

 **THINK!** Can you tell by looking at the pictures which instruments might have a higher range? Lower range? Why?

The special sound quality of each instrument or voice is its **tone color** (or **timbre**).

🔘 **LISTENING** CD 2:1

Blue Moon of Kentucky by Bill Monroe
This bluegrass piece is performed by Bill Monroe and the Blue Grass Boys. It is Kentucky's official state bluegrass song.

Listen to "Blue Moon of Kentucky" and identify the instruments and voices that make the tone colors that you hear.

Meet the Musician

William (Bill) Smith Monroe (1911–1996) came from a family that enjoyed playing music together. He learned to play mandolin and guitar, and sang with a high tenor voice. Monroe also wrote songs. He started out performing with his brothers and later formed a band called the Blue Grass Boys. Other famous musicians in Monroe's band were Earl Scruggs and Lester Flatt. Bill Monroe became known as the Father of Bluegrass Music. He performed for over 60 years.

Bluegrass Tone Colors

Bill Monroe's uncle, James Pendleton Vandiver, was an old-time fiddler. "Uncle Pen" is about this uncle. This bluegrass standard has been recorded by Bill Monroe and other bluegrass musicians. Ricky Skaggs and Kentucky Thunder updated the sound, adding drums and electronic instruments, making the song a Number One country hit in 1984.

Name these pitches with letter names. The last pitch will give you a clue. Then find the pitches in "Uncle Pen."

Sing "Uncle Pen" and name the instruments you hear.

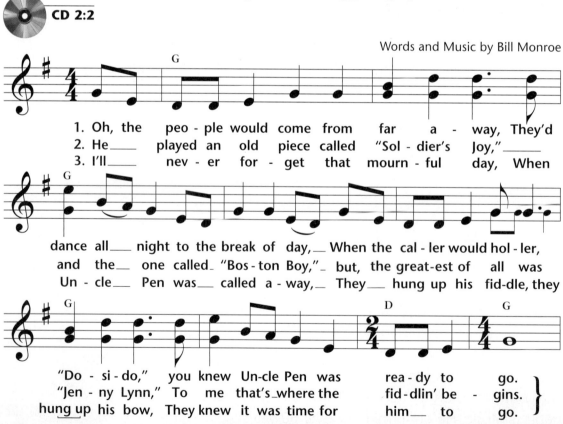

Ode to a Butterfly by Chris Thile

"Ode to a Butterfly" is a contemporary bluegrass piece for fiddle, banjo, mandolin, guitar, and bass. It was composed by Chris Thile of the band Nickel Creek, a bluegrass trio from San Diego, California.

Compare the tone colors of "Blue Moon of Kentucky" with the tone colors of "Ode to a Butterfly."

Meet the Musicians

Nickel Creek is a bluegrass band. The members are Sara Watkins on fiddle, her brother Sean on guitar, and Chris Thile on mandolin and banjo. They formed the band when they were still in elementary and middle school. On this song, Chris's father, Scott, joins in on bass.

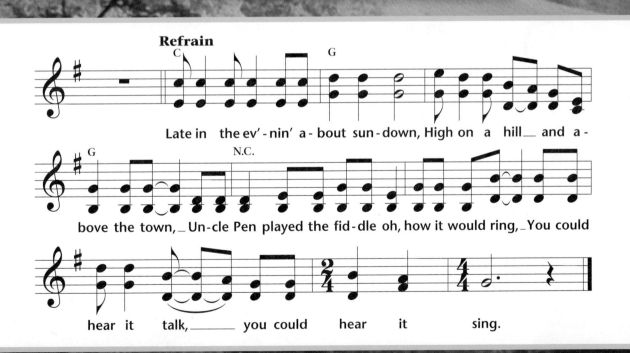

Late in the ev'-nin' a-bout sun-down, High on a hill__ and a-bove the town,__ Un-cle Pen played the fid-dle oh, how it would ring,__ You could hear it talk,_____ you could hear it sing.

CONCEPT
TEXTURE
SKILLS
DESCRIBE,
PLAY, ANALYZE
LINKS
CULTURES,
FINE ART

Hearing and Seeing Textures

The Athabascans are a Native American people who live in Alaska and along the Pacific Coasts of Canada and the United States. They are related to the Navajos, who live in the Southwestern United States.

 LISTENING CD 2:7

Athabascan Song Traditional Athabascan
Bead-Chant Song, arranged by R. Carlos Nakai

"Athabascan Song" is an arrangement of an Athabascan bead-chant song. The music is played on a Native American flute. The melody repeats several times.

Listen to "Athabascan Song" and describe what you hear.

Musical lines occurring at the same time form **texture**. Texture can be described as *thin* or *thick*. When few melodic or rhythmic lines occur, the texture is thin. When many melodic or rhythmic lines occur at the same time, the texture is thick. Each time another line is added, the texture becomes thicker.

Would you describe the texture of "Athabascan Song" as thick or thin?

 Art Gallery

Watching for Dancing Partners
This marble sculpture shows two Native American women waiting to be asked to dance. It was created by Allan Houser 1914–1994, the great-grandson of an Apache chief, in 1979. Textures in sculpture are described as smooth and rough. How would you describe the texture of the various parts of this sculpture?

R. Carlos Nakai playing
Native American flute

Eka Muda Comanche Hand-Game Song

"Eka Muda" has been a popular hand-game song of the Comanche people for many years. Other nations play the same game and sing their own version of the song. The game is popular with people of all ages. In the Comanche language, *eka muda* means "You're no smarter than a red mule." The words are sung to tease members of the other team as the hand game is played.

Athabascan birch bark baskets

Listen for the texture of "Eka Muda."

Which design below represents "Eka Muda"? Which represents "Athabascan Song"? How are the two songs represented in the designs?

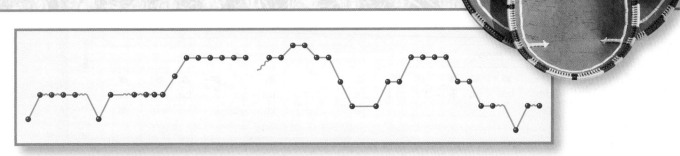

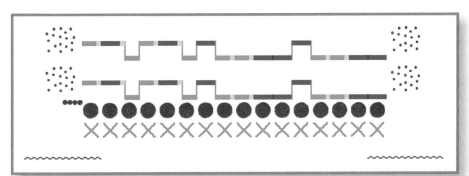

Comanche beaded buckskin bag from Oklahoma

THINK! What kind of design would you use to show thinner texture? What design would you use to show thicker musical texture? Draw them. Look at the textures in the crafts on this page. Which one seems "thinner"? Why?

Make Textures

You can change the texture of "Eka Muda" by adding your own instrumental parts to your singing.

rattles

CD 2:9

Eka Muda

Red Mule

Comanche Hand-Game Song

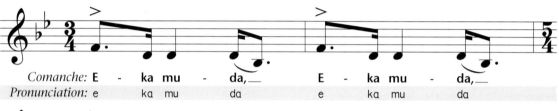

Comanche: E - ka mu - da,___ E - ka mu - da,___
Pronunciation: e ka mu da e ka mu da

He hai - ya E - ka mu - da, He hai - ya E - ka mu - da.
he hai ya e ka mu da he hai ya e ka mu da

Playalong

Play ♫ on a drum throughout the song.

Clap ♩ throughout the song.

Shake rattles or shakers at the beginning and end of the game.

What happened to the texture in "Eka Muda" as you added parts?

drum

Play a Game with "Eka Muda"

The hand game for "Eka Muda" involves competition between two teams of players. For each round of play, one team chooses a "hider," and the other team chooses a "guesser."

1. The hider holds two sticks, one in each hand. One stick has a special mark.

2. As the hider's team sings the song, the hider moves his or her hands through the air and changes the sticks from hand to hand to confuse the guesser.

3. When the hider brings his or her hands forward, the guesser tries to point to the hand that holds the marked stick.

4. If the hand has the marked stick, the guesser's team gets a counting stick. The teams change roles and the singing switches to the other team.

5. If the hand with the marked stick was not selected, the hider's team gets a point and play continues without stopping the song.

Swing into a Form

CONCEPT
FORM
SKILLS
DESCRIBE,
ANALYZE, SING
LINKS
CULTURES,
LANGUAGE ARTS,
PHYSICAL EDUCATION

The order of phrases and sections in music creates **form**. In music, form is described with letters. For example, A and B can represent sections of music that have contrasting melodies.

Identify the two sections of "Uncle Pen" and tell the form.

Listen for the form of "Sing, Sing, Sing."

You probably noticed two sections. The A section occurred twice, followed by the B section, followed by a return of the A section, creating **AABA form**.

Sing, Sing, Sing

CD 2:13

Words and Music by Louis Prima
Adapted by MMH

A Brightly

do

Bm F#7 Bm F#7 Bm F#7 Bm F#7

1. Sing, sing, sing, sing, Ev'-ry-bod-y start to sing___
2. Swing, swing, swing, swing, Ev'-ry-bod-y start to swing_

Bm F#7 Bm F#7 Bm Em F#7 Bm

La - dle - la___ Whoa - ho - ho___ Now you're sing - ing with a swing._
La - dle - la___ Whoa - ho - ho___ Now you're swing - ing while you sing._

A

Bm F#7 Bm F#7 Bm F#7 Bm F#7

Sing, sing, sing, sing, Ev' - ry - bod - y start to sing___
Swing, swing, swing, swing, Ev' - ry - bod - y start to swing_

Bm F#7 Bm F#7 Bm Em F#7 Bm

La - dle - la___ Whoa - ho - ho___ Now you're sing - ing with a swing._
La - dle - la___ Whoa - ho - ho___ Now you're swing - in' while you sing._

Learn About Swing

A style of popular American music is **jazz**. African Americans near the end of the 1800s combined styles such as spirituals, marches, and the blues to create jazz. Jazz often uses syncopation, improvisation, and strong rhythms. A kind of jazz played by big bands is **swing**. It is recognized by its "swinging" rhythm. During the 1930s and early 1940s, swing music was all the rage with young people. The big band sound was everywhere—on the radio, in dance clubs, and even in concert halls.

B

D   A6   D   A   Em11   A7   D

When the mu-sic goes a-round_ ev'-ry-bod-y goes to town,_
When the mu-sic goes a-round_ ev'-ry-bod-y goes to town,_

D   A6   D   A   Em11   A7   D   F#7

but here's some-thing you should know_ ho-ho ba-by ho-ho-ho.
just re-lax and take it slow_ ho-ho ba-by ho-ho-ho.

A

Bm   F#7   Bm   F#7   Bm   F#7   Bm   F#7

Sing, sing, sing, sing, Ev'-ry-bod-y start to sing_

Bm   F#7   Bm   F#7   Bm   Em   F#7   Bm

La-dle-la__ Whoa-ho-ho__ Now you're sing-ing with a swing._

Dance to the Music of Swing

Carnegie Hall is a famous concert hall in New York City. Many famous musicians have performed there, including the King of Swing, Benny Goodman.

Benny Goodman Orchestra

 LISTENING CD 2:16

Sing, Sing, Sing (with a Swing)

(excerpt) by Louis Prima

On January 16, 1938, the Benny Goodman Orchestra, a famous big band, played one of the most famous jazz concerts ever in Carnegie Hall. The musicians just couldn't stop playing "Sing, Sing, Sing." The audience members were out of their seats and dancing in the aisles. The musicians kept improvising right up to the very intense and swinging end.

Listen to "Sing, Sing, Sing" as it was once performed.

What time in history is this poem describing? Can some of the words in the poem describe your favorite music today?

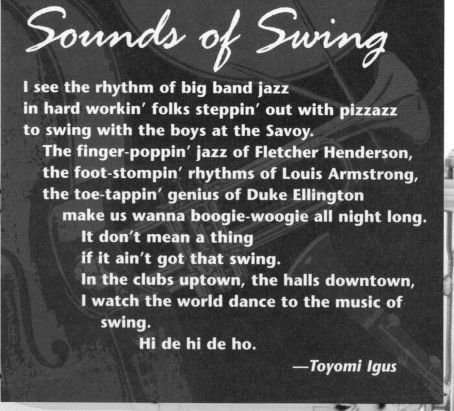

Sounds of Swing

I see the rhythm of big band jazz
in hard workin' folks steppin' out with pizzazz
to swing with the boys at the Savoy.
  The finger-poppin' jazz of Fletcher Henderson,
  the foot-stompin' rhythms of Louis Armstrong,
  the toe-tappin' genius of Duke Ellington
    make us wanna boogie-woogie all night long.
    It don't mean a thing
    if it ain't got that swing.
  In the clubs uptown, the halls downtown,
  I watch the world dance to the music of
    swing.
    Hi de hi de ho.

—*Toyomi Igus*

Swing Dancing Using AABA Form

Swing was also a popular dance. The young people of the 1930s were crazy about this lively dance. Many of the movements were improvised. The jitterbug was one form of this dance.

You can have fun moving to swing music.

Perform these steps with a partner. The steps go with the A sections of "Sing, Sing, Sing." You can move sideways or forward and backward.

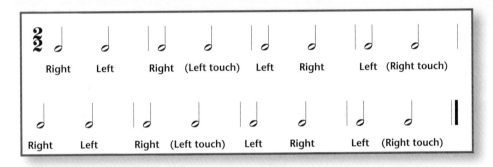

Right   Left   Right   (Left touch)   Left   Right   Left   (Right touch)

Right   Left   Right   (Left touch)   Left   Right   Left   (Right touch)

Create a variation of this step for the B section. Then combine all the steps to make a dance in AABA form.

In swing dancing, dancers change their body facing while doing the steps. *Body facing* in swing dance refers to how body surfaces of one dancer relate to the body surfaces of the other dancer: front to front, side by side, front to back. Try different body facings. Then put the steps and body facings together and have fun swing dancing!

front to front

side by side

front to back

A Dynamic Theme

CONCEPT
DYNAMICS
SKILLS
LISTEN, READ,
COMPOSE
LINKS
HISTORY,
MATHEMATICS

In 1863 Patrick S. Gilmore, an army bandmaster, wrote "When Johnny Comes Marching Home." The words express concern for those away fighting in the Civil War and hope that the men would return home safely.

CD 2:18

Words and Music by Patrick S. Gilmore

1. When John - ny comes march - ing home a - gain, Hur - rah!___ Hur - rah!___
2. Get read - y for the Ju - bi - lee, Hur - rah!___ Hur - rah!___

We'll give him a heart - y wel - come then, Hur - rah!___ Hur - rah!___
We'll give___ the he - ro three times three, Hur - rah!___ Hur - rah!___

The men will cheer,___ the boys will shout. The la - dies they___ will all turn out,
The lau - rel wreath___ is read - y now to place up - on___ his loy - al brow,

and we'll all be glad when John - ny comes march - ing home.___
and we'll all be glad when John - ny comes march - ing home.___

The degrees of strength or loudness of sound are **dynamics**. Here are the dynamics most often used in music.

Dynamics	Symbol	Meaning
fortissimo	*ff*	very loud
forte	*f*	loud
mezzo forte	*mf*	medium loud
mezzo piano	*mp*	medium soft
piano	*p*	soft
pianissimo	*pp*	very soft
crescendo	<	get louder
diminuendo	>	get softer

What dynamics did you hear in "When Johnny Comes Marching Home?"

Morton Gould used "When Johnny Comes Marching Home" as the **theme**, or main musical melody, of *American Salute*. *American Salute* is in a form called **theme and variations**. In each variation, the theme is changed in some way. The use of a theme creates unity, and the variations create variety.

Some of Gould's variations have changes in dynamics. Some variations include kettle-shaped drums called timpani or kettledrums. These percussion instruments are usually struck with mallets that have felt heads. There are usually two to four timpani in an orchestra, each tuned to a different pitch.

timpani

Use Dynamics

Listen to *American Salute* for the dynamics, timpani, and the ways the theme is varied.

 LISTENING   CD 2:17

American Salute by Morton Gould

American Salute is written for orchestra. Morton Gould, a famous American composer of the twentieth century, liked to use the sounds of American folk and popular styles in his music. He combined these sounds with classical forms such as the theme and variations.

Listening Map for *American Salute*

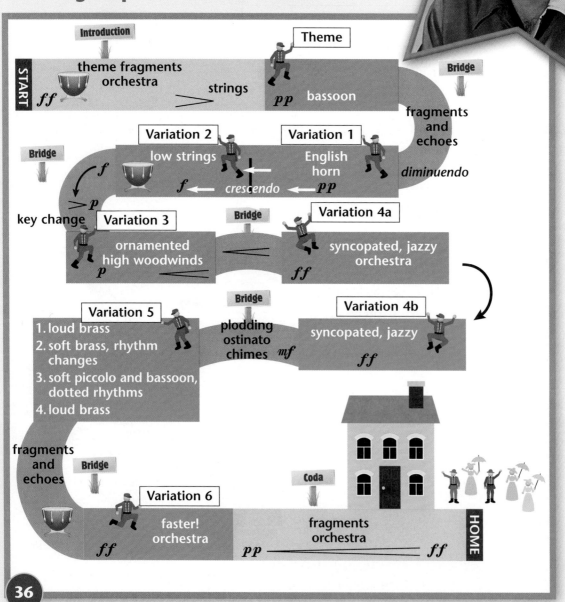

Sing "The Caissons Go Rolling Along."

The Caissons Go Rolling Along

CD 2:21

Music and Words by
Edmund L. Gruber

Verse

O - ver hill, o - ver dale, As we hit the dust - y trail,
In and out, hear them shout, Coun-ter-march and right a - bout,

And the cais - sons go roll - ing a - long.
And the cais - sons go roll - ing a - long.

Refrain

Then it's hi hi hee! In the Field Ar-til-ler - y,

Shout out your num - bers loud and strong;

Wher - e'er you go, You will al - ways know

That those cais - sons go roll - ing a - long.

Compose an eight-beat rhythm using rhythms you know. Play it on a percussion instrument with "The Caissons Go Rolling Along." Use different dynamics as you sing and play.

Spotlight Your Success!

REVIEW

1 Which list of note values goes in order from shortest to longest?

 a. eighth note, half note, sixteenth note, whole note

 b. whole note, quarter note, half rest, eighth note

 c. half note, whole note, quarter note, eighth note

 d. eighth note, quarter note, half note, whole note

2 Which pitches are in a pentatonic scale?

 a. *do re mi fa so*   **b.** *do re mi so ti*   **c.** *do re mi so la*

3 What are the names of these pitches?

 a. C' E G D A C   **b.** C D E G A C'   **c.** D' E' G A B D

4 Which symbols show these rests: half rest, quarter rest, whole rest, eighth rest?

 a. 𝄼 𝄽 — ▬   b. ▬ 𝄽 — 𝄾   c. — ▬ 𝄽 𝄾

READ AND LISTEN

1 **Read** these rhythms. Then listen. Which rhythm do you hear?

 a.

 b.

 c.

 d.

2 **Read** these patterns using pitch syllables. Then listen. Which pattern do you hear?

a.

b.

THINK!

1 How is "In That Great Git'n Up Mornin'" musically the same as "Amazing Grace"?

2 What dynamics would you choose for "Reach"? Why?

3 Tell in your own words the meaning of the lyrics of "Sing, America Sing!"

4 **Write** about one piece of music from the unit. Pretend that you are hearing it for the first time. How would you describe the music using musical terms?

CREATE AND PERFORM

1 Choose ♩, ♩, ♫, and 𝄽 to fill four measures in ⁴⁄₄ meter.

2 **Create** a melody by choosing pitches for your rhythm.

- Use pentatonic pitches in the key of C or G.

- If you choose C, end your melody on C. If you choose G, end your melody on G.

3 **Play** your melody. Use two or more dynamics as you play.

Music News

Meet the Musician
ON NATIONAL RADIO!

Name: Todd Cope   Age: 17
Instrument: Clarinet
Home Town: Dallas, Texas

"I learned through a rather embarrassing experience that I shouldn't move around so much on stage," says seventeen-year-old Todd Cope. Todd was performing in his first music competition. It was the final round, which took place in front of a live audience and several judges.

Todd was playing a solo clarinet piece. He was accompanied by a pianist. There were long sections of the piece where only the pianist played. Instead of standing still at those times, Todd walked behind the piano. "I paced around back there, mumbling to myself, making funny faces, and sucking the spit out of my clarinet," he explains. Afterward, a judge told Todd to work on his stage presence. Todd was embarrassed, but fortunately he'd still played well enough to win the competition!

Since then Todd has performed in several music competitions and thinks they are great learning experiences. "I love competitions because of the journey going into them," he declares. "Whether I win or lose, I've already become a better musician."

 LISTENING   CD 2:25–27   **RECORDED INTERVIEW**

Concerto No. 3 in B flat, Allegro Moderato
by Carl Stamitz

Listen to Todd's performance and interview on the national radio program **From the Top**.

Careers

Judith Palmer, a piano technician, feels that "tuners are like the people on the ground who make sure the planes are safe before they take off." Pilots, not technicians, are the ones who actually fly the planes.

Ms. Palmer took piano lessons from third through sixth grade, then some more in high school. In college she studied psychology and social work, but she chose a different career that allowed her to work more with her hands. Three years after a beginner's class in piano technology and many other courses offered by the Piano Technician's Guild, Ms. Palmer felt she knew enough about tuning pianos to do a good job and get paid for it.

Ms. Palmer's work has many rewards. She enjoys finding and solving a piano's problems, making the instrument sound the best it can, and seeing how grateful her customers are when she's finished.

Did You Know?

Scientists found a 45,000-year-old flute created by a Neanderthal. It was made from a bear's leg bone.

Over 150 years ago, German goldsmith and flutist Theobald Boehm redesigned the flute. With larger holes and a system of pads and keys to cover them, he greatly improved the instrument.

Flutes can be tuned by sliding their three sections farther in or out.

Nose flutes, in which air is blown from the nose instead of the mouth, are common in some cultures.

 LISTENING CD 3:1–2

Badinerie from Suite No. 2 for Orchestra
by Johann Sebastian Bach

Pegasus Suite, First Movement (excerpt)
by N. Bloomer Deussen

Listen to the way these two composers use the sound of the flute with other instruments. In Bach's Badinarie, the flute plays the melody with a string orchestra. In Nancy Bloomer Deussen's music, the flute is accompanied by a piano.

from **The New Colossus**

. . . Give me your tired, your poor,
Your huddled masses yearning to breathe free,
The wretched refuse of your teeming shore.
Send these, the homeless, tempest-tossed to me,
I lift my lamp beside the golden door!

—*Emma Lazarus*

Coming to America

The Statue of Liberty is a symbol of freedom and welcome. The poem "The New Colossus," found at its base, invites people to the United States.

 LISTENING **CD 3:3**

Give Me Your Tired, Your Poor
from *Miss Liberty* by Irving Berlin

Irving Berlin used the poem by Emma Lazarus as the words to his song.

Listen to "Give Me Your Tired, Your Poor."

Coming Attractions

Perform music from many countries.

Play percussion instruments.

Compose music for percussion instruments.

Many people come with
"the power of a dream."
This song, made popular by
Celine Dion, calls attention to the
qualities within that help bring
to reality a person's hopes and dreams.

Sing "The Power of the Dream"
with expression.

Babyface

Celine Dion

The *Power* of the *Dream*

CD 3:5

Words and Music by Babyface,
David Foster and Linda Thompson

1. Deep with-in each heart there lies a mag-ic spark that
(2.) mind will take you far, the rest is just pure heart. You'll

lights the fire of our i-mag-i-na-tion. And
find your fate is all your own cre-a-tion.

since the dawn of man the strength of just "I can" has
Ev'-ry boy and girl, as they come in-to this world, they

brought to-geth-er peo-ple of all na-tions. There's
bring the gift of hope and in-spi-ra-tion. There's

noth-ing or-di-nar - y in the liv-ing of__ each day. There's a

spe-cial part__ ev'-ry one of us will play. Feel the

flame for-ev - er burn, teach-ing les-sons we must learn to bring us

clos-er to__ the pow-er of__ the dream. The world u -

nites in hope and peace, pray that it will al-ways be. It is the

(3rd time) To Coda

pow-er of__ the dream that brings us here.

2. Your here. Feel the

Coda

here to re-al-ize__ the pow-er of the dream.____

Rhythms from Ireland

CONCEPT
RHYTHM
SKILLS
SING, READ, PLAY
LINKS
SOCIAL STUDIES, FINE ART

"The Cliffs of Doneen" is an Irish folk song. It expresses the feelings of Irish immigrants longing for their homeland. The cliffs of Doneen are on the southwest coast of Ireland.

Sing "The Cliffs of Doneen" and listen to the rhythms.

MAP

SCOTLAND

NORTHERN IRELAND

ENGLAND

IRELAND   WALES

The Cliffs of Doneen

 CD 3:8

Irish Folk Song

1. You may trav - el far, far from your own   na - tive land.
2. Take   a   view o'er the moun-tains, fine sights you'll see there.
3. It's   a   nice place to be   on   a   fine   sum - mer's day,
4. Fare thee well to   Do-neen, fare thee well   for   a   while,

Far   a - way o'er the   moun - tains, far a - way o'er the foam.
You'll see   the high, rock - y   moun - tains o'er the west coast of Clare.
Watch - ing   all   the wild flow - ers that__ ne'er do   de - cay.
And   to   all   the kind peo - ple I'm__ leav - ing be - hind.

But of   all   the   fine   pla - ces that   I've ev - er   been,
Oh, the town   of   Kil - kee and   Kil - rush can be   seen,
Oh, the hares and loft - y phea - sants are   plain to be   seen,
To the streams and the mea - dows where late I have   been,

Sure there's none   can com - pare with the cliffs of   Do - neen.
From   the   high, rock - y slopes 'round the cliffs of   Do - neen.
Mak - ing homes for their young 'round the cliffs of   Do - neen.
And   the   high, rock - y slopes 'round the cliffs of   Do - neen.

Look at the rhythm in "The Cliffs of Doneen" to find a quarter note followed by a dot. To read a dotted note, add half the value of the note.

Dotted Notes			
dotted quarter note	♩.	♩. = ♩ + ♪	$1 + \frac{1}{2} = 1\frac{1}{2}$
dotted half note	♩.	♩. = ♩ + ♩	$2 + 1 = 3$

Three beats in a measure with a quarter note lasting one beat is **triple meter**, and it is shown with a $\frac{3}{4}$ **meter** signature.

Clap and count these rhythms to feel the duration of a dotted quarter note in $\frac{3}{4}$ meter. The musical symbol that joins two notes into a single sound equal to their total duration is the **tie** (⌣). For example, ♪ ♪ = ♩

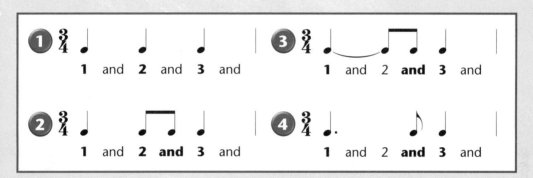

Find the dotted quarter note/eighth note pattern (♩. ♪) as you sing "The Cliffs of Doneen."

When two or more pitches sound at the same time, **harmony** is formed. A harmony part supports the melody.

Play or hum this harmony part with "The Cliffs of Doneen" and notice the dotted half notes.

Playalong

Irish Folk Music

Listen to "Nead na lachan sa mhúta," a folk song for very young children.

LISTENING CD 3:11

Nead na lachan sa mhúta Irish Folk Song

"Nead na lachan sa mhúta" is a slip jig in $\frac{9}{8}$ meter. A jig is a fast lively dance. This piece is in verse and refrain form.

Verses 1 & 5: Nead na lachan sa mhúta (repeat 3x):
    'S cuirfidh mé amach ar an gcuan tú
Verse 2: Béarfaidh mé curach is criú duit (repeat 3x):
    'S cuirfidh mé amach ar an gcuan tú
Verse 3: Ceannóidh mé slat agus d'rú duit (repeat 3x):
    'S cuirfidh mé amach ar an gcuan tú
Verse 4: Ceannóidh mé culaith bhreá nua duit (repeat 3x):
    'S cuirfidh mé amach ar an gcuan tú
Refrain: Haigh di di-dil-di di-dil-di Haigh di daigh di de-ro,
    Haigh-dil-di aigh-dil-di aigh-dil-di Haigh di di-dil-di de-ro.

Verses 1 & 5: The duck's nest is in the moat (or bog);
    I will put you out in the harbor.
Verse 2: I will bring you a curach (small traditional boat) and a crew . . .
Verse 3: I will buy you a rod and line . . .
Verse 4: I will buy a fine new suit . . .
Refrain: Haigh di di-dil-di di-dil-di Haigh di daigh di de-ro,
    Haigh-dil-di aigh-dil-di aigh-dil-di Haigh di di-dil-dil de-ro.

Art Gallery

Chi Rho from *The Book of Kells*

This art is an example of illuminated manuscript. It is called illuminated because the pages seem to glow with the bright colors and gold work. *The Book of Kells* was created around A.D. 800 and is the most elaborate illumination of that time period. Many of the pages contain complex paintings, decorated letters, complicated knotwork or spirals, and figures of humans and animals. The Chi Rho are the Greek letters *X* with an overlapping *P*. This page starts the story of Jesus in the gospel of Matthew.

Learn About Bodhrán

One of the musical instruments brought to the United States is the Irish bodhrán, a frame drum. The bodhrán is traditionally made with a wooden body and a goatskin head. A brace allows the drum to be grasped. A double-headed beater, held in the right hand, strikes the bodhrán. Touching the drumhead with the left hand creates different sounds.

 LISTENING CD 3:12

Maggie in the Wood Traditional Irish Song

A musical group is called an **ensemble**. An Irish ensemble often includes fiddle, flute, pennywhistle, and bodhrán. The bodhrán's rich bass tone and rhythmic drive contrast with the high-pitched melodic instruments.

Meet the Musicians

The Chieftains is the Irish folk ensemble that performed "Maggie in the Wood." The group was formed in 1962 to play and record traditional Irish music. Members of The Chieftains sing or play tin whistle, flute, concertina, fiddle, bodhrán, harp, bagpipes, and tiompán (hammered dulcimer). The ensemble performs often in the United States and around the world.

Echo-clap these rhythms in $\frac{4}{4}$ meter.

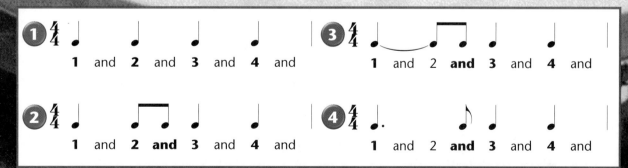

Playalong

Clap or **play** ♩. ♪ ♩ ♩ with "Maggie in the Wood."

CONCEPT
CULTURAL CONTEXT
SKILLS
PLAY, SING,
LISTEN
LINKS
SOCIAL STUDIES,
LANGUAGE ARTS

"**A**rirang" is a Korean folk song that many Americans have come to know and love. "Arirang" is part of Korea's cultural heritage. It is sung in times of joy, sorrow, and celebration. There are as many variations of Arirang as there are emotions that it represents.

Sing "Arirang" and listen for the pentatonic pitches in the melody.

MAP
CHINA
RUSSIA
NORTH KOREA
SOUTH KOREA   JAPAN

CD 3:13

Korean Folk Song
English Words by Marilyn Davidson

Korean: 아 리 랑 아 리 랑 아 라 리 요
Pronounciation: a ɾi rang a ɾi rang a ɾa ɾi yo
English: A - ri - rang, A - ri - rang, A - ra - ri - yo.

아 리 랑 고 개 를 넘 어 간 다
a ɾi rang go ge ɾul nɔ mɔ gan da
You are go-ing far a-way over A-ri-rang hill.

나 를 버 리 고 가 시 는 님 은
na ɾul bɔ ɾi go ga shi nɯn ni mɯn
Oh, my friend, if you leave me here a-lone, may your

십 리 도 못 가 서 발 병 난 다
shim ni do mot ka sɔ bal byɔng nan da
feet be-gin to hurt be-fore you've e-ven walked the first mile!

Name the pitch syllables, letter names, tonal center, and scale of the "Arirang" melody.

Play G and D together to accompany "Arirang."

Mallet Instruments

Many people came to live in the United States before it became a nation, and many still come today. Every day people "knock on the golden door of opportunity," hoping to become American citizens.

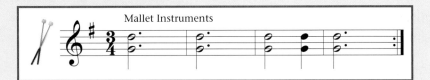

Meet the Musician

Soojin Kim Ritterling taught music in Korea before she came to the United States. Now she is a music teacher in Wisconsin who directs the Samulnori Percussion Ensemble. This ensemble plays Korean percussion music on traditional Korean drums and gongs.

RECORDED INTERVIEW CD 3:18

Listen to Soojin Kim Ritterling talk about how she is introducing Korean culture and music to students in Wisconsin.

Traditional Korean Orchestra

Korean Percussion Rhythms

A musical group made up of only percussion instruments is called a **percussion ensemble**. There are four instruments in a *samulnori*, a Korean percussion ensemble. They are the jing, kkwaenggwari, changko, and puk. These gongs and drums provide distinct Korean tone colors.

A jing is a large, flat, lipped metal gong that is struck with a cloth-covered mallet. It provides the basic beat and has a deep sound.

A kkwaenggwari is a small, flat, lipped metal gong. It is flat and struck with a small wooden mallet with a ball on the end. It plays rhythmic flourishes or ornaments.

A changko is an hourglass-shaped drum made of lacquered wood. The two drumheads are laced together, and each produces a different sound. The higher-sounding right drumhead is played with a thin stick held in the right hand. The lower-sounding left drumhead is played with a mallet-shaped beater held in the left hand.

The puk is a double-headed barrel drum. It is placed on the ground or on the side of the foot when played. A stick in the right hand strikes the right drumhead or the wooden body.

jing

kkwaenggwari

Samulnori Percussion Ensemble: jing, kkwaenggwari, changko, and puk

changko

puk

52

The most common rhythm used in Korean folk music is the **semachi rhythm**. Perform the semachi rhythm using body percussion and speech:

Dong: tap both hands on your thigh
Kung: tap left hand on your thigh
Ta: tap right on your thigh

Play the following rhythms with "Arirang" to imitate the sound of a samulnori.

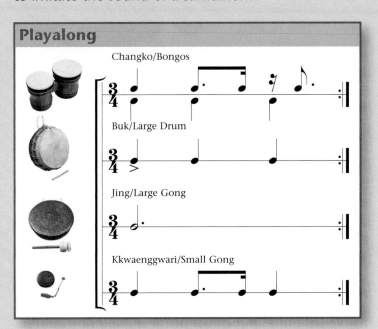

Playalong

Changko/Bongos

Buk/Large Drum

Jing/Large Gong

Kkwaenggwari/Small Gong

changko ▲

 LISTENING CD 3:22

Arirang Korean Folk Song

In Korea, where "Arirang" is a well-known song, the musicians are expected to decorate, or **ornament**, the melody by adding extra notes. The ornamentation varies with each performance, depending on the skill and wishes of the musician. The ornaments are in the voice and the tanso, a Korean bamboo flute. The drum accompaniment is on the changko.

tanso ▶

Listen to the ornamented version of "Arirang."

Improvise a four-measure G-pentatonic melody in ¾ for an introduction, interlude, and coda for "Arirang."

Sing "Arirang" accompanied by all the parts.

53

It's Great to Syncopate!

CONCEPT
RHYTHM
SKILLS
SING, READ,
ANALYZE
LINKS
CULTURES,
DANCE

Often, immigrants bring a musical style that catches on with Americans. A style that began with the Eastern European Jews and is still popular today is **klezmer**. Klezmer bands play traditional music for celebrations, dances, and weddings. The main instruments in a klezmer band are violin, clarinet, accordion, and drums. Other instruments are also used. Listen to "Hava Nagila" performed by the klezmer band, and notice the repeated words.

klezmer band

Sing "Hava Nagila" and notice the rhythms.

Hava Nagila

CD 3:23

Jewish Folk Song
Words by Abraham Zevi Idelsohn

A type of rhythm in which stressed sounds occur between beats instead of on beats is **syncopation**. One common syncopated pattern is ♪ ♩ ♪, which can also be written with a tie as ♫ ♫.

Clap these rhythm patterns while counting the beat.

A circle dance often performed to "Hava Nagila" is the **hora**. The six-beat movement is repeated over and over.

Follow pictures from right to left to learn the hora step.

6	5	4	3	2	1
Hop on right foot as left foot kicks across in front (hop)	Step to right side with right foot (right)	Hop on left foot as right foot kicks across in front (hop)	Step to left side with left foot (left)	Step right foot in back of left foot (back)	Step to left side with left foot (left)

Syncopation Written Two Ways

"Singabahambayo" is a South African freedom song. It represents the unity of blacks as they struggled for freedom and equality in South Africa. This Zulu folk song has become a popular concert piece in the United States because of its rhythmic appeal.

Sing "Singabahambayo" and notice the syncopation.

MAP
BOTSWANA
NAMIBIA
LESOTHO
SOUTH AFRICA

Singabahambayo

Zulu beadwork, Natal, South Africa ▶

Some of the syncopated rhythms in "Singabahambayo" are written with ties.

Clap and count syncopated rhythms 1–3. Then clap and count syncopated rhythms 4–6. They are similar to rhythms 1–3, but have even more syncopation through the use of ties.

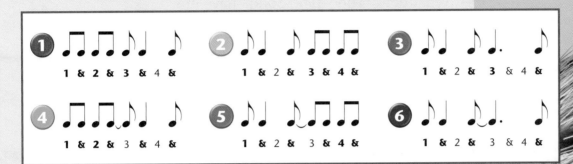

Zulu woman ▼

Syncopation gives energy to both "Hava Nagila" and "Singabahambayo."

Find the syncopation in "Hava Nagila" and "Singabahambayo."

Read and clap the rhythms below. Find the syncopation with and without ties.

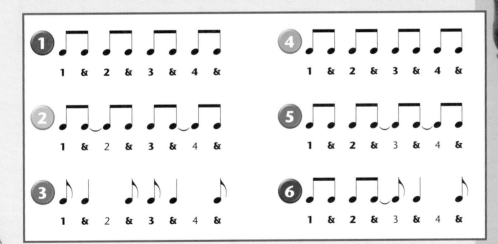

How does the notation of the syncopation differ in each song?

THINK!

What other songs do you know that include syncopation?

CONCEPT
MELODY
SKILLS
SING, ANALYZE,
READ, PLAY
LINKS
CULTURES

"**F**ung Yang Song" is a flower drum song that comes from a very old tradition of Chinese street performers. This Chinese folk song might be heard in street performances in San Francisco or New York. What does "Fung Yang Song" have in common with "Arirang"?

Sing the melody of "Fung Yang Song" and listen for the pentatonic pitches in the melody.

MAP
RUSSIA
MONGOLIA
CHINA
INDIA

CD 4:8

Chinese Folk Song
Arranged by Marilyn Davidson

page 58

Pentatonic Can Start on Different Pitches

Did you discover that "Fung Yang Song" and "Arirang" are both pentatonic melodies? Pentatonic music is found in many parts of the world.

The tonal center of a pentatonic song can be any pitch. "Fung Yang Song" is in D pentatonic. "Arirang" is in G pentatonic.

Fung Yang Song
D pentatonic

la, do re mi so la do'
B, D E F♯ A B D'

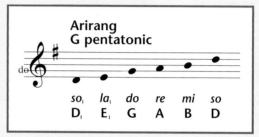

Arirang
G pentatonic

so, la, do re mi so
D, E, G A B D

Name the pitch syllables in each of those pentatonic scales.

Sing "Arirang" using pitch syllables and pitch letter names.

Street performers celebrating the Chinese New Year in San Francisco, California

60

Melodies can be moved to other keys. To perform or write music in a key other than the one in which the music is written is to **transpose**. The melody remains the same, but the pitches will be higher or lower. The tonal center will have a different letter name.

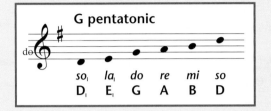

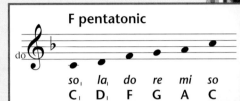

Below is one line of "Arirang" written in G pentatonic and transposed to F pentatonic.

Compare the two examples. What is the difference?

Name the pitches in F pentatonic.

Play these F-pentatonic patterns with "Arirang."

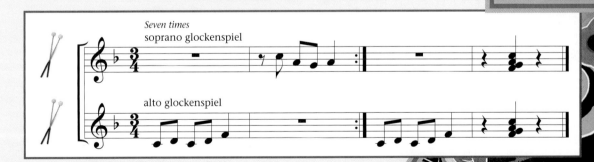

Korean tapestry ▶

THINK! Why might a performer want to transpose a song?

CONCEPT
STYLE

SKILLS
SING, LISTEN, ANALYZE

LINKS
THEATER

Italy has given many styles of music to the United States. "Funiculi, Funicula" is a popular Italian song. Luigi Denza composed it in 1880 to celebrate the opening of a funicular railway, a type of cable car. The funicular carried sightseers to the top of Mount Vesuvius. This joyful song has become popular all over the world.

An exact repeat of a sound or group of sounds is an **echo**. "Funiculi, Funicula" has several echoes. Sing the echoes as you listen to "Funiculi, Funicula."

To make the song more interesting, it can be divided among different groups. When two groups alternate and respond to each other, they sing in an **antiphonal** manner. When the groups join together, they are singing **tutti**.

Sing "Funiculi, Funicula" antiphonally, finishing tutti.

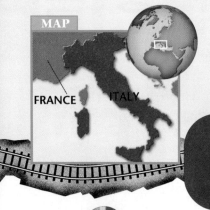

MAP

FRANCE   ITALY

Funiculi, Funicula

CD 4:13

Words and Music by
Luigi Denza

Ⓐ Solo
Some think___ the world is made for fun and frol - ic,___

Group 1   Group 2
and so do I,   and so do I!

Solo
Some think___ it well to be all mel - an - chol - ic,___

Group 1   Group 2
to pine and sigh,   to pine and sigh.

Another Italian Style

A form of storytelling in which all or most of the words are sung is **opera**. Opera appeared in the early 1600s when Italian composers first combined singing with drama. Acting, costumes, and scenery add to the story. An orchestra provides music to set the scene as well as to accompany singing and dancing. Soloists, vocal ensembles, and choruses provide the singing. An extended vocal solo in an opera is called an **aria**.

LISTENING CD 4:16

Nessun dorma (No One Sleeps) from *Turandot*
by Giacomo Puccini

In his opera *Turandot*, Italian composer Giacomo Puccini tells the story of a cold-hearted Chinese princess who does not want to marry. She orders that any prince seeking her hand in marriage must answer three riddles or die. Calàf, a foreign prince in disguise, succeeds in answering the riddles correctly, much to Turandot's dismay. However, instead of holding her to her promise, he offers to die if she can guess his name by morning. Turandot forbids anyone to sleep, sending her troops throughout the city to discover Calàf's name. He sings the tenor aria "Nessun dorma" ("No One Sleeps"). Turandot falls in love with Calàf because of his courage and nobility. The name that he reveals in the morning is not Calàf, but "Love."

Giuseppe Giacomini and Elizabeth Norberg-Schulz perform in a Royal Opera production of Puccini's *Turandot*. September 1994 London, England, UK

Listen to a tenor sing "Nessun dorma" and follow the Listening Map.

Listening Map for Nessun dorma

1.
Nessun dorma,
nessun dorma,

No one sleeps!
No one sleeps!

2.
Tu pure, o Principessa,
nella tua fredda stanza,
guardi le stelle che tremano
d'amore e di speranza.

Even you, oh princess,
in your cold room,
look at the stars that tremble
with love and hope!

3.
Ma il mio mistero
è chiuso in me,
Il nome mio
nessun saprà, No, no,
Sulla tua bocca, io lo dirò
quando la luce splenderà.

But my mystery
it is locked in me.
And my name,
no one will know! No, no!
On your mouth I will say it,
when the light will shine!

4.
Ed il mio bacio
scioglierà il silenzio
che ti fa mia.

And my kiss
will break the silence,
that makes you mine!

5.
Il nome suo nessun saprà
E noi dovrem,
ahimè, morir, morir.

His name no one will know
And we shall have,
alas, to die, to die.

6.
Dilegua, o notte!
Tramontate, stelle!
Tramontate, stelle!
All'alba vincerò!
Vincerò! Vincerò!

Disperse, o night!
Vanish, oh stars!
Vanish, oh stars!
At daybreak, I will win!
I will win! I will win!

How are the styles of "Nessun dorma" and "Funiculi,
Funicula" alike and different?

Latin Rhythms Move North

CONCEPT
RHYTHM

SKILLS
SING, PLAY, COMPOSE

LINKS
CULTURES, LANGUAGE ARTS

CD-ROM

Use *World Instruments* **CD-ROM** to learn more about bongos, claves, congas, güiro, guitarrón, and maracas.

Along the border of Mexico and the United States, the hot, dry, open spaces are well suited to cattle ranching. "Allá en el rancho grande" was inspired by the life of the cowboy. It has been recorded by many famous singers.

Listen to "Allá en el rancho grande." Notice that the song has two sections and is in **A B form**.

A Mexican street band that often includes trumpet, violin, guitar, guitarrón, and vihuela is a **mariachi**.

Sing "Allá en el rancho grande" and listen for the mariachi instruments.

MAP

UNITED STATES

MEXICO

GUATEMALA

Allá en el rancho grande

My Ranch

CD 4:17

Music by Emilio Uranga
Spanish Words by Juan del Moral
English Words by Bartley Costello

Spanish: A - llá en el ran - cho gran - de, a - llá don - de vi - ví -
Pronunciation: a yen el ɾan cho gɾan de a ya ðon de βi βi
English: I love to roam out yon - der, out where the buff' - lo wan -

- a, _____ ha - bía u - na ran - che - ri - ta, que a -
a a byu na ɾan che ɾi ta kea
- der, _____ Free as the ea - gle fly - ing, I'm

le - gre me de - cí - a, que a - le - gre me de - cí - a: _____
le gɾe me ðe si a kea le gɾe me ðe si a
rop - ing and a - ty - ing, I'm rop - ing and a - ty - ing. _____

Notice that the song is in $\frac{2}{4}$ meter. When there are two beats in the measure and the quarter note lasts for one beat, music is in $\frac{2}{4}$ **meter**, also called **duple meter**.

Echo-clap these rhythm patterns:

A silence that lasts as long as an eighth note is an **eighth rest** (ʼ). Name and find these note values or symbols in "Allá en el rancho grande":

mariachi: two trumpets, guitar, vihuela, guitarrón, and another guitar ▼

Te voy a ha - cer tus cal - zo - nes,
te βoi a seɾ tus kal so nes
Give me my ranch and my cat - tle,

co - mo los que u - sa el ran - che - ro;
ko mo los keu sel ɾan che ɾo
Far from the great cit - y's rat - tle,

te los co - mien - zo de la - na,
te los ko myen so ðe la na
Give me a big herd to bat - tle,

te los a - ca - bo de cue - ro.___
te los a ka βo ðe kwe ɾo
For I just love herd - ing cat - tle.___

Percussion Rhythms

CONCEPT
RHYTHM
SKILLS
LISTEN,
PLAY
LINKS
CULTURES,
DANCE

CD-ROM

Use *World Instruments* CD-ROM to learn more about Korean and African instruments.

Korean farmers have a special music and dance for their festivals called **nongak**. It is one of the oldest forms of music and dance that exist in Korea today. Nongak is present at folk celebrations and festivals celebrating the seasons. This folk music is used to make hard work in the fields during planting, weeding, and harvesting of the rice more enjoyable.

Samulnori means "four things (samul) playing (nori)." *Samul* refers to the four instruments used in nongak. The gongs (kkwaenggwari and jing) are symbols of the heavens, and the drums (puk and changko) are symbols of the earth.

 LISTENING CD 4:26

Yongnam Nongak Korean Agricultural Music

This Korean percussion piece is played by Soojin Kim Ritterling's ensemble of American students. This samulnori ensemble plays the jing, puk, changko, and kkwaenggwari.

Follow the changko part as you listen to "Yongnam Nongak" played by a samulnori ensemble.

Samulnori Percussion Ensemble

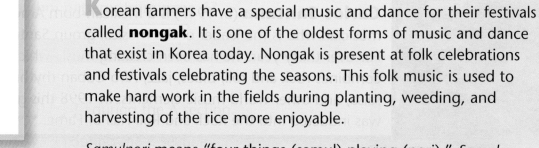

Play the changko part with "Yongnam Nongak" using body percussion or a drum.

Playalong

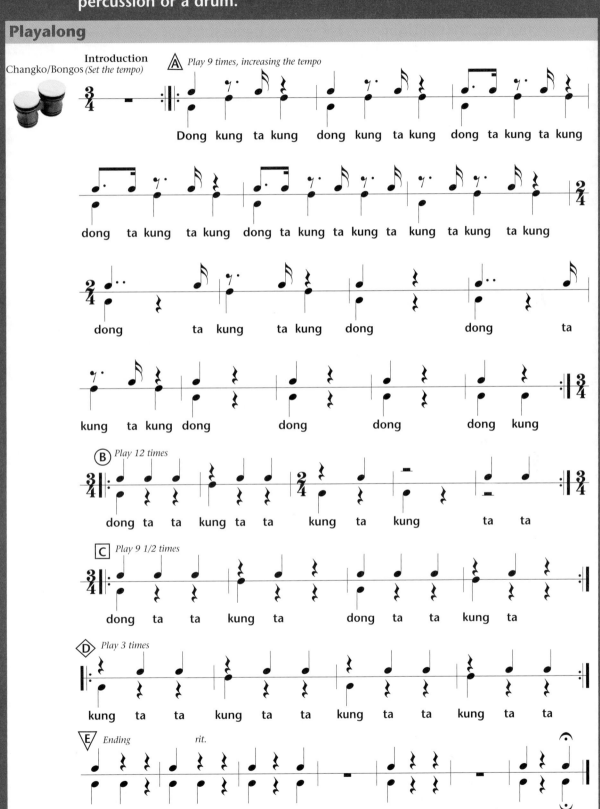

Introduction
Changko/Bongos *(Set the tempo)*

A *Play 9 times, increasing the tempo*

Dong kung ta kung   dong kung ta kung   dong ta kung ta kung

dong ta kung ta kung   dong ta kung ta kung ta kung ta kung ta kung

dong   ta kung   ta kung   dong   dong   ta

kung ta kung dong   dong   dong   dong kung

B *Play 12 times*

dong ta ta kung ta ta   kung ta kung   ta ta

C *Play 9 1/2 times*

dong ta ta kung ta   dong ta ta kung ta

D *Play 3 times*

kung ta ta kung ta ta kung ta ta kung ta ta

E *Ending*   *rit.*

dong kung dong kung   dong   dong   dong   dong dong

Percussion and Rhythms from Ghana

Drums and other percussion instruments are very important in the music of Ghana. Master drummers sometimes begin their study at the age of three or four. It takes many years to master the complicated rhythms of this music.

MAP

MALI BURKINA FASO

IVORY COAST GHANA NIGERIA

TOGO BENIN

WEST AFRICA

Meet the Musician

Kobla Ladzekpo is a master drummer and percussionist of the Anlo-Ewe people of southeastern Ghana. He is from a large family of leading musicians and dancers. Ladzekpo currently teaches African music and dance at UCLA and the California Institute of the Arts. He also leads a professional troupe of dancers and musicians.

RECORDED INTERVIEW CD 5:1

Listen to Kobla Ladzekpo talk about drumming in Ghana.

Sing "Agahu" and do the dance.

Kobla Ladzekpo playing the boba

Agahu

CD 5:2

Ewe Folk Song from Ghana

Call   *Response*

Ewe/French: Bɔŋ sa-va___ J K K Ti-ti a-hɔ-ɖe. Oo___ a-o_a-hɔ-ɖe.

Pronunciation: bong sa va   je ki ki ti ti a hɔ de   o   ao ɔ   de

All

Bɔŋ sa-va___ J K K Ti-ti a-hɔ-ɖe. Oo___ a-o_a-hɔ-ɖe.

bong sa va   je ki ki ti ti a hɔ de   o   ao ɔ   de

Agahu dance-drumming piece from Ghana

"Agahu" is a popular piece among the Anlo-Ewe people of Ghana. It came from Benin but spread to Ghana through trade and the fishers who work along the coast of West Africa.

You heard these Ghanaian percussion instruments in "Agahu."

The gangkogui is a double bell made of iron. Each bell is a different pitch. These pitches vary depending on how and where the bell is struck with a stick.

The atoke is a small bell. It is held flat in the palm and usually plays the beat.

The axatse is a shaker made from a dried gourd. It is surrounded with strings of beads.

The kidi is a drum that is played with sticks.

The sogo is a larger version of the kidi. This drum has a low, booming tone. Musicians play the sogo and kidi seated.

Play these rhythms with "Agahu."

Kuba cloth made of raffia by men in
Kasai region of Congo (formerly Zaire) ▶

gangkogui

atoke

axatse

kidi

sogo

Playalong

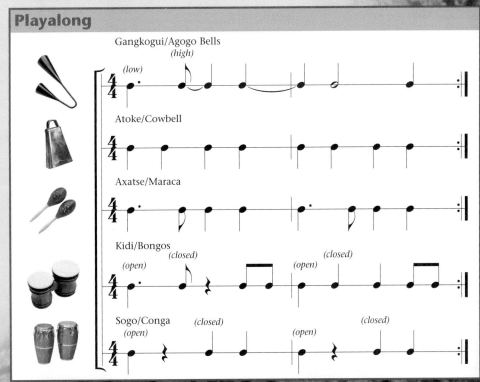

Textures Create Interest

CONCEPT
TEXTURE

SKILLS
SING, ANALYZE,
PLAY

LINKS
CULTURES,
LANGUAGE ARTS

What sounds are mentioned in this poem?

THINK! What kinds of textures might these sounds create?

The Sounds of Africa

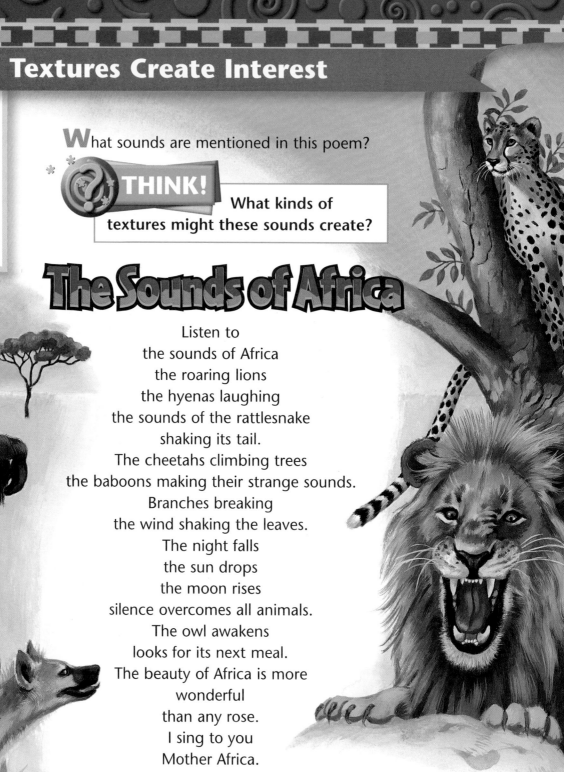

Listen to
the sounds of Africa
the roaring lions
the hyenas laughing
the sounds of the rattlesnake
shaking its tail.
The cheetahs climbing trees
the baboons making their strange sounds.
Branches breaking
the wind shaking the leaves.
The night falls
the sun drops
the moon rises
silence overcomes all animals.
The owl awakens
looks for its next meal.
The beauty of Africa is more
wonderful
than any rose.
I sing to you
Mother Africa.
—*Wandile,* age 10

In music, playing or singing the same thing at the same time is a different texture from playing or singing different things at the same time. All musicians who perform the same part perform in **unison**. Solo singing and unison singing, if unaccompanied, has a thin texture. Texture becomes thicker when a musical background, or **accompaniment**, is added. Another way to make the texture thicker is to add vocal harmony parts.

Add Instruments for a Thicker Texture

Listen for unison and part singing in "Singabahambayo."

How many vocal parts do you hear in "Singabahambayo"?

Sing "Singabahambayo" in unison accompanied by percussion instruments.

djembe

slit drum

shekere

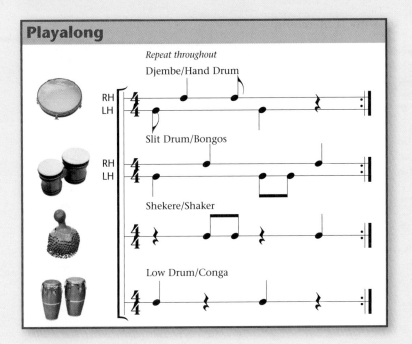

Playalong

Repeat throughout

Djembe/Hand Drum

RH
LH

Slit Drum/Bongos

RH
LH

Shekere/Shaker

Low Drum/Conga

Art Gallery

Imbenge Baskets

The Zulu people in South Africa are known for their basket making. Some baskets are so tightly woven that they can hold liquids. The traditional imbenge basket is made of hand-dyed grasses or palm leaves. In urban areas these baskets have been made of recycled telephone wire. The baskets often have swirling designs. No two are the same. The Zulu people believe that these pots give pride, warmth, and dignity to a home.

low drum

Texture Gets Thicker

Sing each part in "Singabahambayo," then sing all parts together to make a thicker texture. Then add the percussion parts.

Singabahambayo

CD 4:1

An Army Is Marching

South African Zulu Folk Song
Arranged by Cheryl Lavender

Zulu: 1. Sin - ga - ba - ham - ba - yo thi - na. Ku - lom - hla - ba.___ Ke - pha si -
Pronunciation: sing a ba ham ba yo ti na ku lom ɬa ba ke pa si
English: (2.) ar - my is march - ing. We're go - ing home.__ Our hearts are

ne - kha - ya.___ e - Zul - wi - ni.___ Sin - ga - ba - Zul - wi - ni.___ } Ha -
ne ka ya e zul wi ni sing a ba zul wi ni
filled with song.__ We sing out strong.__ On earth an sing out strong.__ } Ha -

76

B

Si - thi_____ Si - thi
su ti   su ti

Part 1   *Last time rit.*

le - lu - ya!___ Ha - le - lu - ya!___ Ha - le - lu - ya! Ha - le - lu - ya! Ha -

Part 2   *Last time rit.*

le - lu - ya!___ Ha - le - lu - ya!___ Ha - le - lu - ya! Ha - le - lu - ya! Ha -

Part 3   *Last time rit.*

le - lu - ya!___ Ha - le - lu - ya!___ Ha - le - lu - ya! Ha - le - lu - ya! Ha -

1.   *2.*
                                              Last time

Si - thi_____
su   ti

                                              Last time

le - lu - ya!___   Ha - le - lu - ya!___

                                              Last time

le - lu - ya!___   Ha - le - lu - ya!

                                              Last time

le - lu - ya!___   Ha - le - lu - ya!

Unit 2 Coming to America   **77**

Spotlight Your Success!

REVIEW

1 A dotted quarter note and eighth note is written as

a. ♩. ♩   b. ♩. ♩   c. ♩. ♪   d. ♩ ♪

2 Which of the following is a musical instrument?

a. changko   b. hora   c. ornament   d. tie

3 Which of the following show syncopation without a tie?

a. 4/4 ♪ ♩ ♪ ♪ ♩ ♪   b. 4/4 ♩ ♫ ♫   c. 4/4 ♪ ♩ ♪ ♫ ♩

4 Which of the following is an Irish musical instrument?

a. jing   b. puk   c. kkwaenggwari   d. bodhrán

5 What is the key of this melody?

a. G pentatonic   b. F pentatonic   c. C major   d. B minor

READ AND LISTEN

1 **Read** these rhythms. Then listen. Which rhythm do you hear?

a.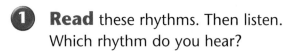

b. 3/4 ♩ ♩ ♫ ♩

2 **Read** these rhythms. Then listen. Which rhythm do you hear?

a.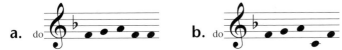

b.

c.

3 **Read** these patterns. Then listen. Which pattern shows this G pentatonic pattern transposed to F pentatonic?

a.   b.

THINK!

1 Name and describe at least two different styles that you heard in this unit and name or describe two other styles that you know.

2 Name at least two percussion instruments in this unit and tell how they are alike and different.

3 How do pitch syllables or pitch letter names help you to sing pentatonic melodies?

4 Describe the texture of a song from the unit.

CREATE AND PERFORM

1 **Create** a four-measure rhythm that uses ♪ ♩ ♪ and ♩. ♪ and other rhythms that you know.

2 **Write** a melody for this rhythm in G pentatonic.

3 **Transpose** your melody to F pentatonic.

4 **Play** your melody.

Music News

Meet the Musician
ON NATIONAL RADIO!

Name: Jewell "Tre" Fortenberry
Age: 15
Instrument: Piano
Home Town: Atlanta, Georgia

Fifteen-year-old Tre Fortenberry loves to compete. "Whether I'm playing in a piano competition or just playing a video game, I like the rush I get," he explains. Tre feels he performs best under pressure. "That's when my brain kicks in and I do really well," he states.

At piano competitions, Tre likes to hear other pianists because their performances fuel him to reach higher. He goes into competitions expecting to win but preparing to lose. "That way, I never get too disappointed," he says. Tre also likes to compete through sports. He especially loves playing basketball,

although he doesn't play very often because he doesn't want to risk hurting his hands. He also looks forward to a good game of Monopoly® or cards with his friends.

Tre has many friends, but one of the most important people in his life is his grandma. "I can talk to her about anything." Tre visits his grandma in Mississippi for several weeks each summer, and he especially looks forward to her great cooking. Tre's grandma even bought a piano so he can enjoy practicing whenever he visits.

 LISTENING CD 5:9–10  **RECORDED INTERVIEW**

Etude in C-sharp minor, Op. 10, No. 4
by Frédéric Chopin

Listen to Tre's performance and interview on the national radio program From the Top.

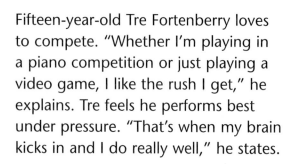

A Tip from the Top
"Competition is an opportunity to grow!"
Tre Fortenberry feels energized when he takes part in contests. Seeing his competitors perform their best inspires Tre to improve his own abilities. Whether or not he comes home with an award, he's won because he's increased his skill.

Spotlight on the French Horn

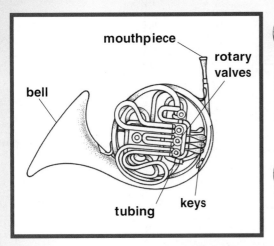

mouthpiece

rotary valves

bell

tubing

keys

LISTENING CD 5:11

Symphony No. 5, Second Movement (excerpt)
by P. Tchaikovsky

LISTENING CD 5:12

Till Eulenspiegel's Merry Pranks
by Richard Strauss

Listen to how Tchaikovsky
wrote this section of the symphony
for the mellow sound of the French horn.
In contrast, Strauss's famous French horn solo
displays the wide range of the instrument, going from
high notes all the way down to the very bottom of the horn's range.

Did You Know?

The French horn actually originated in Germany.

A French horn player mutes his or her instrument by inserting the right hand into the bell.

The French horn has a double set of metal tubing. One set produces a low, warm sound, while the other set is used for high, bright notes.

An uncoiled French horn would be 30 feet long.

The Old Becomes the New

Change is a good thing! What would it be like if everything always stayed the same? Musicians think about change. By changing certain musical elements, a musician can make a piece of music sound brand new. You will learn about these kinds of musical changes in Unit 3.

Coming Attractions

Perform different arrangements.

Listen to famous works by Beethoven and Dvořák.

Sing in a variety of old and new styles.

Choose a musical element such as pitch, rhythm, or tone color, and notice how it changes or stays the same as you listen to and sing "Change Is Good."

Change Is Good

CD 5:13

Words and Music by Ed Kaecher, Jim Tullio and Rick Danko

1. Change is then,__ change is now, Change is what, change__
2. Change is yes,__ change is no, Change is ev'-ry-where__
3. Change is high,__ change is low, Chang-es come and chan-

___ is how,_____ Change is this, change is__ that,__
___ you go,_____ Change is right, change is__ wrong,__
- ges go,_____ Change is this, change is__ that,__

Change is where change is__ at,__ } Change is__ good._____
Change is here, change is__ gone,_ } Change is__ good._____
Change is where change is__ at,__ }

2., 3. *Verse 2: to Refrain*
A   *Verse 3: to* %   **Refrain**

good._____ You can change your life,_ find a

new way to_ go,_ You can change your world,_ And you don't e-ven_ know_

Meter Makes a Difference

CONCEPT
METER
SKILLS
SING, LISTEN, READ
LINKS
SOCIAL STUDIES

The words in "The Star-Spangled Banner" were written as a poem after a battle with the British in the War of 1812. Later this poem was set to the melody of a British tune.

Sing "The Star-Spangled Banner" and identify the meter.

 LISTENING CD 5:17

The Star-Spangled Banner Music attributed to J. S. Smith, Words by F. S. Key, arr. by M. Hogan

When a composer rewrites a piece of music for a new performing group, the result is an **arrangement**. Moses Hogan based this vocal arrangement on another arrangement done by Boyz II Men, a popular American singing group.

Sing this inspiring song and listen for the meter.

Boyz II Men

Lift Every Voice and Sing

CD 5:18

Music by Rosamond Johnson
Words by James Weldon Johnson

Lift ev'-ry voice and sing, till earth and heav-en ring,

Ring with the har-mo-nies of lib-er-ty.

Lift Every Voice and Sing by James Weldon Johnson
and J. Rosamond Johnson

Gospel music is a style of religious music, started by African Americans, which includes improvisation and strong feelings. Notice how this gospel arrangement changes the song.

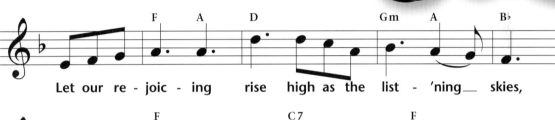

Let our re - joic - ing   rise high as the list - 'ning___ skies,

Let it re - sound loud as the roll - ing sea.

Sing   a   song full of the faith that the dark past has taught us;

Sing   a   song full of the hope that the pres-ent has brought us;

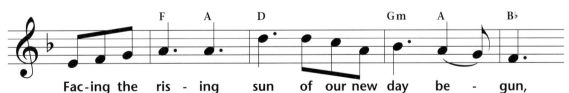

Fac-ing the ris - ing   sun   of our new day   be - gun,

Let   us march on   till vic - to - ry_____ is won.

Meet $\frac{6}{8}$ Meter

"Lift Every Voice and Sing" is exciting to sing. Its strong beat and rhythm fit the deep meaning of the lyrics. This song is in $\frac{6}{8}$ meter.

The dotted quarter note (♩.) receives the beat in $\frac{6}{8}$ **meter**. Each of these beats can be divided into three parts (♪♪♪). When the beats are divided into three parts (♩. = ♪♪♪), the music is in **compound meter**.

Say the words below as you point to the beats.

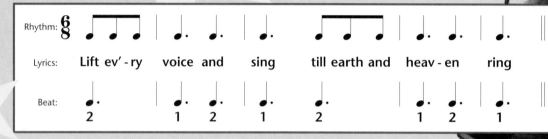

Rhythm:	$\frac{6}{8}$
Lyrics:	Lift ev'-ry voice and sing till earth and heav-en ring
Beat:	2 1 2 1 2 1 2 1

Clap the rhythm of the words while tapping with the beat.

Another song in $\frac{6}{8}$ is "De colores." Through the years the words remained almost the same, but the melody has changed.

De colores

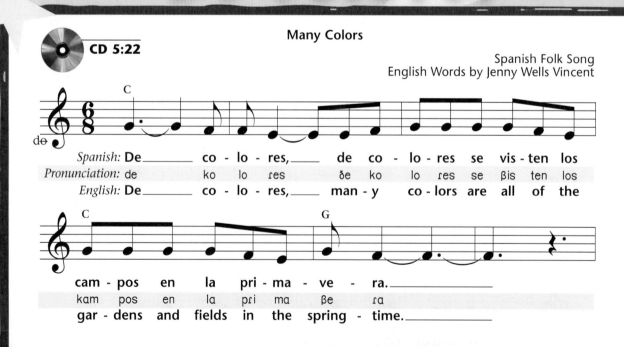

CD 5:22

Many Colors

Spanish Folk Song
English Words by Jenny Wells Vincent

Spanish: De_____ co - lo - res,_____ de co - lo - res se vis - ten los

Pronunciation: de ko lo res ðe ko lo res se βis ten los

English: De_____ co - lo - re,_____ man - y co - lors are all of the

cam - pos en la pri - ma - ve - ra._____

kam pos en la pri ma βe ra

gar - dens and fields in the spring - time._____

THINK!

What other songs do you know that are important to a group of people? Why are they important?

Steps of the Major Scale

"Mango Walk" is a song from Jamaica. You will hear steel drums, which are pitched percussion instruments made from old oil barrels.

Listen for steel drums in "Mango Walk."

Usually a melody is built on a scale and has a tonal center. The tonal center pitch is the letter name of the scale.

Sing "Mango Walk" and identify the final pitch and tonal center.

MAP

CUBA

JAMAICA   HAITI

CD 5:27

Jamaican Calypso

My   moth - er deed - a   tell   me that you   go man - go walk,

you   go man - go   walk,   you   go man - go   walk.

My   moth - er deed - a   tell   me that you   go man - go walk

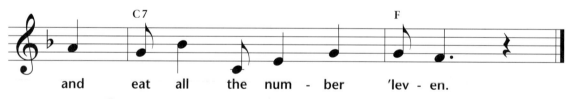

and   eat   all   the   num - ber   'lev - en.

Play these parts with "Mango Walk."

hand drum

bass xylophone

Pitches that move in order without skipping, move in a scalewise manner.

Sing or play these scalewise pitches.

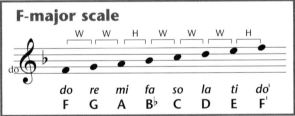

Notice that *fa* and *ti* are not part of a pentatonic scale. A scale that includes the pitches *do re mi fa so la ti do*' is a diatonic scale. When the tonal center of the diatonic scale is *do,* the scale is a **major scale**.

The distance from one pitch to any other pitch is an interval. The smallest interval in most Western music is a **half step**. An interval equal to two half steps is a **whole step**. An interval from one letter name to the very next letter name is a second.

A major scale is a scale made of whole steps and half steps in the order: whole, whole, half, whole, whole, whole, half.

F-major scale

Since the pitches in "Mango Walk" include all the pitches of the major scale and the tonal center, *do,* is on F, the name of its scale and also its key is F major.

steel drums

Add a Major Countermelody

A melody that sounds good with another melody is called a **countermelody** . Notice the scalewise pitches in this countermelody.

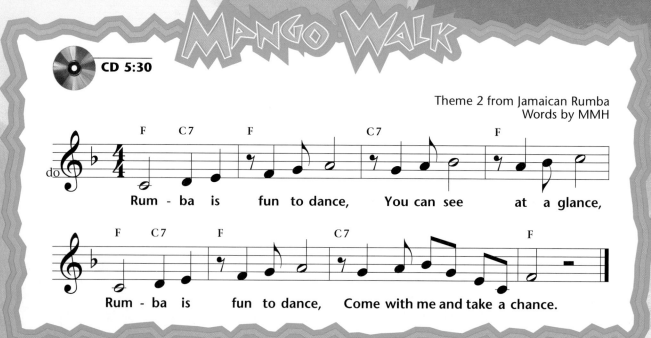

Countermelody for
MANGO WALK

CD 5:30

Theme 2 from Jamaican Rumba
Words by MMH

Rum - ba is fun to dance, You can see at a glance,

Rum - ba is fun to dance, Come with me and take a chance.

LISTENING CD 6:1

Jamaican Rumba by Arthur Benjamin

Arthur Benjamin transformed the melody of "Mango Walk" into Theme 1 of "Jamaican Rumba." The countermelody for "Mango Walk" is similar to Theme 2.

Theme 1

Theme 2

"Jamaican Rumba" uses several orchestral percussion instruments. You will hear three mallet instruments—marimba, vibraphone, and orchestral bells.

marimba

vibraphone

orchestral bells

Listen to "Jamaican Rumba" and follow the listening map.

Listening Map for Jamaican Rumba

CONCEPT
RHYTHM
SKILLS
SING, READ, CREATE, LISTEN
LINKS
SOCIAL STUDIES

⁶⁄₈ Meter and Rhythms

The old English song "Pop! Goes the Weasel" is about a tailor who must *pop* (pawn or sell) his *weasel* (pressing iron) in order to spend "a penny for a spool of thread, a penny for a needle," just to stay in business. What new problem would the tailor have if he sold his weasel?

Sing "Pop! Goes the Weasel" and tap the beat in ⁶⁄₈

CD 6:2

English Ring Game

1. All a-round the cob - bler's bench, The mon-key chased the wea-sel.
2. A half a pound of tu-pen-ny rice, A half a pound of trea-cle.

The mon-key said 'twas all___ in fun.   Pop!   goes the wea-sel.
Mix it up and make_ it nice.   Pop!   goes the wea-sel.

A pen-ny for a spool_of thread, a pen-ny for a nee-dle,
Up and down the Lon - don road,   in and out_of the Ea-gle,

That's the way the mon - ey goes.   Pop!   goes the wea - sel.
That's the way the mon - ey goes.   Pop!   goes the wea - sel.

Two hundred years after the English sang about their money problems in "Pop! Goes the Weasel," pioneers on the plains of America were laughing at their daily hardships in the song "My Government Claim."

Sing "My Government Claim" and tap the beat in $\frac{6}{8}$.

My Government Claim

CD 6:5

English Folk Tune (The Irish Washerwoman)
Traditional Kansas Words

Lively

1. Hur-rah for Lane Coun-ty, the land of the free,___ The
2. My__ house it is built on the na-tion-al soil,___ The
3. My__ clothes they are rag-ged, my lan-guage is rough,_ my

home of the grass-hop-per, bed-bug and flea;___ I'll
walls are e-rect-ed ac-cord-ing to Hoyle;_ The
head is case-hard-ened. It's sol-id and tough;_ But

sing of her prais-es, And boast of her fame;___ A-
roof has no pitch,___ It's lev-el and plain.___ I
I have a good time and live on my ease___ on

starv-ing to death on my gov-ern-ment claim.
al-ways get wet when it hap-pens to rain.
com-mon sop sor-ghum, old ba-con and cheese.

Create and Perform $\frac{6}{8}$ Rhythms

"Pop! Goes the Weasel" and "My Government Claim" have more in common than just their hardships. Look at these rhythm patterns from the two songs:

Look at the meter signatures in the songs. Both songs are in $\frac{6}{8}$ meter. In $\frac{6}{8}$ meter there are two beats in each measure, and each beat is divided into three smaller beats. When two beats in the measure are divided into three parts, it is **compound duple meter**.

Below are four $\frac{6}{8}$ rhythm patterns. Which ones can you find in the songs?

Perform the patterns first with body percussion and then on drums.

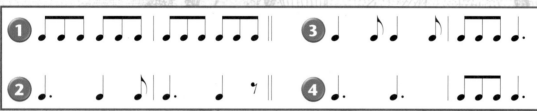

Create a four-measure ostinato using rhythms found in the two songs.

Perform your ostinato as you sing each of the songs.

 LISTENING CD 6:8

Variations on the Theme
"Pop! Goes the Weasel" by Lucien Caillet

"Pop! Goes the Weasel" has been transformed many times during the past four hundred years. In 1938, Lucien Caillet, a French-born American composer, wrote a set of orchestral variations based on this old song. The variations include various historical dances. The "Pop" sound is made with different instruments, including popgun and slide whistle.

Listen for the beat and meter as you follow the listening map for Variations on the Theme "Pop! Goes the Weasel."

Listening Map for Variations on the Theme "Pop! Goes the Weasel"

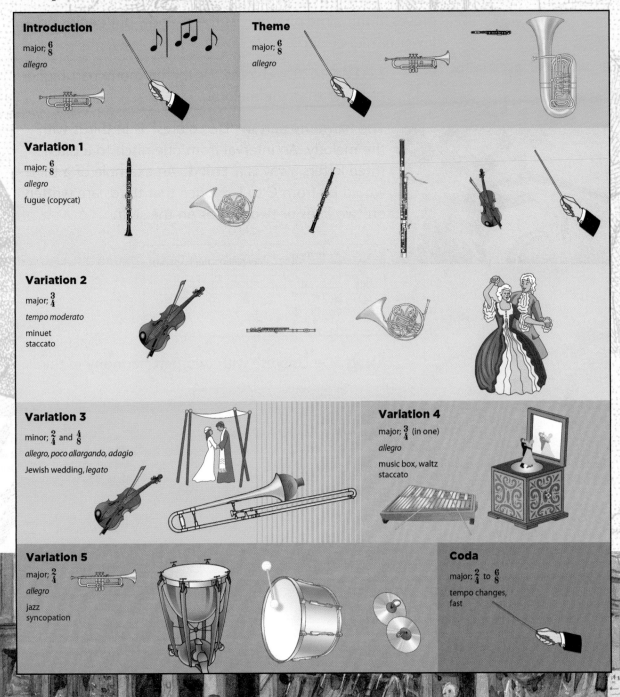

Introduction
major; $\frac{6}{8}$
allegro

Theme
major; $\frac{6}{8}$
allegro

Variation 1
major; $\frac{6}{8}$
allegro
fugue (copycat)

Variation 2
major; $\frac{3}{4}$
tempo moderato
minuet
staccato

Variation 3
minor; $\frac{2}{4}$ and $\frac{4}{8}$
allegro, poco allargando, adagio
Jewish wedding, *legato*

Variation 4
major; $\frac{3}{4}$ (in one)
allegro
music box, waltz
staccato

Variation 5
major; $\frac{2}{4}$
allegro
jazz
syncopation

Coda
major; $\frac{2}{4}$ to $\frac{6}{8}$
tempo changes,
fast

THINK! Can you play your $\frac{6}{8}$ ostinato with any of the variations? Why or why not?

LESSON 4

Transform with Harmony

CONCEPT
HARMONY

SKILLS
SING,
READ

LINKS
FINE ART,
LANGUAGE ARTS

You can transform a song by singing a harmony part. One kind of harmony part is a countermelody such as the one you sang with "Mango Walk." Another kind of harmony part moves in the same direction as the melody, but begins on a lower or higher pitch.

Listen to "De colores." Is the harmony part higher or lower than the melody?

The harmony part in "De colores" is in thirds with the melody. An interval from one pitch to a pitch three letters away is a **third**. An example of a third would be from C to E. Notice that thirds are written on two lines or two spaces on the staff.

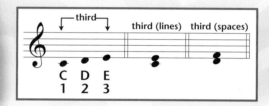

third   third (lines)   third (spaces)

C D E
1 2 3

Sing "De colores" with two-part harmony in thirds.

De colores

Many Colors

CD 5:22

Spanish Folk Song
English Words by Jenny Wells Vincent

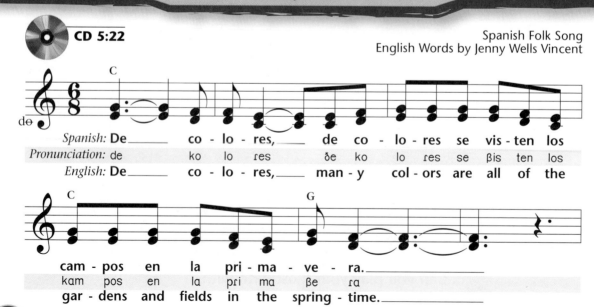

Spanish: De_____ co - lo - res,_____ de co - lo - res se vis - ten los
Pronunciation: de ko lo res ðe ko lo res se βis ten los
English: De_____ co - lo - res,_____ man - y col - ors are all of the

cam - pos en la pri - ma - ve - ra._____
kam pos en la pri ma βe ra
gar - dens and fields in the spring - time._____

98

Sing in Harmony with Thirds

"De colores" is built on the C-major scale. This scale has all the pitches between C and C^{I}, *do* to *do*^{I}. The song also has a pitch that is not part of the C-major scale. This extra note is marked with an accidental. A sharp, flat, or natural sign next to a note and is not in the key signature is an **accidental**.

Accidental	Symbol	What It Does
sharp	♯	raises the pitch a half step
flat	♭	lowers the pitch a half step
natural	♮	removes a sharp or flat

Identify and locate the accidental in the song that is not part of the C-major scale.

Sing the C-major scale with pitch letter names, then with pitch syllables.

Now make the scale longer by singing two notes higher, C to E^{I}, *do* to *mi*^{I}. Sing this longer C-major scale.

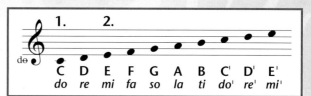

Sing this same scale in two-part canon in thirds. Part 2 starts on C, *do* as Part 1 sings E, *mi*.

Learn About the Rainbow

A rainbow is an arc of colors in the sky. Sunlight passes through water droplets in the air. The light spreads into different colors as it is bent and reflected. Rainbows appear different to each viewer.

Use Colors

Portrait of Dolores Olmeda

This oil painting was created by Diego Rivera (1860–1957) in 1955. Both Rivera and his artist wife Frida Kahlo (1907–1954) were famous Mexican artists. Dolores Olmedo Patino was a Mexican art collector and model for many paintings by Diego Rivera. She turned her hacienda into a museum for the works of Rivera and Kahlo. Notice the many colors in the clothing. Which colors are found in a rainbow? Do you wear the same colors? How is this clothing different from what you normally wear?

Picture the many colors of the rainbow as you read this poem.

COLORES DE CARACOL

Colores de caracol
arco iris en el cielo
es la bandera del sol.

The rainbow showing
through the rain
says the sun
will shine again.

—Ernesto Galarza

Changes in Style

CONCEPT ◄
STYLE

SKILLS
SING, DESCRIBE,
PLAY, LISTEN

LINKS
HISTORY

CD-ROM

Use *Orchestral Instruments* **CD-ROM** to learn more about the instruments of the orchestra.

In 1823 Ludwig van Beethoven included a choral section in his Symphony No. 9. Its famous melody is known as "Ode to Joy."

 LISTENING CD 6:9

Symphony No. 9 in D minor, Op. 125 ("Choral"), Fourth Movement (excerpt)
by Ludwig van Beethoven

A musical work for orchestra, usually with three or four movements, is a **symphony**. This was a popular musical form during the time of Beethoven. This excerpt starts with the orchestra playing the "Ode to Joy" melody. There is a transition and male solo. This leads to the melody sung by the singer, joined by the adult chorus.

Listen for "Ode to Joy" in Beethoven's Symphony No. 9.

The "Ode to Joy" melody was later adapted into a hymn tune. In 1907 Henry van Dyke wrote the words to the hymn "Joyful, Joyful, We Adore Thee." He wanted the words sung to the music of Beethoven's "Ode to Joy." This hymn is still sung today.

Meet the Musician

Ludwig van Beethoven (1770–1827) was a German composer. He began composing when he was eleven years old. As a skilled pianist, Beethoven gave many public performances of his works. Beethoven believed in composing music the way he liked it, rather than conforming to the tastes of his patrons. He wrote nine symphonies and many other types of music. In his mid-twenties, he began to notice problems with his hearing. This became very serious in his early thirties, and by the end of his life he was completely deaf. In spite of this, Beethoven wrote many of his greatest works after he became deaf. He has been a musical hero for many composers.

Sing "Joyful, Joyful, We Adore Thee" and describe what you hear.

Joyful, Joyful, We Adore Thee

CD 6:10

Music Arranged from Ludwig van Beethoven
Words by Henry van Dyke
Words Adapted by Judy Bond

1. Joy - ful, joy - ful we a - dore Thee, God of glo - ry,
2. All Thy works with joy sur - round Thee; Earth and hea - ven re -
3. Mor - tals join the might - y chor - us, Which the morn - ing

God of love, Hearts un - fold like flow - ers be - fore Thee,
flect Thy rays, Stars and an - gels sing a - round Thee,
stars be - gan. All cre - a - tion joins to - geth - er,

Open - ing to the sun a - bove. Melt the clouds of
Cen - ter of un - bro - ken praise. Field and for - est,
Son and daugh - ter, wom - an, man. Ev - er sing - ing,

sin and sad - ness, Drive the dark of doubt a - way.
vale and moun - tain, Flow - 'ring mead - ow, flash - ing sea.
march we on - ward, Vic - tors in the midst of strife.

Giv - er of im - mor - tal glad - ness, Fill us with the light of day.
Chant - ing bird and flow - ing foun - tain, Call us to re - joice in Thee.
Joy - ful mu - sic lifts us sun - ward, In the tri - umph song of life.

Playalong

Play phrases 1, 2, and 4 of the "Ode to Joy" melody on a keyboard.

Style Changes Continue

Beethoven's symphony and "Joyful, Joyful, We Adore Thee" share the same melody. There are big differences in the sound and style, however. These differences reflect the ideas of composers, poets, and performers as well as the time, place, and purpose of the music. The different ways in which the elements of music have been used have created the different styles. Over the past few years, Beethoven's melody has been arranged in very different styles.

The hymn style of "Joyful, Joyful, We Adore Thee" was transformed into a more modern style in "Joyful, Joyful" (from *Sister Act 2: Back in the Habit*). Compare both treatments of Beethoven's original melody. How are they the same and how are they different?

Sing "Joyful, Joyful." Notice how its rhythm, melody, and tempo are different from the original.

THINK! What other musical styles would work well for an arrangement of Beethoven's "Ode to Joy"? What would need to be changed?

Sister Act 2: Neighborhood fund-raiser for students to perform in the state choir competition

Joyful, Joyful

from the movie *Sister Act 2*

Music based on Ludwig van Beethoven's
Symphony No. 9
Words by Henry van Dyke
Arranged by Mervyn Warren

CD 6:13

Joy-ful, joy-ful,__ Lord,__ we a - dore__ Thee. God of glo-ry,__ Lord__ __ of love.__ Hearts un-fold like__ flow-ers be-fore Thee, hail__ Thee__ as the sun a - bove. Melt the clouds of__ sin, sin and sad - ness.__ Drive the__ dark of doubt a - way,__ Giv-er of im - mor - tal glad-ness, fill__ us, fill us with__ the light of__ day. Light of day.

Unit 3 The Old Becomes the New

105

Melodies Use Different Scales

CONCEPT
MELODY
SKILLS
LISTEN,
READ
LINKS
HISTORY

Many composers have used folk melodies as themes in larger works. Sometimes the opposite occurs, and a melody from a larger work is later transformed into a song.

 LISTENING CD 6:16

Largo from Symphony No. 9 in E minor, Op. 95 "From the New World" (excerpt)
by Antonín Dvořák

Antonín Dvořák wrote his great Symphony No. 9 in E minor, "From the New World," while he was living in the United States. The symphony's second movement has a beautiful melody that is well known. The movement is identified by its tempo, **largo**, which means very slow. This symphony gives Dvořák's impressions of America. According to Dvořák, the "Largo" was based on Henry Wadsworth Longfellow's poem "Hiawatha."

Listen for the famous melody in "Largo."

 **THINK!**
What emotions do you think are expressed in "Largo"?

New York City,
late 1800s

 Meet the Musician

Antonín Dvořák (1841–1904) was a very successful and popular Czech composer. He composed many kinds of music, including symphonies, string quartets, and orchestral works. Dvořák included the sounds of Czech folk music in his music. In 1892 and 1893 he lived in New York City where he composed his Symphony No. 9. This symphony reflects the sounds of African American and Native American music. Dvořák's melodies are his own, but they reflect the spirit and style of folk tunes. This style of composition, which included national characteristics and was popular among composers in the late 1800s, is **nationalism**.

Timpani can make longer sounds by playing very fast notes on one pitch. This is called a **roll**. You heard timpani rolls toward the beginning and end of "Largo."

Listen to "Largo" and follow the listening map. Then describe what you heard.

Listening Map for Largo

From Symphony to Song

 **THINK!**

How could Dvořák's "Largo" be transformed?

One of Dvořák's favorite American students was William Arms Fisher. Fisher adapted Dvořák's "Largo" melody so that it would work as a song. Fisher wrote the "Goin' Home" words in the style of a spiritual. William Arms Fisher became a music editor and music historian.

Listen to "Goin' Home" and describe how the music was transformed.

Goin' Home

CD 6:17

Music by Antonín Dvořák (adapted)
Words by William Arms Fisher

Go - in' home, Go - in' home. I'm a - go - in' home;

Qui - et - like, some still day, I'm jes' go - in' home.

It's not far, jes' close by, Through an o - pen door;

Work all done, care laid by, Goin' to fear no more.

Pentatonic or Diatonic Melody?

Look at the last pitch of "Goin' Home" and tell its letter name.
This pitch is *do*.

On the staff at right are the pitches in "Goin' Home."
What are the pitch syllables?

do re mi so la ti do' re' mi'
C D E G A B C' D' E'

Compare the tonal centers, pitches, and use of *fa* and *ti* in "Goin' Home," "Joyful, Joyful, We Adore Thee," and the countermelody for "Mango Walk."

Pitches in "Joyful, Joyful, We Adore Thee"

so, do re mi fa so
D, G A B C D

Pitches in Countermelody for "Mango Walk"

so, la, ti, do re mi fa so
C D E F G A B♭ C

C   G7

Moth - er's there 'spect - in' me,   Fa - ther's wait - in' too;

C   G/B   Am   C   F   C

Lots   o' folk   ga - ther'd there,   All   the friends I knew,

F   C   F   C

All   the friends I knew,   All   the friends I   knew.

LESSON
7

CONCEPT
RHYTHM
SKILLS
SING, CREATE,
PLAY
LINKS
HISTORY,
DANCE

Transform by Adding ⁶⁄₈ Rhythms

Change "My Government Claim" by adding vocal harmony parts.

My Government Claim

CD 6:20

English Folk Tune (The Irish Washerwoman)
Traditional Kansas Words

Lively

1. Hur - rah for Lane Coun - ty, the land of the free,___ The
2. My__ house it is built on the na - tion - al soil,___ The
3. My__ clothes they are rag - ged, my lan - guage is rough,___ my

Gov - ern - ment

Oh, no! Woe is me!

home of the grass - hop - per, bed - bug and flea;___ I'll
walls are e - rect - ed ac - cord - ing to Hoyle;___ The
head is case - hard - ened. It's sol - id and tough;___ But

claim,

my way to

Oh, no! Woe is me!

You can continue to transform "My Government Claim" by adding instrument parts.

Create and perform a two-measure percussion ostinato for "My Government Claim." Use these $\frac{6}{8}$ rhythms: ♫♪ , ♩♪ , ♩. , ♩ ♪

Play vocal Parts 2 and 3 on mallet instruments. For a challenge, play Part 1 also.

sing of her prais - es, And boast of her fame;___ A -
roof has no pitch,___ It's lev - el and plain.___ I
I have a good time and live on my ease___ on

fame! Oh what a

Oh, no! Woe is me!

starv - ing to death on my gov - ern - ment claim.
al - ways get wet when it hap - pens to rain.
com - mon sop sor - ghum, old ba - con and cheese.

shame, this gov - ern - ment claim!

Oh, no! Woe is me!

Unit 3 The Old Becomes the New   111

$\frac{6}{8}$ Rhythms to Dance and Write

A sheet of music in the British Library, dated March 14, 1853, describes a new dance performed at a ball for the Queen. And what was the music? "Pop! Goes the Weasel"! This music, which began as a song about problems of ordinary people, had found its way into the royal court. Noble men and women were dancing to it!

Perform a new version of the dance "Pop! Goes the Weasel."

DANCE FOR "POP! GOES THE WEASEL"

Formation

CD 6:23

A section

Formation: longways set of 6 couples

Two facing lines, boys in one line, girls in the other. Partners standing across from each other.

4 beats: Head couple holds hands and slides down the set.

4 beats: Head couple does two-handed swing around once.

4 beats: Head couple slides back up the set.

4 beats: Everyone claps partner's hands in a double "high five," claps own hands, pats knees twice.

Change the Dance

Describe and explore movements that can be done to "Pop! Goes the Weasel," and notate the rhythm of each movement.

Create and write the rhythm for two eight-beat movement phrases. **Perform** the new movements for the A section followed by the original movements for the B section.

Art Gallery

Princess Baryatinskaya's Ball

This picture is made with watercolor on paper. It is by the Russian artist Grigori Grigorevich Gagarin (1810–1893). The painting shows a ball, which is a large fancy dance. Notice the evening dress and uniforms on the dancers, and the elaborate room. Balls were popular with the nobility in Europe in the 1800s. Have you ever seen a similar ball in a movie, a play, or a picture?

B section

8 beats: Head couple separates, casting off to right and left, leading their lines down outside of set. At the foot, head couple forms an arch.

4 beats: Couple 2 skips under the arch and back up to the head of the set leading rest of students. Couple forming the arch stays at the foot of the set and Couple 2 becomes the new head couple.

4 beats: Everyone does previous clapping pattern.

LESSON
8

CONCEPT
EXPRESSIVE
QUALITIES

SKILLS
SING, DESCRIBE,
LISTEN

LINKS
LANGUAGE ARTS

Express Yourself!

The manner of communicating feeling or meaning through music is called **expression**.

Listen for and look for elements of expression, such as tempo, dynamics, and tone color, in "We Are the Children of Tomorrow."

We Are the Children of Tomorrow

Words and Music by Terre McPheeters

CD 6:24

1. To-geth-er we can make a dif-f'rence.___ To-
2. We can change the land to-geth-er.___ We'll

geth-er we can make a start.___ So put your hand___ in my___
make the world a bet-ter place___ with peace and love___ for-ev-

___ hand, this song comes straight from the heart
-er,___ friend-ship will lead___ the way.___ We'll

Noth-ing can stand___ be-tween___ us.___ U-
teach the next___ gen-er-a-tion.___

nit-ed we___ are strong.___ With you my friend___ be-side___
We be-lieve___ we can.___ Join in our___ cel-e-bra-

Parts 1 and 2 E♭m   G♭   to Coda   D♭   B♭m   G♭   D.S. al Coda

We won't let a thing____ stand in our way.____

Coda   D♭   B♭m

We won't let a thing____

E♭m   G♭   B♭m   E♭m   rit.

____ stand in our way.____   We won't let a thing____

G♭/A♭   rubato   D♭   B♭m   G♭   G♭/A♭   D♭
                    a tempo

____ stand in our way.____

Means of Expression

One means of expression is tempo. You can perform fast or slow or change the tempo for variety.

Tempo	Symbol	Meaning
accelerando	accel.	speed up
ritardando	rit.	slow down
rubato	rubato	take liberties with tempo
fermata	⌢	hold a note longer
a tempo	a tempo	go back to the original tempo

Find *rubato, fermato, ritardando,* and *a tempo* in the song.

Dynamics is another means of expression. You can play loud or soft. You can make a crescendo or a decrescendo (diminuendo).

Find the dynamic markings in the song.

Expression can also be shown with tone color. Specific instruments and voices are used. The way the sound is produced such as a muted trumpet or a raspy alto voice extends the possibilities.

CD-ROM

Use *Orchestral Instruments* **CD-ROM** to learn more about the instruments of the orchestra.

The manner of expressing individual notes is **articulation**. Notes can be connected **(legato)** or detached **(staccato)**. You can play a note louder than other notes **(accent)**.

Describe the articulation in the song.

Find the description of the way the song should be sung.

Sing the song again and add more of these elements of expression.

timpani

 LISTENING CD 6:28

Lift Every Voice and Sing by J. W. and J. R. Johnson, arr. by R. Carter

Roland Carter wrote this arrangement of "Lift Every Voice and Sing." The performance by the Brazeal Dennard Chorale and the Detroit Symphony Orchestra (shown below) is a wonderful example of how a chorus and orchestra perform the expressive qualities in a musical arrangement.

Listen for the wide range of dynamics, tempo changes, tone colors, and articulations in "Lift Every Voice and Sing."

Meet the Musician

Roland Carter (b. 1942) is an African American composer, conductor, and pianist. He has made important contributions to performing and preserving African American music. His arrangement of "Lift Every Voice and Sing" is often used in formal settings.

Spotlight Your Success!

REVIEW

1 What is created when a piece of music is changed so that it has different instruments or voices from the original?

    a. a largo   **b.** an arrangement   **c.** a countermelody

2 What is the style of religious music, started by African Americans, that includes improvisation and strong feelings?

    a. gospel   **b.** symphony   **c.** bluegrass

3 Which diatonic scale has the tonal center of *do*?

    a. minor scale   **b.** pentatonic scale   **c.** major scale

4 What is the interval from one letter name to the very next letter name?

    a. third   **b.** second   **c.** octave

READ AND LISTEN

1 Read these rhythms. Then listen. Which rhythm pattern is in compound meter?

    a.    b.

2 Read these rhythms. Then listen. Which rhythm do you hear?

    a.   b.

3 Read these pitches. Then listen. Which pattern includes *fa* and is the diatonic C-major scale?

    a.   b.

THINK!

1. How are duple and compound duple meter different?

2. Choose a song. How would it sound different without *fa* or *ti*?

3. How has "Ode to Joy" been transformed since it was created?

4. **Write** about a favorite musical change in this unit. What elements were changed and why was it interesting?

CREATE AND PERFORM

1. **Play** or sing the C-major scale in $\frac{4}{4}$ with quarter notes.

2. **Arrange** the scale by changing it in one or more ways. You might change the tone color, rhythm, meter, tempo, or rearrange the pitches. You might add harmony, dynamics, or articulation.

3. **Play** or sing your arrangement.

Meet the Musician

ON NATIONAL RADIO!

Name: Toni Marchioni
Age: 17
Instrument: Oboe
Home Town:
Mechanicsburg, Pennsylvania

One of the worst days in seventeen-year-old Toni Marchioni's life turned out to be one of the luckiest. She was playing field hockey in gym class. During an especially rowdy moment, a hockey stick came down hard on Toni's hand. Her pinky was seriously injured and she required eleven stitches.

As a result of her injury, Toni was unable to play oboe for an entire month. During that time she realized just how much she missed it. "I credit that one field hockey game with helping me decide that music was what I wanted to do for the rest of my life," she explains. "Nothing makes me happier than playing music!"

Toni admits there is one aspect of being an oboist she doesn't especially like: making her own reeds. To make an oboe reed, Toni carves and shapes a piece of cane. Sometimes after she shapes it, it's not quite right and she has to start all over again. "It can take a long time, but it has to be done," states Toni.

LISTENING CD 7:1–2

Concerto in C minor, Second Movement (Adagio)
by Alessandro Marcello

RECORDED INTERVIEW

Listen to Toni's performance and interview on the national radio program **From the Top**.

Spotlight on a Piano Trio

Did You Know?

The instruments in a piano trio are piano, violin, and cello.

Music written for a piano trio is called *chamber music*. Chamber music is meant to be performed by a few musicians in a small space like a home or small auditorium, not a large concert hall.

The piano, violin, and cello all have strings. The piano is a member of the percussion family because the strings are struck rather than plucked or bowed. Unlike violinists and cellists, pianists do not touch the strings with their fingers.

 LISTENING CD 7:3–4

Trio for Piano, Violin, and Cello, Op.11, Third Movement (Presto Leggiero)
by C. Chaminade

Concerto for Piano, Violin, and Cello in C Major, Op. 56 ("Triple Concerto"), Third Movement (excerpt)
by Ludwig van Beethoven

Listen to how Cécile Chaminade uses the high and low voices of violin and cello with the piano. The same combination of solo instruments is used with orchestra in this famous concerto by Beethoven.

UNIT 4

A Tale to Be Told

Often music tells a story or communicates feelings. Read how one poet describes this.

Music

Music is a tale told in sounds
Of such infinite reach
All time, all life, all tongues
Are in its speech.
Music is the sound of events
So moving, in its classic or
    its blue,
The heart nods recognition:
    "I was there.
And I have felt that, too . . ."
        —Mary O'Neill

Coming Attractions

Listen to music that tells stories from different countries.

Sing songs about the Underground Railroad.

Create music using sixteenth notes and triads.

Sometimes, composers write music for stories. Some of these stories have been told for generations. The song "Beauty and the Beast" was composed for the Walt Disney animated film that retells the classic French fairy tale "Beauty and the Beast."

Sing "Beauty and the Beast."

Beauty and the Beast

from the movie *Beauty and the Beast*

CD 7:5

Music by Alan Menken
Lyrics by Howard Ashman

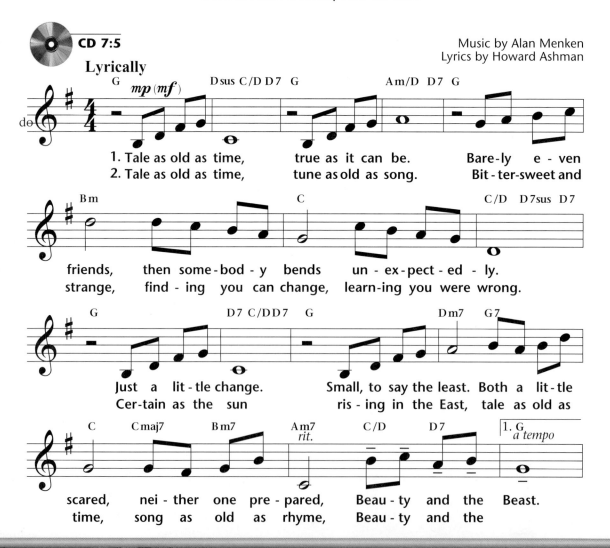

Lyrically

G   *mp* (*mf*)   Dsus C/D D7 G   Am/D D7 G

1. Tale as old as time,   true as it can be.   Bare-ly e - ven
2. Tale as old as time,   tune as old as song.   Bit - ter-sweet and

Bm   C   C/D D7sus D7

friends,   then some-bod - y bends   un - ex-pect - ed - ly.
strange,   find - ing you can change,   learn-ing you were wrong.

G   D7 C/D D7   G   Dm7 G7

Just a lit - tle change.   Small, to say the least. Both a lit - tle
Cer-tain as the sun   ris - ing in the East, tale as old as

C   Cmaj7   Bm7   Am7   C/D   D7   1. G
                         rit.   *a tempo*

scared,   nei - ther one pre - pared,   Beau - ty and the Beast.
time,   song as old as rhyme,   Beau - ty and the

THINK! How does the song "Beauty and the Beast" add to the telling of the story?

Meet the Musicians

Alan Menken (b. 1949), shown at right, is a theater and film composer and **Howard Ashman** (1951–1991) was a lyricist. They are known for their music in Disney's animated movies, such as *The Little Mermaid, Aladdin,* and *Beauty and the Beast.*

 LISTENING CD 7:8

Short Ride in a Fast Machine
by J. Adams

Program music tells a story with sounds. The music suggests images or events. What kind of machine do you think of as you listen to this music?

Listen to "Short Ride in a Fast Machine."

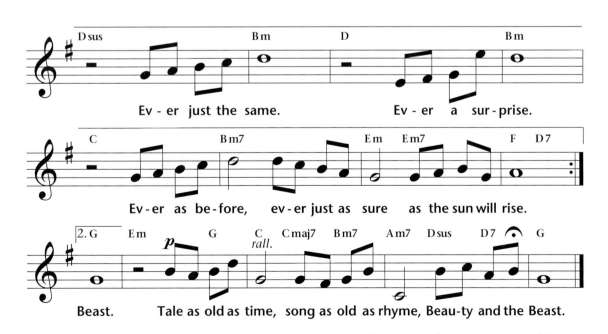

Ev - er just the same.   Ev - er a sur - prise.

Ev - er as be - fore,   ev - er just as sure   as the sun will rise.

Beast.   Tale as old as time, song as old as rhyme, Beau-ty and the Beast.

Moving Rhythms

Spirituals often tell a story. "Joshua Fit the Battle of Jericho" tells of an ancient battle for Jericho, a city near the border between what are today the countries of Israel and Jordan.

Sing "Joshua Fit the Battle of Jericho" and notice the rhythm.

Joshua Fit the Battle of Jericho

CD 7:9
With a swing
Refrain

African American Spiritual

Josh - ua fit the bat-tle of_ Jer - i - cho,_ Jer - i - cho,_ Jer - i - cho._

Last time to Coda

Josh - ua fit the bat-tle of_ Jer - i - cho_ and the walls came tum-bl-in' down.

Verse

1. You may talk a - bout your king of Gid - e - on,_____ You may
2. Up to the walls of Jer - i - cho_____ He_
3. Then the ram horns_ they be - gan to blow,_ And the

talk a - bout your man of Saul. There's none like good ol'
marched with a spear in hand, "Go blow those ram horns,"
trum-pets_ be - gan to sound, Then Josh-ua_com - mand - ed the

D.C. al Coda

Josh - u - a_____ At the bat-tle of Jer - i - cho._
Josh - ua cried,_ "'Cause the bat-tle is in my hand."_
chil-dren_ to shout, And the walls_ came tum-blin' down._

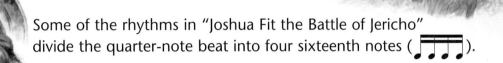

Some of the rhythms in "Joshua Fit the Battle of Jericho" divide the quarter-note beat into four sixteenth notes (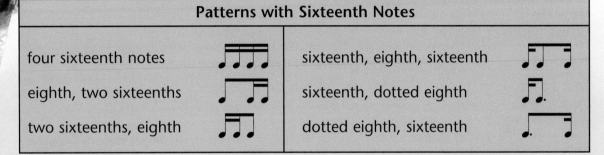).

Patterns with Sixteenth Notes			
four sixteenth notes		sixteenth, eighth, sixteenth	
eighth, two sixteenths		sixteenth, dotted eighth	
two sixteenths, eighth		dotted eighth, sixteenth	

Identify the sixteenth-note patterns in "Joshua Fit the Battle of Jericho."

 LISTENING CD 7:12

Joshua Fit the Battle of Jericho, African American Spiritual

This arrangement, sung by Mahalia Jackson, uses slightly different pitches and rhythms from those that you sang. Listen for the sixteenth notes.

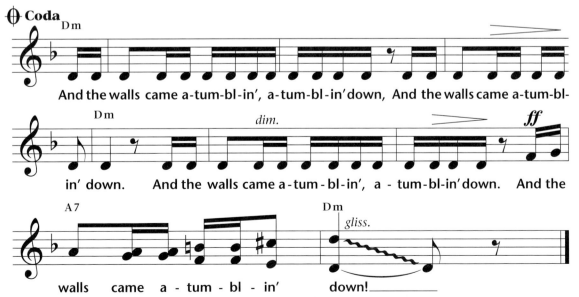

Sixteenths in a Turkish Song

"Üsküdar" is a well-known song in Turkey, a country in southwestern Asia. It was written in the early 1900s. In the verse below, the lyrics give part of a story. Think of what might happen next in the story.

Listen to "Üsküdar" and identify the rhythm patterns with sixteenth notes.

"Üsküdar" and "Joshua Fit the Battle of Jericho" share some of the same rhythms. What pattern in "Üsküdar" is not found in "Joshua Fit the Battle of Jericho"?

Tap the beat with your foot and pat the sixteenth notes with your hands as you listen to "Üsküdar." Then sing the song.

Popular Turkish Folk Song
English Words by MMH

Turkish: Üs - kü - dar' a gi - der_ i ken al - di - da bir yağ mur.
Pronunciation: üs kü dar a gi dɛr i kɛn al di da bir ya mur
English: Üs - kü - dar, a dis - tant_ cit - y. I walk a-long the road.

Ka - ti - bi - min se - tre - si u - zun e - te - gi - ça -
ka ti bi min sɛ trɛ si u zun ɛ te gi ja
On a rain - y morn - ing____ there_ I_ met_ my_

mur. e - te - gi - ça - mur.
mur ɛ te gi ja mur
friend there_ I____ met____ my____ friend.

Another way to experience sixteenth notes is by dancing. Prepare for this dance by walking to the beat during "Üsküdar."

1 Preparation

Formation: Circle, holding hands, facing CCW
Movement: Walk CCW, starting with the left foot.

2 Dance

Formation: Circle, holding hands at shoulder height, facing counterclockwise
Movement:
Beat 1: Left foot step forward (CCW)
Beat 2: Right foot step back (CW) then do a small hop
Beat 3: Left foot step forward (CCW)
Beats 4–8: Continue stepping forward (CCW)
Repeat beats 1–8 for the entire song.

With practice you will be able to dance as you sing the song.

Play an ostinato with "Üsküdar."

Playalong

Üsküdar Station, Istanbul, Turkey ▼

History in a New Key

CONCEPT
TONALITY
SKILLS
LISTEN, SING
LINKS
HISTORY

Music with *la* as the tonal center is in a **minor key**. A diatonic scale with *la* as the tonal center is a **minor scale**. A minor key is based on minor scale. A key can set the musical mood.

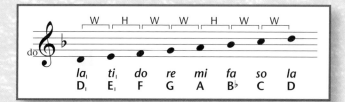

Ride Like the Wind

🔘 **CD 7:17**

Music and Words by Mary Donnelly
Arranged by George L.O. Strid

Spirited

1. He was just fif-teen and an or-phan child.
(2. It was) pour-ing rain when he left St. Joe,

Ride like the wind!__ { He was lean and lank and a
And he had one hun-dred__

lit-tle wild._____
miles to go._____

Ride like the wind!__ { He
Through

want-ed to put__ his cour-age to the test;__ he
per-ils and dan-gers on the West-ern trail__ he

Minor and Major Keys

The teenager riding for the Pony Express in "Ride like the Wind" had a very different life story than that of the mule driver in "Erie Canal." Picture yourself as a mule driver in upstate New York sometime between 1825 and 1850. Your mule is towing a flat-bottomed boat along the Erie Canal.

Sing "Erie Canal," listening for the part that is in minor.

CD 7:22

Thomas S. Allen

Freely

1. I got a mule, her name is Sal, Fif-teen miles on the
2. Git up there Sal, we passed that lock, Fif-teen miles on the

E - rie Ca - nal!__ She's a good old work-er and a good old pal,
E - rie Ca - nal!__ And__ we'll make Rome__ 'fore_ six o-'clock,

Fif-teen miles on the E - rie Ca - nal!__ We've hauled some barg - es
Fif-teen miles on the E - rie Ca - nal!__ Just one more trip and

in our day, Filled with lum-ber, coal and hay, And we know ev'-ry
back we'll go, Through the rain and sleet and snow, 'Cause we know ev'-ry

inch of the way From Al - ba-ny__ to__ Buf - fa-lo.__
inch of the way From Al - ba-ny__ to__ Buf - fa-lo.__

Erie Canal at Little Falls, New York

This oil on canvas painting was created in 1884 by William Rickarby Miller (1818–1893). What object is the center of interest? How does the painter draw your eye to that object?

A minor key with the same key signature as the major key three half steps higher is the **relative minor**. A major key with the same key signature as the minor key three half steps lower is the **relative major**. Compare F major and D minor.

F-major scale

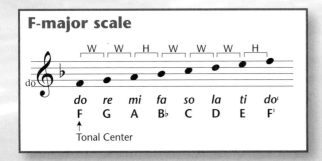

D-minor scale

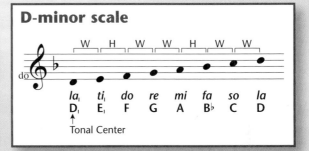

Refrain

Low bridge, ev'-ry-bod-y down, Low bridge, 'cause we're com-ing to a town;

And you'll al - ways know your neigh - bor, You'll al - ways know your pal,

If you ev - er nav - i - gat - ed on the E - rie Ca - nal.

Unit 4 A Tale to Be Told

Story Rhythms

CONCEPT
RHYTHM
SKILLS
CREATE, SING, MOVE
LINKS
SOCIAL STUDIES, DANCE

Whether a song retells a folk tale or a battle story, it has rhythm. Often the rhythms are determined by the words. In "Üsküdar," the rhythm of the lyrics *I walk a-long the road* follows the rhythm of the words as you would speak them.

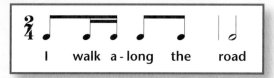

The word *Üsküdar* uses a dotted eighth and sixteenth rhythm followed by an eighth note.

Üs - kü - dar

The **dotted eighth and sixteenth** (♩▭) lasts for one beat.

$$♩. ♪ = ♬♬ = \tfrac{3}{4} \text{ beat}, \tfrac{1}{4} \text{ beat}$$

Other times the words are made to fit the rhythms. On the words *dis-tant cit-y*, each of the first two syllables is sung with two sixteenth notes. These notes are connected with a **slur** (⌣), which means the notes are connected smoothly. When a slur is sung, a single syllable sounds on more than one note.

dis - tant cit - y

Find other English words in "Üsküdar" that have two or more sixteenth notes for each syllable.

Anatolian musicians and dancers at Topkapi Palace, Istanbul, Turkey

The rhythms in both "Üsküdar" and "Joshua Fit the Battle of Jericho" feature eighth notes and sixteenth notes. Find the rhythms that are the same in both songs.

Play this ostinato with "Üsküdar."

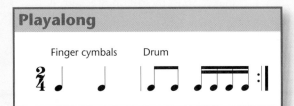

Goreme Muslim woman making carpet, Cappadocia, Turkey

Compose a four-beat ostinato from the rhythms you found in both songs or from the rhythms given below. Perform your ostinato with the two songs.

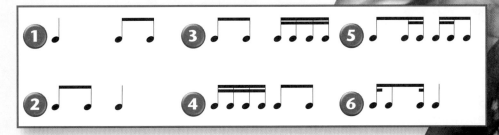

THINK! Does your ostinato work equally well with each song? Why or why not?

Art Gallery

Turkish Carpet

Turkish carpets often have distinctive styles that identify them with particular areas. Some designs have been handed down for generations. These carpets provide three purposes: home furnishing, religious, and/or artistic. The most valuable carpets have the most knots per square inch. Carpets are part of the cultural tradition of Turkey.

Simple Gifts

CD 8:1

Shaker Song by Joseph Brackett, Jr.

'Tis the gift to be sim-ple, 'tis the gift to be free,

'Tis the gift to come down where we ought to be.

And when we find our-selves in the place just right,

'Twill be in the val-ley of love and de-light.

When true sim - pli - ci - ty is gained,

To bow and to bend we shan't be a-shamed.

To turn, turn will be our de-light,

Till by turn-ing, turn-ing we come 'round right.

Notice the eighth-and-sixteenth patterns, including the dotted eighth and sixteenth pattern in "Simple Gifts." Sometimes the patterns are written with beams and sometimes with flags.

"Simple Gifts" is the musical expression of a religious group called Shakers. In the middle 1800s, Shakers would have danced to some of their religious songs as they sang them during their church services. Shakers also believed in a simple life.

"Simple Gifts" Dance
Formation: Form column of boys and column of girls. Each column faces the other. Columns are made up of rows of three students, side by side. All phrases start with the right foot. All steps to the beat, except the "tip tap."

Dance

A Section (Measures 1–8)

Measures 1–2: 3 steps forward and close
Measures 3–4: 4 steps to circle right in place
Measures 5–6: 3 steps backward and close
Measures 7–8: 4 steps to circle left, in place

B Section (Measures 9–16)

Measure 9: step-close-step ♪♪♪ (tip tap)
Measure 10: step-close-step ♪♪♪
Measures 11–12: 2 beats to bow, 2 beats to straighten up
Measures 13–14: 4 steps to circle right
Measures 15–16: 4 steps to circle left

Interlude: (Measures 17–18) 4 counts to face forward in original position.

Coda (4 measures) Bow at the end of the third time through.

Create a four-beat percussion ostinato for the B section using rhythms from the song. Include eighth and sixteenth notes.

Perform the song in three groups: one singing, one dancing, one playing the percussion ostinato.

Art Gallery

Shakers Near Lebanon
This lithograph was produced by Nathaniel Currier and James Ives in 1872 from a stipple-and-line engraving created around 1830.

LOG ON

To research Shakers, see **music** **.mmhschool.com**

LESSON 4

Triad Messages

CONCEPT
MELODY

SKILLS
SING, IMPROVISE, PLAY

LINKS
CULTURES

Story songs can be about many different topics. In the Scottish song "Loch Lomond," the singer remembers a *bonnie* (beautiful) place. As you listen to the song, picture yourself sitting on the banks of that *loch* (lake).

Is "Loch Lomond" in major or minor?

MAP

NORTHERN IRELAND
SCOTLAND
IRELAND
ENGLAND
WALES

LOCH LOMOND

CD 8:4

Scottish Folk Song
Words attributed to Lady John Scott

do

F — Dm — B♭ — C

1. By____ yon bon - nie banks and by yon bon - nie braes,
2. 'Twas____ there that we part - ed in yon shad - y glen,
3. The____ wee bird - ies sing and the wild flow - ers spring,

F — Dm — B♭ — Am

Where the sun shines bright on Loch Lo - mond;
On the steep, steep side o' Ben Lo - mond,
An' in sun - shine the wa - ters are sleep - in';

B♭ — F — B♭

Where me and my true love were ev - er wont to gae,
where pur - ple in hue____ the Hie - land hills we view,
But the bro - ken heart it kens____ nae, se - cond spring a - gain,

F — B♭ — C — F

On the bon - nie, bon - nie banks of Loch Lo - mond.
And the moon____ com - ing out in the gloam - in.
And the wae - fu' may____ cease frae their greet - in',

138

Three or more pitches sounding together form a **chord**. A chord with three pitches is a **triad**. A triad is formed of two thirds. The pitches of a triad can sound separately, as a melody, or can sound at the same time, as a chord.

Find the highlighted triads in the song and sing them. What are the letter names of those pitches?

Improvise Using Triads

Triads can be major or minor. Sing the pitches of these minor and major triads. Notice the difference in the way half and whole steps are organized in the thirds.

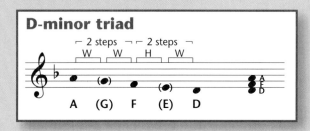

D-minor triad

⌐ 2 steps ¬ ⌐ 2 steps ¬
W   W   H   W

A   (G)   F   (E)   D

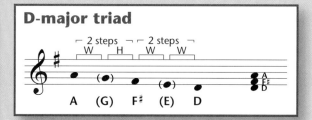

D-major triad

⌐ 2 steps ¬ ⌐ 2 steps ¬
W   H   W   W

A   (G)   F♯   (E)   D

Find the D-minor triad in "Ride like the Wind."

Find the D-major triad in "Simple Gifts."

Let's Improvise

To make up the music as you perform it is to **improvise**. Improvise a "triad message" with pitches found in "Ride like the Wind," "Simple Gifts," or "Loch Lomond."

1 Create a two-line poem. Repeat the words until you find an easy rhythm. Say these words and rhythms of a sample triad message.

Ride   like   the   wind   through the   star - ry   night,

Ride   like   the   wind,   Hold   on   tight.

2 Choose pitches of a D-minor triad if your message is from a Pony Express rider, pitches of a D-major triad if it is from a young Shaker, or pitches from an F-major triad if it is from Scottish person.

3 Sing or play the word rhythms of your message on one pitch of your triad. Repeat on two pitches, then on all three. Sing or play the pitches in any order. Use repeated notes, skips, or leaps. End on the bottom pitch of the triad, the **root**. Play or sing these sample patterns to get ideas.

please come vis - it

repeated notes

please come vis - it

skip

please come vis - it

leap

Improvise your melody.

Three Songs Tell One Story

CONCEPT
BACKGROUND
SKILLS
SING, LISTEN
LINKS
SOCIAL STUDIES

The Underground Railroad was a secret system of safe houses in the 1800s. It helped enslaved African Americans escape to the North. "Follow the Drinkin' Gourd" is a code song that instructed enslaved people to follow the Big Dipper (drinking gourd) constellation. From this constellation they could find the North Star, which pointed north.

FOLLOW THE DRINKIN' GOURD

CD 8:7

Traditional African American
Adapted by Paul Campbell

Slowly, but rhythmically

1. When the sun comes back and the first quail calls,___
2. Now the riv-er bank-'ll make__ a might-y good road;___ The
3. Now the riv - er ends__ be - tween two hills;___

Fol - low_____ the Drink - in' Gourd.__ Then the
dead trees - 'll show you the way. And the
Fol - low_____ the Drink - in' Gourd.__ And____

Old Man is a - wait - in' for to car - ry you to
left____ foot,__ peg - foot,__ trav - el - in'____
there's an - oth - er riv - er on the oth - er____

free - dom,__ Fol - low the Drink - in' Gourd.
on; just you fol - low the Drink - in' Gourd.
side, just you fol - low the Drink - in' Gourd.

Listen to "Follow the Drinkin' Gourd" and identify the tonal center and key.

The meter that has two beats in a measure and the half note getting one beat is **cut time**. Find the cut time (¢) meter signature. Cut time is also shown as $\frac{2}{2}$. Sing "Follow the Drinkin' Gourd," noticing the feeling of cut time.

Play or sing this syncopated ostinato with "Follow the Drinkin' Gourd."

Drink-in' gourd

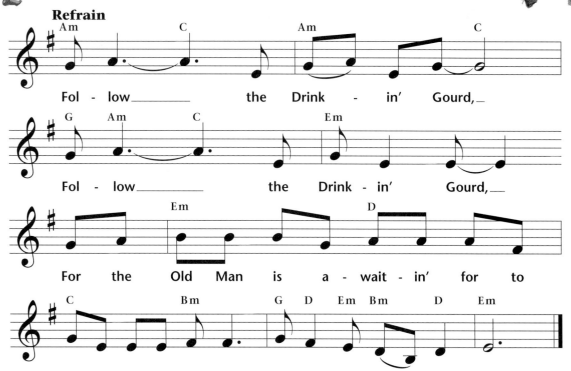

Refrain

Fol - low_____ the Drink - in' Gourd,_

Fol - low_____ the Drink - in' Gourd,_

For the Old Man is a - wait - in' for to

car - ry you to free - dom, Fol - low the Drink - in' Gourd.

Unit 4 A Tale to Be Told 143

The Story Continues

Bloodhounds were often used to pick up the scent of escaping enslaved African Americans. By "wading in the water," these people would throw the dogs off their trail. This is one of the meanings of the words to "Wade in the Water." Originally songs like this were learned "by ear" and passed from one person to another.

 LISTENING CD 8:10

Wade in the Water
(African American Spiritual)
arr. by M. Hogan

As spirituals became part of the American folk tradition, arrangers started making new settings of these songs. This arrangement is for a four-part adult choir made up of sopranos, altos, tenors, and basses. The choir performs **a cappella**, which means without instrumental accompaniment.

Listen to the choral arrangement of "Wade in the Water."

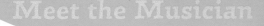
Meet the Musician

Moses Hogan (1957–2003) was a composer, pianist, conductor, and arranger. He is well known for his arrangements of spirituals. Hogan created the arrangement of "Wade in the Water" that you heard. His Moses Hogan Chorale has performed at many famous concert halls.

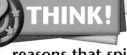 **THINK!** What might be the reasons that spirituals were originally sung a cappella?

144

Harriet Tubman was one of the most famous conductors of the Underground Railroad. She led hundreds of enslaved African Americans to freedom. "The Ballad of the Underground Railroad" tells a story of her work.

Sing only the refrain of "The Ballad of the Underground Railroad" as you listen to the complete song.

The Ballad of the Underground Railroad

CD 8:11

Words and Music by René Boyer-Alexander

Allegro with enthusiasm

Refrain

The Un - der - ground Rail - road, the Un - der - ground Rail - road,

ev' - ry - bod - y get on board! ___ So,

come on chil - dren, we're bound for free - dom. We'll

make it by the help of the Lord. _____

Tales in Different Cultures

CONCEPT ▶
CULTURAL CONTEXT
SKILLS ▶
SING, LISTEN
LINKS ▶
CULTURES

There are many ways a song can tell a tale. One way is through the lyrics. A poem or song that tells a story with short simple verses is a **ballad**. It has a setting, characters, plot, and mood. "John Henry" is a ballad that tells the story of a man against a machine. Discover who won the contest and at what price.

MIDI

For another activity with "John Henry," see *Spotlight on MIDI*.

John Henry

CD 8:16

West Virginia Folk Ballad

Vocal Introduction

C   Am

do   Lis-ten to my sto-ry.___ 'Tis a sto-ry___ true,

C

'Bout a might-y man, John Hen-ry was his name,

C

Hen-ry was a steel-dri-ver too, Lord, Lord,

C/G   C

Hen-ry was a steel-dri-ver too.

Verse

C

1.,5. Now the man that in-vent - ed the steam drill   He
2. Well, the Cap-tain said___ to John___ Hen-ry,
3. Well, John Hen-ry said_____ to the Cap-tain,   "A
4. John___ Hen-ry told_____ his___ Cap-tain,

thought___ he was might_____ fine;
"Gon - na bring that steam drill 'round.
man_____ ain't_____ no - thin' but a man;
"Look - a yon - der what I see.

But John Hen - ry___ drove_____ fif - teen__ feet
Gon - na bring that_____ steam_ drill___ out___ on the job.
But be - fore I'd let your steam_ drill___ beat__ me___ down,
Your__ drill's_ done_ broke_ and your holes__ done_ choke,

The steam___ drill___ on - ly made___ nine, Lord, Lord, The
____ Gon - na whup that steel_ on___ down, Lord, Lord,___
I'd die_____ with a ham-mer in my hand, Lord, Lord, I'd
It can't___ drive_ steel_ like___ me, Lord, Lord, It

D.S. to Verse

steam_____ drill_____ on - ly made___ nine.
Gon - na whup that steel_____ on_____ down."
die_____ with a ham - mer in my hand."
can't____ drive____ steel_____ like_____ me."

6. John Henry hammered in the mountains,
   His hammer was striking fire;
   But he worked so hard it broke his poor heart,
   And he laid down his hammer and he died, Lord, Lord . . . .

7. They took John Henry to the graveyard,
   And they buried him in the sand;
   And ev'ry engine comes a-roaring by
   Whistles, "There lies a steel-driving man, Lord, Lord . . . .

8. Well, every Monday morning,
   When the bluebirds begin to sing,
   You can hear John Henry a mile or more.
   You can hear his hammer ring, Lord, Lord . . . .

Another Tale with a Hammer

"John Henry" and "Anvil Chorus" have similar topics. In each, mountains provide the setting as workers swing their hammers. In "Anvil Chorus," gypsy men sing as they work with hammer and anvil.

"Anvil Chorus" from *Il Trovatore*

 LISTENING CD 8:19

Anvil Chorus from *Il Trovatore* by Giuseppe Verdi

"Anvil Chorus" is part of a longer story told in the Italian opera *Il Trovatore*, or "The Troubador." This opera was written in 1853. It has an exciting plot with dreadful events and a sad ending, and it includes famous arias and choruses.

Listen for the ring of hammers in "Anvil Chorus."

Meet the Musician

Giuseppe Verdi (1813–1901) was a popular Italian opera composer. Verdi played organ as a child. He then became a town music master. Verdi had a gift for writing stirring melodies. He wanted to show the full force of an opera's drama in his music. Besides writing operas, he often directed them. Verdi was concerned about Italy's struggle for freedom and unity. He was involved in Italian politics, eventually becoming a senator.

Instrumental sounds create a musical atmosphere. Lyrics give some details of a story. You fill out the story in your mind. What story ideas do the lyrics of "Kojo No Tsuki" suggest to you?

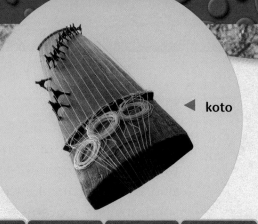

Sing "Kojo No Tsuki" and listen for the koto.

◀ koto

MAP
RUSSIA
CHINA
NORTH KOREA
JAPAN
SOUTH KOREA

Kojo No Tsuki
Moon at the Ruined Castle

CD 8:20

Music by Rentaro Taki
Words by Doi Bansui
English Words by Audrey Snyder

Legato

Japanese: は ろ こ う ろ う の は な の え れ
Pronunciation: ha ɾu ko ɾo no ha na no e ŋ
English: In the moon-light sha - dows the ru - ined cas - tle dims,

め ぐ ろ け か ず ほ か げ け し て
me gu ɾu sa ka zu ki ka ge sa shi te
Once in sun-lit splen - dor, it now no long - er glows.

ち よ の ま つ が ゑ わ け い で し
chi yo no ma tsu ga e wc ke i de shi
Lone - ly are the an - cient pines, re - call - ing bright - er days.

む か し の ひ か り い ま い で こ
mu ka shi no hi ka ɾi i ma i zu ko
Where is the glo - ry now, that light from long a - go?

Play these parts with "Kojo No Tsuki."

4   Recorder   Keyboard

Unit 4 A Tale to Be Told (149)

Tales in Movement

CONCEPT
CULTURAL CONTEXT

SKILLS
LISTEN, SING,
MOVE

LINKS
DANCE,
CULTURES

Use **World Instruments CD-ROM** to learn more about instruments of Oceania.

Global Voices

Some music uses movement to help tell a story. Music is very important in the Maori culture. People sing about events of everyday life, and many of the songs include movement.

🔘 LISTENING CD 9:1

Ake Tonu Maori Song

"Ake Tonu" is a Maori welcome song from New Zealand. Movement helps the singers express the meaning of the song.

Tena koutou e nga ropu ë (Boys: püpü pu ta)
Kei te mihi tonu i runga (e) te aroha
Ko wai mätou (e) karanga nei
Ngä tamariki o whanau Awhina' ë
Powhiritia, karangatia,
Tena koutou (Boys: ngä tängata)

Greetings to you. We greet you in love. Who are we? We are the children of Te Whanau Awhina'. Welcoming, calling, and greeting you.

Listen to "Ake Tonu." What kind of movements fit the music and meaning of the song?

🔘 LISTENING CD 9:2

Po Atarau Maori Song

One of the most famous Maori songs has a mixed-up history! This farewell song started in 1913 as a piano piece. Maori words were added and the meter changed to become "Po Atarau." The lyrics were changed further, making it "Haere Ra." In 1948 it had become the Top Ten song "Now Is the Hour."

MAP

AUSTRALIA

NEW ZEALAND

Sing "Haere Ra"
(Now Is the Hour).

Haere Ra

Now Is the Hour

Music by Maewa Kaihan
Based on "Swiss Cradle Song" by Clement Scott
Maori Words Traditional and by Maewa Kaihan
English Words as sung by Bing Crosby

CD 9:3

Refrain

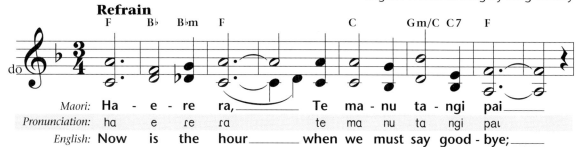

Maori:	Ha	- e - re	ra,	Te	ma - nu	ta - ngi	pai
Pronunciation:	ha	e ɾe	ɾa	te	ma	nu	ta	ngi	paɪ
English:	Now	is	the hour	when we	must say	good - bye;

E	hae - re	a - na,	Koe ki	pa - ma - mao.
e	hae ɾe	a na	kwe ki	pa ma mao
Soon	you'll be	sail - ing	far a - cross the	sea.

Ha	- e - re	ra,	Ka	ho - ki mai	a - no,
ha	e ɾe	ɾa	ka	ho ki maɪ	a no
While	you're a - way,	O,	then re - mem - ber	me,

Ki	- te tau,	E	ta - ngi	a - tu	nei.
ki	te to	e	ta ngi	a	tu	neɪ
When	you re - turn,	you'll find	me	wait - ing	here.

A Story Without Words

You have learned that a ballad is a song that tells a story. But even without words, music can tell a story. One art form that tells a story through music and movement is **ballet**. Aaron Copland wrote several ballets.

Martha Graham, noted innovator in modern dance, as the young bride in her ballet *Appalachian Spring* ▼

Meet the Musician

Aaron Copland (1900–1990) was an American composer. He learned to play piano from his older sister. Copland studied composition in New York City and then in France. He tried to find a serious style that sounded American, rather than European. Some of his music was based on American life, such as the ballets *Billy the Kid* and *Appalachian Spring.* Other works used elements of jazz, folk music, and other twentieth-century styles. Copland wrote music for ballets, orchestral music, choral music, and movie scores. He also conducted, gave lectures, taught, and wrote books. Copland helped make modern American classical music more popular.

 **LISTENING** CD 9:8

Variations on "Simple Gifts" from *Appalachian Spring*
by Aaron Copland

Aaron Copland wrote this ballet score, and the dancer Martha Graham choreographed it. Graham gave the ballet its name, *Appalachian Spring*. The ballet, first performed in 1944, celebrates a newly married pioneer couple moving into a home built for them by people in their community. The spirit of working together and helping each other is expressed through movement and music. Copland used "Simple Gifts" as the theme for several variations.

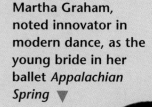

152

Martha Graham performs her signature dance, *Appalachian Spring*, at a theater in Manhattan, 1944. ▶

Listen to Variations on "Simple Gifts" and follow the listening map.

Listening Map for Variations on "Simple Gifts"

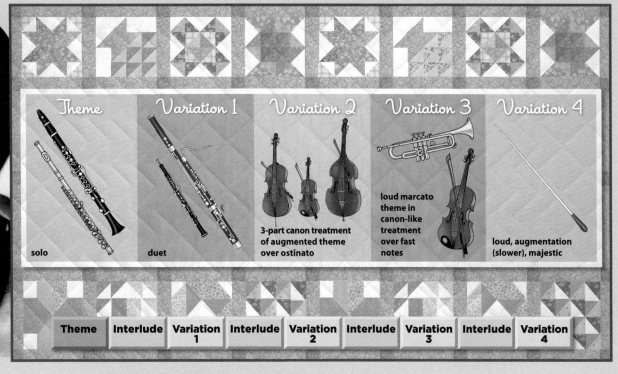

Theme	Variation 1	Variation 2	Variation 3	Variation 4
solo	duet	3-part canon treatment of augmented theme over ostinato	loud marcato theme in canon-like treatment over fast notes	loud, augmentation (slower), majestic

Theme	Interlude	Variation 1	Interlude	Variation 2	Interlude	Variation 3	Interlude	Variation 4

Improvise a Dance

Perform "Simple Gifts" and its dance.

Improvise movement for Variations on "Simple Gifts." Use the "Simple Gifts" dance as a starting point to improvise movement during the orchestral variations. Show the changes you hear in the music. Use different movements for each variation.

Texture Gets Thicker

CONCEPT
TEXTURE
SKILLS
SING
LINKS
SOCIAL STUDIES

Picture Harriet Tubman traveling from plantation to plantation collecting enslaved people who want to escape to freedom.

Songs that can be sung at the same time are **partner songs**. They sound good together because they use the same harmony. Variants of "Follow the Drinkin' Gourd" and "Wade in the Water" are partner songs within "The Ballad of the Underground Railroad." Listen for the different textures in this song.

The Ballad of the Underground Railroad

CD 8:11

Allegro

Words and Music by René Boyer-Alexander

The Un-der-ground Rail - road, the Un-der-ground Rail - road,

ev'-ry-bod-y get on board! So, come on chil - dren, we're

bound for free - dom. We'll make it by the help of the Lord.

1. The

2., 3., 4., 5.   to Verse   6.   to Coda

We'll

2. The
3. They
4. The

B Verse

1. Har-ri-et Tub-man showed them where to ___ go. ___ She
slaves be-came the pas-sen-gers on board the Free-dom train. The
let the North Star guide them there be-neath the drink-in' gourd, that was
wa-ter cov-ered signs of them; their smells and scents were gone. The

led them through the wil-der-ness, ev'-ry-one should know. She
jour-ney was most chal-leng-ing, not ea-sy to ex-plain. They
out-lined oh, so clear-ly by their great and power-ful Lord, When the
pow'r of song ___ saved their souls, but chilled them to the bones. The con-

was a might-y wom-an ___ who al-ways said, "I can." She
slept by day and moved by night, this seemed the on-ly way! Through
sounds of dogs came near-er, you could hear a qui-et hum, to
duc-tor would ___ soon ar-rive, her car-go safe in hand, in a

Verse 1 D.S. refrain to 3rd ending
Verse 2 D.S. refrain to 4th ending
Verse 3 to C
Verse 4 to ◇D

did her best to lead the slaves from E-gypt's ___ land. ___ The
wind and rain, ___ cold and heat, they slept in fields of hay! The
wade in the wa-ter chil-dren, in the wa-ter you'll o-ver-come.
place where slaves would all be free like an-y oth-er man.

More

Unit 4 A Tale to Be Told

155

Notice the harmony in the verse. This harmony uses two intervals, the third and the fourth. A fourth is the distance between two pitches that are four pitches apart. Count the first pitch as "one."

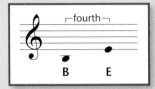

Notice the harmony at letter . It uses two different chords.

Practice singing the first chord, then the second chord.

For a challenge, sing the whole song with all the parts.

THINK! What is the easiest part of the song to sing? The most difficult? Why?

Learn About Harriet Tubman

Harriet Tubman (c.1820–1913) was born into slavery in Maryland. Around 1844 she ran away from the plantation, afraid that she would be sold. In Philadelphia, Tubman found a job, saved her money, and returned to Maryland to take her sisters to freedom. During a ten-year period, Tubman made nineteen perilous trips into the South, bringing 300 enslaved African Americans to freedom. Harriet Tubman became known as "Moses" and is perhaps the most famous of all the Underground Railroad's "conductors."

Spotlight Your Success!

REVIEW

1 What note values are in this rhythm?

   a. half, quarter, quarter

   b. eighth, sixteenth, sixteenth

   c. dotted eighth, sixteenth, whole

2 How many sixteenth notes fit in one quarter note?

   a. 2   **b.** 3   **c.** 4   **d.** 16

3 What kind of chord is made up of three pitches?

   a. root   **b.** chord pattern   **c.** triad

4 What kind of key has half steps between steps 2 and 3 and 5 and 6?

   a. minor   **b.** pentatonic   **c.** major   **d.** tonal

5 Which chord is minor?

   a. *do mi so*   **b.** *la do mi*   **c.** *fa la do*

READ AND LISTEN

1 **Read** these rhythms. Then listen. Which rhythm do you hear?

   a.   **b.**

2 **Read** these rhythms. Then listen. Which rhythm do you hear?

   a.    **b.**

3 **Read** these pitches. Then listen. Which scale is minor?

  a. *do re mi fa so la ti do*ᴵ

  b. *la, ti, do re mi fa so la*

  c. *so la do re mi so*ᴵ *la*ᴵ *do*ᴵ

THINK!

1 What is the difference between a ballad and a ballet?

2 Can you sing a triad with others? How did that make you feel?

3 What uses could you find for relative minor and relative major keys?

4 **Write** Choose a story song and tell its story in your own words.

CREATE AND PERFORM

1 Choose a major or minor triad.

2 **Create** an eight-beat rhythm that uses at least two sixteenth-note patterns.

3 Select pitches from your triad for the rhythm.

4 **Play** or sing your piece.

FROM THE TOP

Meet the Musician

ON NATIONAL RADIO!

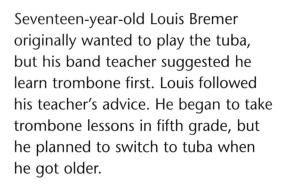

Name: Louis Bremer
Age: 17
Instrument: Bass Trombone
Home Town: Kingsport, Tennessee

Seventeen-year-old Louis Bremer originally wanted to play the tuba, but his band teacher suggested he learn trombone first. Louis followed his teacher's advice. He began to take trombone lessons in fifth grade, but he planned to switch to tuba when he got older.

The more Louis played trombone, the more he enjoyed it. He tried bass trombone, which has a similar range to a tuba, and before long, Louis didn't want to play tuba anymore. "The bass trombone has a nice mellow sound, and it's exciting," he declares.

Louis loves playing in his school band. "There are over 300 people in the band," says Louis. "It's huge!" He feels lucky to go to a school where so many people play music.

In the future, Louis is looking forward to being a father and having his own family. "My own parents are great," he states. "Every morning when my dad takes me to school, he says, 'Be good, do good, and have a good day.'"

Louis enjoys working with young children. He explains, "When I see them learn and grow through whatever I'm helping them with, it's very satisfying."

LISTENING CD 9:10–11 **RECORDED INTERVIEW**

Sonata for Bass Trombone, First Movement (Andantino)
by P. McCarty

Listen to Louis's performance and interview on the national radio program **From the Top**.

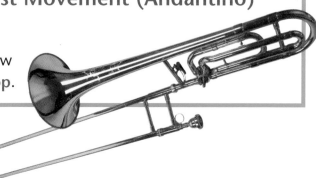

Spotlight on the Double Bass

Did You Know?

The double bass can produce two different types of sound. A bow can be pulled across the strings (*arco*), or the strings can be plucked with the fingers (*pizzicato*).

The double bass is used in both classical and jazz music.

The double bass can be five or six feet tall. Players either sit on high stools or stand to perform.

 LISTENING CD 9:12–13

Symphony No. 1 "Titan," Third Movement (excerpt)
by Gustav Mahler

Concerto for Double Bass No. 2, First Movement (excerpt)
by Giovanni Bottesini

Listen to the low, mournful notes of the double bass in this "funeral march" by Mahler. It sounds like a minor-key version of the familiar round "Frère Jacques." Then listen for both high and low pitches in the concerto.

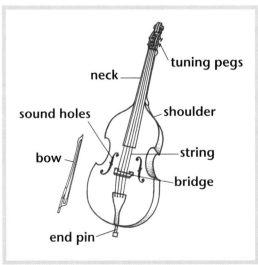

neck — tuning pegs — shoulder — sound holes — bow — string — bridge — end pin

UNIT 5

Expressions in Song

Have you ever found yourself humming or whistling a tune for no special reason? Do you sometimes have a tune that just won't leave your mind? Your special tune might be a melody you have heard, or it could be something you created.

Think of times when a melody has stayed in your mind. Talk about this experience with a partner.

Coming Attractions

Play I, IV, V chord accompaniments.

Sing several blues songs.

Perform a circle dance with a canon.

and describe the message

Listen to "There're's a Song in Me."
and mood.

Sing the

ERE'S A SONG IN ME

CD 9:14

Music and Words by Cristi Cary Miller

Verse
mp

do

1. There's a song in me that runs through my head. It's a
(2.) sing it when I'm feel - in' sad, and I
3. Oh you have one, too; a mel - o - dy. If you
(4.) sing it when you're feel - in' sad. You can

mel - o - dy I'm hum - min'. When I
sing it when I'm hap - py. It's the
lis - ten close, you'll hear it. It is
sing it when you're hap - py. And you'll

start to doubt, I sing it in - stead. Oh, I
kind of tune that makes me feel glad, and I
in your heart, just look and you'll see. Oh, it's
find that it will make you feel glad, as you

1., 3.
Dsus D   2., 4.
              Dsus D
         mp

hear it all day long. 2. And I
know I can't go wrong.
there for you to know. 4. You can
sing where - 'er you go.

What important message have you heard in a song? Did the song's mood or arrangement help to give the message?

LISTENING   CD 9:18

Vocal Expressions (montage)

Listen for the different moods and the ways of expressing them in these opera excerpts. *Die Zauberflöte*: The Queen of the Night is angry at her husband. *Pagliacci*: Canio, a clown, finds out his wife doesn't love him. He's very sad and cries. *La Traviata*: Alfredo and others are happy. They are having a party with friends.

There's a song in me. I want to share it with you. It's a mel - o - dy that keeps me mov - in' on. Mu - sic fills my head with glad - ness and it helps me car - ry on, so I'll spend my time just sing - in' my song.

(1st time) Go to Verse 3
(2nd time) D.S. al Fine
Fine

Chords from the Islands

People everywhere express themselves through singing. Imagine yourself on an island beach in Jamaica or Trinidad. Just close your eyes and you can almost hear the sound of people singing.

Sing "Mary Ann," expressing a happy mood.

MIDI

For another activity with "Mary Ann," see *Spotlight on MIDI.*

MAP

CUBA

JAMAICA

TRINIDAD

CD 9:19

West Indian Calypso

All day, all night, Miss Ma-ry Ann,_____

Down by the sea - shore sift-ing sand._____

1. E - ven lit - tle chil - dren join in the band_____
2. Young and old, all come now, join in the band_____
3. Ev - 'ry-bod - y, come now, join in the band_____

Down by the sea - shore sift-ing sand._____

Notice the chord symbols above the staff. These letters and other symbols tell what chords to play. Chords can also be labeled with Roman numerals.

Primary Chords (main chords in a major key)		
Roman Numeral	**Chord Name**	**Chord Root**
I ("one")	**tonic**	First pitch of major scale
IV ("four")	**subdominant**	Fourth pitch of major scale
V ("five")	**dominant**	Fifth pitch of major scale

Many songs can be accompanied by only primary chords. The F and C chords in "Mary Ann" are the I and V chords.

Play the chords with "Mary Ann." Play on the first beat of each measure.

Playalong

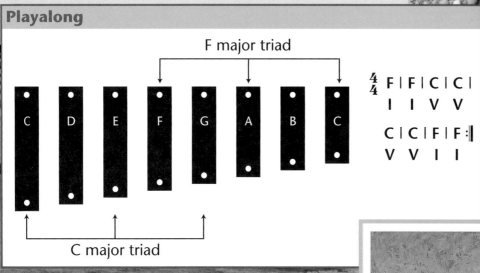

F major triad

C major triad

$\frac{4}{4}$ F | F | C | C |
    I I V V

C | C | F | F :‖
V V I I

Art Gallery

Barcas de Pesca
This painting was created by Gail Wells-Hess in 2000. The title means "small fishing boats." Wells-Hess is interested in capturing the light and color of real places. She works with pastels and oils. Pigment is used to capture the mood and character of the landscape.

Play Three Chords

As you listen to "Cuando salí de Cuba," think of how you would feel if you had to move away from your country.

Cuando salí de Cuba

I Went Away from Cuba

CD 9:22

Words and Music by Luis Aguile
English Words by Linda Worsley

Spanish: Nun - ca___ po - dré mo - rir - me   mi co - ra - zón no___ lo ten - go_a-

Pronunciation: nun ka   po ðɾe mo ɾiɾ me   mi ko ɾa son no   lo teng goa

English: I know___ I can - not die now,   My heart is gone, and___ I can not

quí,   Al - guien___ me_es - tá_es - pe - ran - do   me_es - tá_a - guar -

ki   a yi   mes taes pe ɾan do   mes ta gwaɾ

stay,   My heart___ is   wait - ing there now,   A - wait - ing

dan - do___ que vuel - va_a - llí.   Cuan - do sa - lí de Cu -

ðan do   ke βwel βa yi   kwan do sa li ðe ku

my___   re - turn some day.   I went a - way from Cu -

- ba   de - jé mi vi - da de - jé mi_a - mor,___

βa   ðe xe mi βi ða ðe xe mia moɾ

- ba,   My life, my love   I left in des - pair.___

cuan - do sa - lí de Cu - ba   de - jé_en - te - rra - do mi co - ra - zón.___

kwan do sa li ðe ku βa   ðe xen te ɾ̃a ðo mi ko ɾa son

I went a - way from Cu - ba,   and now my poor heart is bur - ied there.___

"Cuando salí de Cuba" has the three primary chords. Which chords are the I, IV, and V chords in the key of C?

autoharp

Playalong

Play a primary-chord accompaniment as you sing "Cuando salí de Cuba." Use the chord symbols above the staff as your guide. Play on beat 1 or make up a rhythm.

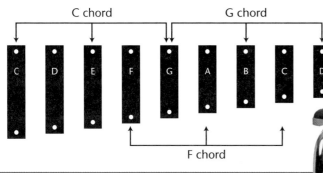

C chord

G chord

C D E F G A B C D

F chord

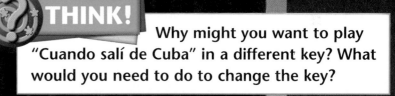

THINK!

Why might you want to play "Cuando salí de Cuba" in a different key? What would you need to do to change the key?

Harmony on the Move

CONCEPT
HARMONY
SKILLS
LISTEN, PLAY, SING
LINKS
CULTURES, DANCE

"Tzena, Tzena" was composed in 1948 to celebrate the nation of Israel. The steady beat and strong rhythm of this song make it just right for dancing the hora. The chords in "Tzena, Tzena" repeat over and over in the following order: C (I), F (IV), G (V), C (I).

Listen to "Tzena, Tzena" and notice the chords.

The letter name of a chord is the pitch on which the chord is built, the root. A chord formed in the order root, third, fifth is in **root position**. Pitches used in more than one chord are called **common tones**. Find the common tones in the three primary chords.

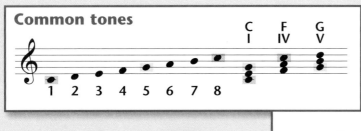

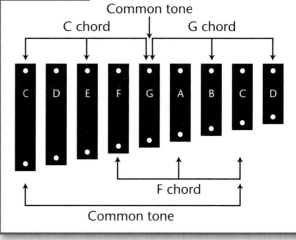

Playalong

Play "Tzena, Tzena" following the chord symbols. One person plays the chord roots, another person plays the other chord pitches. Play on the first beat of the measure.

Tzena, Tzena

CD 9:26

Music by Issachar Miron and Julius Grossman
Words by Mitchell Parish

A C / F

Hebrew/English: Tze - na, tze - na, tze - na, tze - na, Hear the hap - py sounds of danc - ing,
Pronunciation: tsɛ na tsɛ na tsɛ na tsɛ na

Tze - na, tze - na, tze - na, tze - na, Ev - 'ry - one can sing a - long, so

G 1. C 2. C **B**

come____ and dance a - long. La la la la,
join____ us in our song.

F G C

la la la la la la, Join us as we dance to - geth - er, sing - ing.

C F G

La la la la, la la la la la la, Join us in our hap - py

C **C** F

song. Clap your hands and (clap) raise your voic - es high - er,

G C

Make a cir - cle while we dance a - round the fire.__ Dance the ho - ra

F G C

(clap) to your heart's de - sire.__ All the world sings Tze - na, tze - na, tze - na.

Chords in a Different Key

Chord progressions built on the I, IV, and V chords are found in songs from many parts of the world. "The Lion Sleeps Tonight" was originally composed by Solomon Linda from South Africa. The song was made popular in the United States by folk singer Pete Seeger.

Listen to "The Lion Sleeps Tonight" and follow the chord symbols in the key of G: G (I), C (IV), G (I), D (V).

Notice that the chords in the vocal parts are not all in root position. When the root is not the bottom of the chord, the chord is in an **inversion**.

Chords and Their Inversions

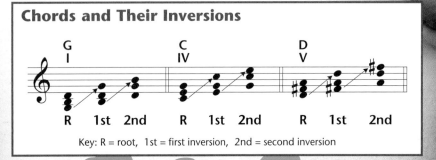

Key: R = root, 1st = first inversion, 2nd = second inversion

The Lion Sleeps Tonight

CD 10:1

Words and Music by Solomon Linda
Arranged by Robert J. de Frece

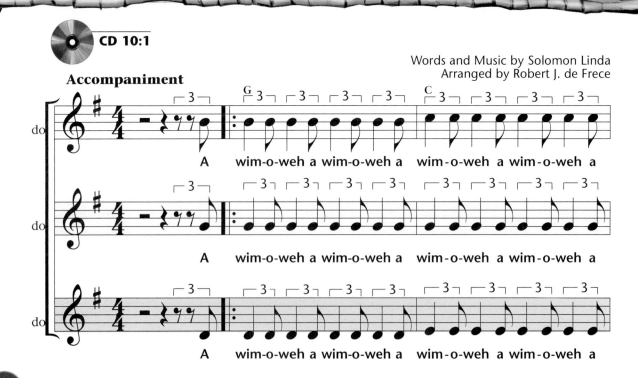

172

How Blue Are You?

CONCEPT
HARMONY
SKILLS
SING, LISTEN, PLAY
LINKS
SOCIAL STUDIES

Music can express feelings of sadness. African Americans in the 1860s began a new style of music. It often had a slow $\frac{4}{4}$ meter, a 12-bar chord progression, three lines of lyrics, and certain altered pitches. This style was the **blues**. The words of blues songs usually express sad feelings, but they also express hope and courage in the face of life's challenges.

 LISTENING CD 10:7

Backwater Blues by Bessie Smith

Bessie Smith is known as "Empress of the Blues." She was the greatest of the classic blues singers in the 1920s. In 1927, a frightening storm in the South produced a flood that forced thousands of people from their homes in the Delta of the Mississippi River. "Backwater Blues" tells this story.

Listen to the "Empress of the Blues," Bessie Smith, sing "Backwater Blues."

Bessie Smith

Art Gallery

Empress of the Blues

This collage was created in 1974 by the artist Romare Bearden (1911–1988). A collage is made by fastening materials together on a surface. Bearden used colored paper and magazine cutouts as well as acrylic and lacquer on board. Bessie Smith is shown, backed up by a blues band swaying to the music.

Art © Romare Bearden Foundation/Licensed by VAGA, New York, NY

One of the characteristic chord progressions in the blues is the **12-bar blues**. It is twelve bars, or measures, long and includes the I, IV, and V chords in the following order:

I	I	I	I	IV	IV	I	I	V	IV	I	I

Read the chord symbols and follow the 12-bar blues chord progression as you listen to "Backwater Blues." The chords B♭, E♭, and F are the I, IV, and V chords.

Backwater Blues

CD 10:8

Words and Music by Bessie Smith

B♭

1. When it rained five days and the skies turned dark as night.__
2. Then they rowed a lit-tle boat 'bout__ five miles 'cross the farm.__
3. Then I went out and stood on some high old lone-some hill.__
4. Back-wa-ter blues done caused me to pack my things and go.__

E♭7   B♭

When it rained five days and the skies turned dark as night.__
Then they rowed a lit-tle boat 'bout__ five miles 'cross the farm.__
Then I went out and stood on some high old lone-some hill.__
Back-wa-ter blues done caused me to pack my things and go.__

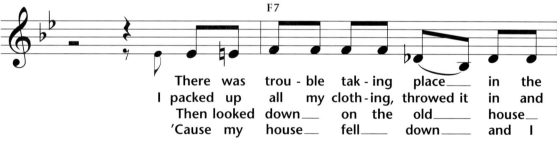

F7

There was trou-ble tak-ing place__ in the
I packed up all my cloth-ing, throwed it in and
Then looked down__ on the old__ house__
'Cause my house__ fell__ down__ and I

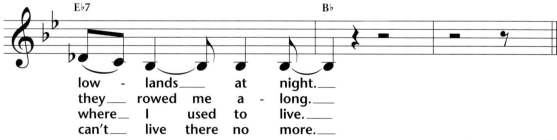

E♭7   B♭

low - lands__ at night.__
they__ rowed me a - long.__
where__ I used to live.__
can't__ live there no more.__

Playing the Blues

The blues has a distinctive musical flavor that comes from singing or playing pitches that have been "bent." These bent pitches, called **blue notes**, are lowered and the notes usually appear with accidentals. The blue notes create the sound of the **blues scale**, which is similar to the major scale with the third, seventh, and sometimes fifth degrees of the scale often lowered to become blue notes.

F Major scale

1   2   3   4   5   6   7   8

F Blues scale

1   2   3   4   5   6   7   8

  **THINK!** Which instruments can bend pitches? How do they do it?

LISTENING CD 10:11

Good Mornin', Blues
by Huddie Ledbetter

Huddie Ledbetter is known by his nickname, "Leadbelly." Like many other musicians, Leadbelly accompanied himself on the guitar while he sang the blues. He played accompaniments using mostly the three primary chords. He recorded hundreds of blues and other African American songs, making him one of the most important blues performers in the history of the United States.

Listen to Leadbelly sing "Good Mornin', Blues."

Sing "Good Mornin', Blues," and identify the blue notes.

Good Mornin', Blues

CD 10:12

Words and Music by Huddie Ledbetter

1. Good morn - in', blues;
2. I lay down last night,

Blues, how do you do?
turn-in' from side to side.

Good morn - in', blues; Blues, how do you do?
Yes, I was turn-in' from side to side.

I'm do-ing all right, good morn - in', how are you?
I was not a - sleep, but I was dis - sat - is - fied.

Playalong

Play the 12-bar blues chord progression to accompany "Good Mornin', Blues." Follow the chord symbols above the staff or on this chart. Each chord is one measure long.

F F F F   B♭ B♭ F F   C B♭ F F

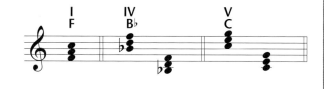

I   IV   V
F   B♭   C

Singin' the Blues

CONCEPT
HARMONY
SKILLS
SING, CREATE, PLAY
LINKS
LANGUAGE ARTS

Improvisation is an element important to the blues. The earliest blues singers passed on their songs from one to another without writing them down. Each singer improvised variations of the lyrics and the melody. One thing remained unchanged: the 12-bar blues pattern of chords supporting the melody.

Learn About Vocal Sounds

Your voice is a very personal musical instrument. You can create a wide variety of vocal sounds. To do this, various parts of your body are used. The size and shape of your open mouth affect the sound. The position and use of your tongue help form letters and other sounds. Your lips also help form the sounds of letters. Air from your lungs makes vocal cords in your larynx vibrate, creating sound. Sounds may be smooth, refined, raspy, or come out as a growl. Different sounds are needed for different styles of music.

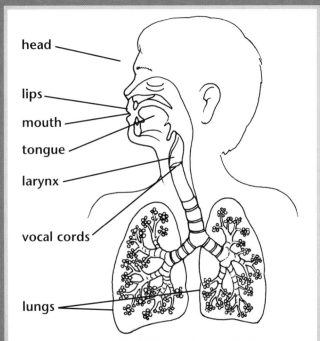

head
lips
mouth
tongue
larynx
vocal cords
lungs

Sing "Every Day I Have the Blues."

EVERY DAY I HAVE THE BLUES

CD 10:15

Music and Words by Peter Chapman

Ev - 'ry-day, Ev - 'ry day, Ev - 'ry day, Ev - 'ry day I have the

blues. Ev - 'ry day, Ev - 'ry day, Ev - 'ry

day, Ev - 'ry day I have the blues. I

don't know why it's hap' - nin' 'cause I got no more to lose.___

No - bod - y loves me. No - bod - y seems to care.___ I said,

No - bod - y loves me. No - bod - y seems to care.___

Speak-in' of wor-ries and trou-bles, I know I've had my share.___

Words in the Blues

Notice the pattern of the lyrics in the 12-bar blues in "Every Day I Have the Blues" and "Good Mornin', Blues." There are always three phrases, the second identical to the first, then a third that ends with a rhyming word to the first two, an *a a a* rhyme scheme. Often the first two phrases have the same melody and the third phrase is different, creating an a a b form.

Sing "Every Day I Have the Blues" and make up your own words and tune for the third phrase.

Listen for the long note at the end of each phrase and fill these measures by improvising a rhythm or melody to happen at the same time.

Play these parts below with "Good Mornin', Blues" or "Every Day I Have the Blues."

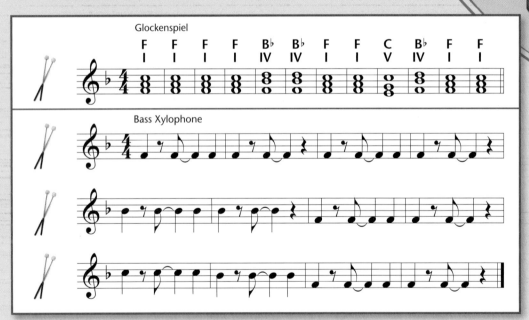

Play these chords with "Backwater Blues."

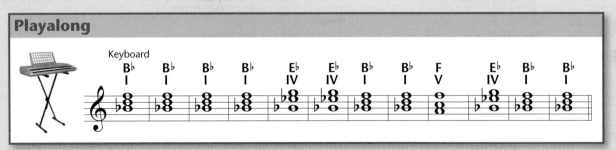

Bound No'th Blues

Goin' down de road, Lawd,
Goin' down de road.
Down de road, Lawd,
Way, way down de road.
Got to find somebody
To help me carry dis load.

Road's in front o' me,
Nothin' to do but walk.
Road's in front o' me,
Walk...and walk...and walk.
I'd like to meet a good friend
To come along an' talk.

Road, road, road, O!
Road, road...road...road, road!
Road, road, road, O!
On de No'thern road.
These Mississippi towns ain't
Fit fer a hoppin' toad.

—Langston Hughes

Sing in Two Parts

CONCEPT
HARMONY
SKILLS
SING, IMPROVISE,
PLAY
LINKS
LANGUAGE
ARTS

Blues musicians often improvise melodies using pitches of the blues scale. The blue notes decorate or embellish the melody.

Find the blue notes on the scale below.

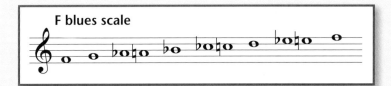

F blues scale

You can improvise using the pitches of the blues scale. Select some of the pitches to use for your improvisation, for example:

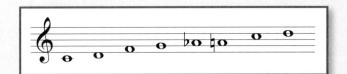

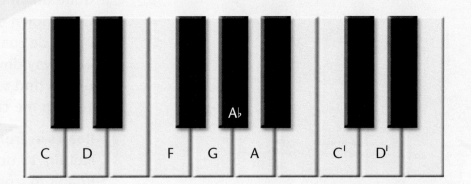

Improvise melodies using the pitches of the blues scale. Use the rhythm below or make up another rhythm the same length.

Look at the end of phrases in the blues you have sung. This is a favorite spot for improvisation.

Play your melodies during the long note at the end of each phrase in "Every Day I Have the Blues." Then sing your improvisation using the lyrics you made up in Lesson 4. You could also use scat syllables such as *du dut-en du*.

The composer of "There's a Song in Me" created a light and happy feeling in this song. After "singing the blues," this music provides a change of mood.

Notice the added harmony part. Sometimes Part 1 sings the harmony and sometimes Part 2. Learn this part, then sing the song in two parts and listen to the harmony. Do you hear any blue notes?

When you sing a song in two parts, listen very carefully to the other part while you are singing your own part.

Sing "There's a Song in Me" in two parts.

THERE'S A SONG IN ME

CD 9:14

Music and Words by Cristi Cary Miller

With feeling

Verses 1 and 2: all sing Melody (Part 2)
Verses 3 and 4: Parts 1 and 2

Part 1

There   is   a   song,_____

Melody
Part 2 *mp*

1. There's a   song   in   me   that   runs through my head. It's a
   (2.) sing   it   when   I'm   feel - in' sad, and I
3. Oh you have one, too; a   mel - o - dy. If you
   (4.) sing   it   when you're   feel - in' sad. You can

there   is   a   song,_____

mel - o - dy I'm   hum - min', When I
sing   it   when   I'm   hap - py. It's the
lis - ten   close, you'll   hear   it. It is
sing   it   when you're   hap - py. And you'll

More →

Unit 5 Expressions in Song   183

LESSON 6

A Moving Form

CONCEPT
FORM

SKILLS
LISTEN, SING, MOVE

LINKS
CULTURES

See **music .mmhschool.com** to research George and Ira Gershwin.

A musical **phrase** is like a sentence: It expresses a complete thought. Often phrases are identified by small letters. The first phrase is called *a*. If a phrase is different from *a*, it is given a different letter, such as *b*. If a phrase is similar to another, it is written with the same letter and a prime sign, such as *a¹*.

This is the first phrase of "Mary Ann."

All day, all night, Miss Ma-ry Ann,____

Which form matches "Mary Ann"?

Ella Fitzgerald ▼

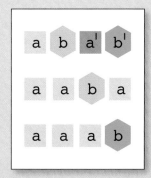

A combination of two or more related phrases is a **section**. A musical section is like a paragraph. Often a section is identified by a capital letter.

LISTENING CD 10:18

Fascinating Rhythm from *Lady, Be Good*
Music by George Gershwin and Words by Ira Gershwin

This song was created by two brothers. It is sung by Ella Fitzgerald, a famous jazz singer, and it is played by a big band. Listen for the phrases and sections in this song and a short ending called a **tag**. See if you can hear this form:

George (left) and
Ira (right) Gershwin

Instrumental introduction		Vocal introduction		
Ⓐ	Ⓑ	Ⓐ	Ⓑ♩	turnaround
instrumental		vocal		
Ⓐ♩	Ⓑ♫	Ⓐ	Ⓑ♫	tag
instrumental tag				

Identify the form of "I Got Rhythm."

186

I Got Rhythm

from the musical *Girl Crazy*

Music by George Gershwin
Words by Ira Gershwin

A I____ got rhy - thm,____ I____ got mu - sic,____

I____ got my friends,____ Who could ask for an - y-thing more?

A I____ got dai - sies____ In____ green pas - tures,____

I____ got my friends,____ Who could ask for an - y-thing more?

B Old__ Man Trou - ble,__ I____ don't mind him,__ You__ won't

find him__ 'Round__ my door. **A** I____ got star - light,__

I____ got sweet dreams,__ I____ got my friends,__ who could

ask for an - y-thing more, Who could ask for an - y-thing more?

Unit 5 Expressions in Song   187

Familiar Forms

Guadalajara is a beautiful city in Jalisco, a state in western Mexico. "¡Ay, Jalisco no te rajes!" expresses great love for the city and for the state. Listen for the form as you sing this song.

MAP
UNITED STATES
MEXICO
BELIZE
GUATEMALA

¡Ay, Jalisco no te rajes!

Ay, Jalisco, Never Fail Her!

CD 10:22

Words and Lyrics by
Manuel Esperón and Ernesto Cortázar
English Words by Linda Worsley

Verse

Spanish: ¡Ay! Ja - lis - co, Ja - lis - co, Ja - lis - co, tú tie - nes tu
Pronunciation: ai xa lis ko xa lis ko xa lis ko tu tye nes tu
English: Ay, Ja - lis - co, Ja - lis - co, Ja - lis - co, Your love is the

no - via que_es Gua - da - la - ja - ra.
no βya kes gwa ða la xa ɾa
cit - y of Gua - da - la - ja - ra.

Mu - cha - cha bo - ni - ta, la per - la más ra - ra de
mu cha cha βo ni ta la peɾ la mas ɾa ɾa ðe
A la - dy so love - ly, like dia - monds she spar - kles, in

to - do Ja - lis - co_es mi Gua - da - la - ja - ra.
to ðo xa lis koes mi gwa ða la xa ɾa
all of Ja - lis - co, my Gua - da - la - ja - ra.

188

Meet the Musicians

Manuel Esperón (b. 1911) is a Mexican composer. He played piano accompaniment for silent movies and later wrote orchestra scores for films. Esperón wrote music for 548 films and over 300 songs. Mariachi musicians refer to him as the "Father of Mexican music."

Ernesto Cortázar (1897–1953) was a Mexican composer and pianist. After a string of hit songs, he teamed up with Manuel Esperón. Together the two musicians wrote many hit songs and toured the world.

Move with the A section of "¡Ay, Jalisco!" in a Right-together-Right, Left-together-Left pattern. Create contrasting movement for the B section.

Refrain

¡Ay,_____ Ja - lis - co no te ra - jes!_____
ai xɑ lis ko no te ɾɑ xes
Ay,_____ Ja - lis - co, nev - er fail her._____

____ me sa - le del al - ma_____ gri - tar con ca - lor,_____
me sɑ le ðel al ma gɾi tɑɾ kon kɑ loɾ
____ I feel it so deep-ly,_____ I call from my soul._____

____ a - brir to-do el pe - cho pa'e- char es - te gri - to: ¡Qué
ɑ βɾiɾ to ðoel pe cho pɑe char es te gɾi to ke
____ And now shall I say it once more with my whole heart, my

lin - do es Ja - lis - co, pa - la - bra de ho - nor!
lin ðoes xɑ lis ko pɑ la βɾɑ ðeo noɾ
love - ly Ja - lis - co, I'll nev - er for - get.

Unit 5 Expressions in Song

189

CONCEPT
TONE COLOR

SKILLS
SING, PLAY,
LISTEN

LINKS
DANCE

Tone color helps you to tell the difference between different kinds of instruments and voices. What tone colors do you hear in "Och Jungfrun Hon Går I Ringen"?

MAP
NORWAY
SWEDEN
RUSSIA

Och Jungfrun Hon Går I Ringen

A Girl with a Shiny Ribbon

CD 11:1

Swedish Dance Song
English Words by Linda Worsley

Swedish: Och jung - frun hon går i ring - en med rö - dan gull -
Pronunciation: o yung frun hon gor i ring ən mɛd rö dən gul
English: A girl with a shin - y rib - bon went danc - ing one

band, och jung - frun hon går i ring - en med rö - dan gull -
band o yung frun hon gor i ring ən mɛd rö dən gul
night, a girl with a shin - y rib - bon went danc - ing one

band. Det bin - der hon om sin kä - ras - tes
band dɛh bɪn dər hon om sin she ras tɛs
night. She danced with her beau and tied him up

arm, det bin - der hon om sin kä - ras - tes arm.
arm dɛh bɪn dər hon om sin she ras tɛs arm
tight, she danced with her beau and tied him up tight.

Create an accompaniment using unpitched instruments that have different tone colors.

glockenspiel

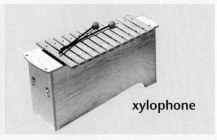

xylophone

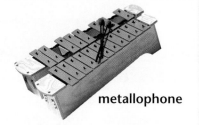

metallophone

Play the parts below with "Och Jungfrun Hon Går I Ringen."

 LISTENING CD 11:5

Och Jungfrun Hon Går I Ringen,
Swedish Dance Song

This arrangement is sung by the St. Olaf Choir.

Listen to "Och Jungfrun Hon Går I Ringen" and compare it to the version you sang.

A Norwegian Tale

Meet the Musician

Edvard Grieg (1843–1907) was a Norwegian composer. He was also a conductor, teacher, and performer. In 1875 Grieg wrote music to a play by Henrik Ibsen called *Peer Gynt*. Later Grieg choose eight of the pieces and arranged them for full orchestra and formed them into two suites. A **suite** is a group of related pieces. These suites became very popular. His *Concerto in A Minor* for piano is also well known. Grieg was interested in the folk music of Norway and used some of it in his compositions.

Michael Sheen (Peer) and Paola Dionisotti (Peer's mother) appear in a Royal Shakespeare Company production of "Peer Gynt"

 LISTENING CD 11:6

Solveig's Song from *Peer Gynt Suite No. 2*, Op. 55 by E. Grieg

Edvard Grieg wrote music for the dramatic story of Peer Gynt, a legendary Norwegian farm boy who was full of tricks and mischief. The story tells of Peer's sometimes frightening adventures as he traveled far away from home. When Peer finally returns he is an old man. Solveig, the girl he danced with in his youth, has waited for him all this time. She sings the beautiful "Solveig's Song" for Peer.

Listen to "Solveig's Song." Compare the vocal tone color of an adult soprano with the vocal tone color of a young person's voice.

Use *Orchestral Instruments* **CD-ROM** to learn more about stringed instruments.

arco

LISTENING CD 11:7

Anitra's Dance from *Peer Gynt Suite No. 1*, Op. 46 by E. Grieg

One of the people Peer meets during his travels is a Moroccan dancing girl, Anitra. Listen for the different instrumental tone colors in "Anitra's Dance." How do they contrast? The strings are played two ways: **arco** (with the bow) and **pizzicato** (by plucking).

pizzicato

Listen to "Anitra's Dance" and follow the listening map.

Listening Map for Anitra's Dance

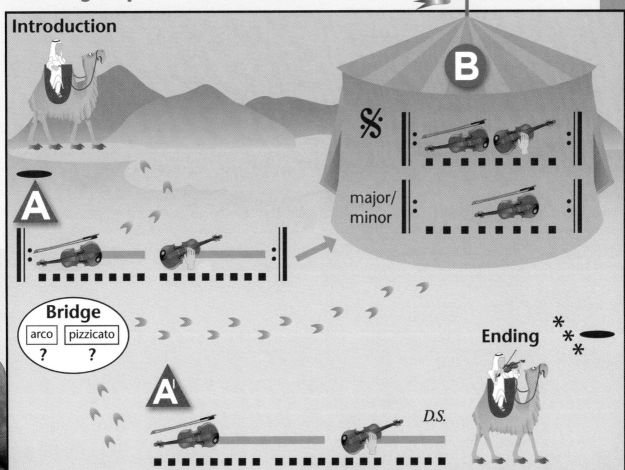

Unit 5 Expressions in Song   **193**

LESSON 8

CONCEPT
ARTICULATION
SKILLS
SING, MOVE, LISTEN
LINKS
DANCE

Articulating in Circles

"**T**umbai" is in a minor key. You can express feelings of joy in this song by singing and dancing it with a strong rhythmic quality.

Sing "Tumbai" in unison and then as a canon.

Tumbai

CD 11:8

Israeli Folk Song

mf

1 Em   B 7   Em

do

Hebrew: בִּי - טוֹם בִּי - טוֹם בִּי - טוֹם בִּי - טוֹם   טוֹם בִּי - טוֹם בִּי - טוֹם בִּי

Pronunciation: tum bai tum bai tum bai tum bai   tum bai tum bai tum bai

2 Em

Tra la la   la la la la la   la la la la la la.

3 Am   Em   B 7   E 7

Tra la la la   la   la   la la la   la   la la la la la   la.

"**Tumbai" Dance** (for unison version)

Formation: circle, partners standing next to each other.

Song

Phrase 1: three steps right, reverse facing on beat 4, repeat to the left.

Phrase 2: right, back, right, hop; left, back, left, hop

Phrase 3: move forward 3 steps and clap, back 3 steps and clap.

Instrumental section

Create 16 beats of movement to do with a partner.

Global Voices

MAP

BOTSWANA

NAMIBIA

LESOTHO

SOUTH AFRICA

LISTENING CD 11:13

Ngikhumbula
Swazi Song

"Ngikhumbula" is a Swazi love song from South Africa. Swazi are a people of east central Africa. They speak Swazi, a Bantu language. This traditional song might be sung whenever Swazi people get together. In this case, it is performed by the KaNyamazane Township Choir and it is formalized for their performance. It is typical of the kind of song they might sing after a wedding ceremony when the families perform for one another.

The KaNyamazane Township is near Kruger National Park, a wildlife preserve. On a visit to the park, you are likely to see giraffes, elephants, kudu, hyenas, and chimpanzees. On a good day, you might sight a lion or tiger. This is what the words mean:

Ngikhumbuli langa ngiznikela kuwe
Sasihleli sisobabili ngiznikela kuwe
We mama we mama (nonsense syllables)

I remember the day I handed myself to you
We were seated together the day I handed myself to you
We mama we mama (nonsense syllables)

Listen to "Ngikhumbula" and describe the articulation. What else did you hear?

A Smooth Circle

Compare the mood and message of "Circle of Friends" with the mood and message of "Tumbai."

Sing "Circle of Friends" legato.

Circle of Friends

Words and Music by Roger Emerson

 **CD 11:14**
1st time: Part 2
2nd time and D.C.: Parts 1 and 2

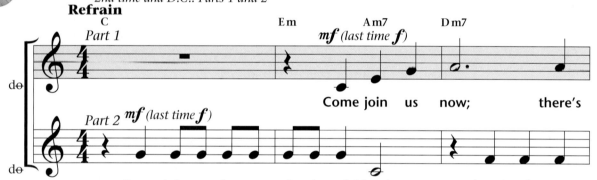

Refrain

Part 1 — Come join us now; there's

Part 2 — Come join us in our cir-cle of friends; there's al-ways

room for one___ more. It ne-ver ends just

room for one more. A cir-cle that nev-er ends, all you do is

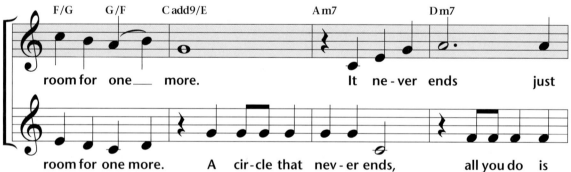

o - pen up the door.___

o - pen up the door.

Verse

1. Have you ev-er been
2. When you're on___ the

Spotlight Your Success!

REVIEW

1 Which chord symbols represent moving from the tonic to the dominant chords?

    a. V I   **b.** IV I   **c.** I V   **d.** I IV

2 What chords are shown here?

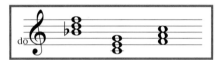

    a. IV V I   **b.** I IV V   **c.** V I IV   **d.** IV I V

3 Which group of chords contain only primary chords?

    a. I ii IV V   **b.** I ii iii V   **c.** IV V vii   **d.** I IV V

4 Which chords are inverted?

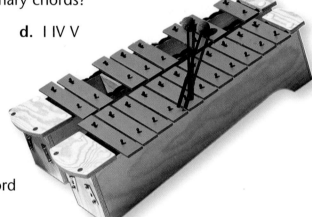

    a. G chord   **b.** C chord   **c.** D chord

5 Which of the following is a blues scale?

    a.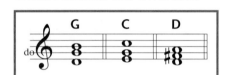

    b.

READ AND LISTEN

1 Read these pitches. Then listen. Which pitches do you hear?

    a.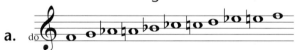

    b.

2 Read these pitches. Then listen. Which chord do you hear?

a.

b.

THINK!

1 Choose a song. What would happen if different chords were used in the accompaniment?

2 Which do you think is easier to sing—legato or staccato? Why?

3 What are your favorite tone colors? Explain why.

4 **Write** Why do you think the 12-bar blues form is popular?

CREATE AND PERFORM

1 **Create** a 12-bar blues melody to these words:

I lost my homework, I feel so awful blue.
I lost my homework, I feel so awful blue.
Did anybody find it? I don't know what to do.

2 **Use** the pitches in the F-blues scale.

3 **Sing** your melody over the 12-bar blues chord progression in the key of F.

Meet the Musician
ON NATIONAL RADIO!

Name: Elena Urioste
Age: 15
Instrument: Violin
Home Town:
North Wales, Pennsylvania

People carry all sorts of good luck charms, but have you ever heard of someone carrying a banana for good luck? That's what fifteen-year-old violinist Elena Urioste used to do whenever she performed.

Elena's first violin teacher was very creative. Before Elena went onstage, her teacher would give her a "magical" banana for good luck. "I was usually too nervous to eat the banana so I'd just place it beside my case when I played," explains Elena. That same teacher also taught Elena to say "rhinoceros" when taking a bow to make sure she stood onstage long enough to accept the audience's applause.

It has been a long time since Elena relied on lucky bananas, but she does fondly recall the creativity of her first teacher. Now when she performs, Elena concentrates on sharing the music with the audience. "I try to have fun and make the audience feel something."

 LISTENING CD 11:19–20 **RECORDED INTERVIEW**

Carmen Fantasy for Violin and Piano, Op. 25
by P. de Sarasate

Listen to Elena's performance and interview on the national radio program **From the Top**.

Careers

Jesse "Chuy" Varela says "When you get an opportunity to try something, *try* it! You never know where it's going to lead."

When he was young, Mr. Varela's uncles used Mexican folk music to teach him the guitar. As a teenager, he played in garage bands, then Mexican dance bands. Hearing the high school jazz band inspired him to take lessons.

The radio bug bit Mr. Varela on a fifth-grade field trip to a local station. A broadcaster let him record and hear his own voice. In college, after serving in the military, Mr. Varela volunteered at public radio stations. This led to work as a deejay, on-air host, reporter, foreign correspondent, and writer.

Now music director of KCSM at the College of San Mateo, California, Mr. Varela selects the music for their 24-hour, 7-day-a-week jazz radio station. He especially enjoys "passing the torch" to a younger generation. By guiding station tours and mentoring college students, he shares what he continues to learn about jazz and public radio.

Did You Know?

"Xylophone" is Greek for "wood sound."

The xylophone keys are wooden bars arranged from the longest (lowest notes) to shortest (highest notes). When the keys are struck with a mallet, they vibrate to make a sound.

Because they are struck to make sounds, xylophones belong in the percussion family.

 LISTENING CD 11:21–22

The Golden Age of Xylophone (excerpt)
by Watson, Brewer, Howgill, Innes, Simpson, and Skull

Music for Strings, Percussion, and Celesta (excerpt)
by B. Bartók

Listen to a playful section of a concerto for xylophone. Then listen to how the repeated pitches of the xylophone add to the quality of Bartók's music.

Music for Changing Times

You live in changing times. Air travel and instant communication have made your life different from that of your grandparents or great-grandparents when they were your age.

Music, too, has changed over the years. Think of the musical choices available on radio, television, films, the Internet, and recordings. New music continues to be created in new and old styles.

Coming Attractions

Sing
in new meters.

Conduct
several songs.

Listen to
songs from around
the world.

Even with all the changes that happen over the years, some things have stayed the same. Music can still connect you—to the past and the present, to other people and various cultures. The song "The Times They Are A-Changin'" connects you with the 1960s and the idea of changing times.

Sing "The Times They Are A-Changin'."

The Times They Are A-Changin'

CD 11:23

Words and Music by Bob Dylan

1. Come gath-er 'round peo-ple where-ev-er you
writ-ers and crit-ics who proph-e-size with your

roam,_____ And ad-mit that the wa-ters a-
pen,_____ And__ keep your eyes wide, the chance

round you have grown. And ac-cept it that soon you'll be
won't come a-gain. And don't speak too soon, for the

drenched to the bone._____ If your time to
wheel's still in spin._____ And there's no tell-in'

Life

Life is a gift for you and me,
To see what great people we can come to be.
Solving your problems day by day,
Helping others and lighting the way.
You can be someone famous, or someone unknown,
But we find our destiny along the way, by the things that we've been shown.
We're all different, we're each one of a kind,
And in that way, we each have our own minds.
Sometimes we need help from others, to guide us to our goal,
But then the whole thing may turn around, so you're helping the other soul.
It's important to do good deeds in life, for others all around,
Like if another person falls, you should help them off the ground.
So remember to live your life to the fullest, no matter what your sorrows,
Because you never know what could come from what happens tomorrow.

—*Sydney DeShetler* (age 11)

you is worth sav-in',_____ then you bet-ter start
who that it's nam-in',_____ for the los-er_____

swim-min' or you'll sink like a stone. } For the times
now_____ will be lat-er to win. }

they are a-chang - in'! 2. Come in'!_____

THINK! How does this song connect you to the past, and what does it say about the present or future?

Turn the Beat Around

CONCEPT
RHYTHM
SKILLS
SING, PLAY
LINKS
MATH,
CULTURES

When you listen to the radio or television, the music you hear usually sounds familiar. One reason for this is the familiar meters in which most American music is written: $\frac{2}{4}$, $\frac{3}{4}$, $\frac{4}{4}$, and $\frac{6}{8}$. You may not be aware of the meter when you hear the music, but it sounds "right."

Sing "Dance for the Nations" in unison and identify the meter.

Dance for the Nations

CD 11:26

Words and Music by John Krumm

'Round and 'round we go! We hold___ each oth-er's hands and

weave our - selves in a cir - cle. The

time is gone, the dance goes___ on!___

Art Gallery

Dance of Youth

This line drawing is by Pablo Picasso (1888–1973), a Spanish artist. Notice the dancers in four different colors and the dove of peace in the center. They are not shown realistically but were created with simple lines and colors. How does Picasso show movement with the figures?

Listen to "Dance for the Nations" and perform these ostinatos. Feel the $\frac{2}{4}$ meter.

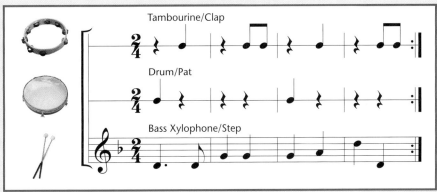

Perform the ostinatos as you sing the song.

An Irregular Meter

Try to identify the number of beats in each measure of this song.
Sing the refrain after verses 3 and 6.

Turn the World Around

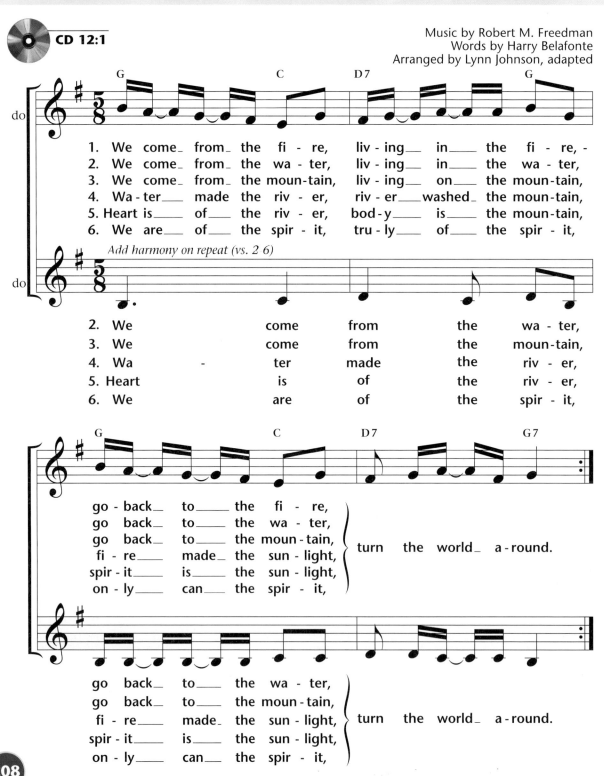

CD 12:1

Music by Robert M. Freedman
Words by Harry Belafonte
Arranged by Lynn Johnson, adapted

1. We come from the fi - re, liv - ing in the fi - re, -
2. We come from the wa - ter, liv - ing in the wa - ter,
3. We come from the moun-tain, liv - ing on the moun-tain,
4. Wa - ter made the riv - er, riv - er washed the moun-tain,
5. Heart is of the riv - er, bod - y is the moun-tain,
6. We are of the spir - it, tru - ly of the spir - it,

Add harmony on repeat (vs. 2 6)

2. We come from the wa - ter,
3. We come from the moun-tain,
4. Wa - ter made the riv - er,
5. Heart is of the riv - er,
6. We are of the spir - it,

go - back to the fi - re,
go back to the wa - ter,
go back to the moun-tain,
fi - re made the sun - light,
spir - it is the sun - light,
on - ly can the spir - it,

turn the world a - round.

go back to the wa - ter,
go back to the moun-tain,
fi - re made the sun - light,
spir - it is the sun - light,
on - ly can the spir - it,

turn the world a - round.

208

"Turn the World Around" is in $\frac{5}{8}$. There are five beats in the measure and the eighth note receives one beat in $\frac{5}{8}$ **meter**. The meter $\frac{5}{8}$ is an irregular meter. The organization of beats in sets of 5 or 7 is **irregular meter**.

Perform these rhythms with "Turn the World Around." Replace the pat and clap with two percussion instruments.

Playalong

1 $\frac{5}{8}$

pat clap clap clap clap

2 $\frac{5}{8}$

pat clap clap pat clap

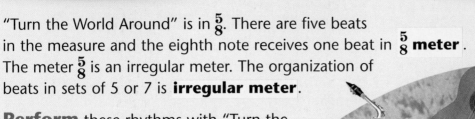

Refrain

G   C   D7   G   C   D7   G

Do   you know   who   I   am?   Do   I   know   who   you   are?
Oh,____ oh,   so   is   life,   Ah____ hah!   so   is   life;

(add on the repeat)

Ah_____   ah   ah   ah_____   ah   ah

G   C   D7   G   C   D7   G

See   we   one an-oth-er clear-ly,   Do   we   know   who   we   are? -
Oh,____ oh,____ so   is   life,   Ah____ hah!   so   is   life.

Ah_____   ah   ah   ah_____   ah   ah

Meter in Three and Five

"**E**l vito" is a folk song from Spain. The meter signature for "El vito" is $\frac{3}{8}$. There are three beats to the measure with the eighth note receiving one beat in $\frac{3}{8}$ **meter**. When the song is performed at a fast tempo, the measure is felt in one rather than three.

MAP
FRANCE
PORTUGAL
SPAIN
MOROCCO   ALGERIA

CD 12:5

Spanish Folk Song
English Words by MMH

Very fast
Refrain

Spanish: Con el vi - to, vi - to, vi - to,_____ con el
Pronunciation: kon el bi to βi to βi to kon el
English: How the days are swift - ly fly - ing,_____ while my

vi - to vi - to va._____
bi to βi to βa
heart is deep - ly sigh - ing._____

Verse

Yo no quie - ro - que me mi - ren_____ que me
yo no kye ɾo ke me mi ɾen ke me
In the dark - ness, I am hid - ing._____ In the

pon - go co - lo - ra - do.
pong go ko lo ɾa ðo
shad - ows, I am cry - ing._____

Many Spanish folk songs are accompanied by foot stamping and hand clapping.

Practice this pattern and then perform it with "El vito."

Beat Groupings

What do you see around each 5 in this art?

Art Gallery

X-5

This geometric pop art is by American artist Robert Indiana (b. 1928). The art shows the number 5 within an X. Find the shapes: X, square, circle, pentagon, star, triangle.

Sometimes meters contain groups of beats. A meter of $\frac{5}{8}$ may have groups of 3 + 2 or 2 + 3.

Listen for the meter as you say these words. What grouping did you hear?

$\frac{5}{8}$ Step to the rhy-thm, Step to the beat.

Come feel the rhy-thm, It's in your feet.

It's not in four-four, it's in five.

It's got me mov-in', me-ter in five.

Add this ostinato to the words. Choose two instrument sounds to play it.

$\frac{5}{8}$ pat clap clap pat clap

Dave Brubeck Quartet

LISTENING CD 12:9

Take Five by Paul Desmond

Paul Desmond's "Take Five" is one of the most famous tunes in jazz. Paul Desmond was the saxophone player in the Dave Brubeck Quartet. This group made "Take Five" a huge hit in the late 1950s and early 1960s. The piece is still popular today. The $\frac{5}{4}$ meter is a feature of "Take Five." There are five beats in a measure and the quarter note receives one beat in $\frac{5}{4}$ **meter**.

Listen to the $\frac{5}{4}$ meter in "Take Five" played by the Dave Brubeck Quartet.

Perform the $\frac{5}{4}$ ostinato with "Take Five." Notice how it is similar to the $\frac{5}{8}$ ostinato on page 212.

Paul Desmond

Playalong

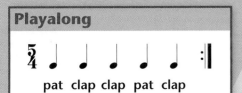

pat clap clap pat clap

Meet the Musician

Dave Brubeck (b. 1920) is an American jazz pianist and composer. He started performing professionally by the age of 13. Brubeck experimented with time signatures through much of his career. His Dave Brubeck Quartet performed in the 1950s and 1960s. Brubeck continues to compose and perform. He has done a lot of work to bring jazz to college audiences.

LESSON 3

Meters That Change

CONCEPT
METER

SKILLS
SING,
CONDUCT

LINKS
CULTURES

MAP
FLORIDA
CUBA
HAITI
DOMINICAN
REPUBLIC

"**G**uantanamera" is a Cuban song that has been popular for a long time in the United States. It is written in $\frac{4}{4}$ meter with the strong beat falling on the first beat of the measure, the **downbeat**. Many songs are composed in this common meter. Sometimes the $\frac{4}{4}$ meter signature is written with the **common time** symbol ₵. These two meter signatures mean the same thing.

Conduct "Guantanamera" using relaxed hand and arm movements. The downbeat is always a downward movement in a conducting pattern.

Guantanamera

CD 12:10

Words and Music by José Fernandez Dias
Music adapted by Julian Orbon and Pete Seeger
Lyrics adapted by Julian Orbon based on a poem by José Martí
English Words by John Higgins

Refrain

Spanish: Guan-ta-na-me-ra,   gua-ji-ra Guan-ta-na-me-ra,
Pronunciation: gwan ta na me ɾa   gwa xi ɾa gwan ta na me ɾa

Guan-ta-na-me-ra,   gua-ji-ra Guan-ta-na-me-ra.
gwan ta na me ɾa   gwa xi ɾa gwan ta na me ɾa

Verse

Yo soy un hom-bre sin-ce-ro   de don-de cre-ce la pal-ma,
yo soi un om bɾe sin se ɾo   de ðon de kɾe se la pal ma
English: For I am sim-ple and truth-ful   and from a land rich with palms.

Yo soy un hom-bre sin-ce-ro   de don-de cre-ce la pal-ma,
yo soi un om bɾe sin se ɾo   de ðon de kɾe se la pal ma
For I am sim-ple and truth-ful   and from a land rich with palms.

Y_an-tes de mo-rir-me quie-ro,   E-char mis ver-sos del al-ma.
ian tes ðe mo ɾiɾ me kye ɾo   e chaɾ mis ßeɾ sos ðel al ma
Be-fore my days end, I sing my song,   I sing the ver-ses of my soul.

Unit 6 Music for Changing Times

215

Changing Meters

Have you ever started off in one direction and changed your mind about where you wanted to go? Meters can change in the same way. The alternation between two or more meters in a piece of music is **changing meters**.

A look at the music of "No despiertes a mi niño" will show you that the meter changes often. What are the meters in this song?

Practice the $\frac{2}{4}$ and $\frac{3}{4}$ conducting patterns.

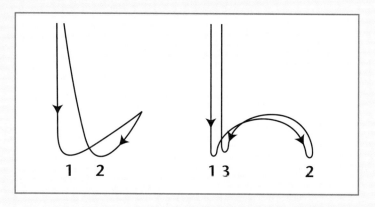

Notice that "No despiertes a mi niño" starts on Beat 2. The beginning of a phrase that does not start on beat 1 is an **upbeat**. Sometimes an upbeat is less or more than a beat.

Conduct "No despiertes a mi niño" as others sing.

THINK! Both "Guantanamera" from Cuba and "No despiertes a mi niño" from Spain have Spanish lyrics. In what ways is the music different? In what ways is it similar?

No despiertes a mi niño

Do Not Wake My Little Son

CD 12:14

Spanish Folk Song
Transcribed by Theo Alcantara
English Words by Linda Worsley

Lento

Spanish: Pa - ja - ri - to que can - tas, En las la - gu - nas,
Pronunciation: pa xa ɾi to ke kan tas en las la gu nas
English: Lit - tle bird sing-ing sweet - ly out by the wa - ter,

No des - pier - tes a mi ni - ño, Que es-tá en la__ cu - na,__
no ðes pyeɾ tos a mi ni nyo kes taen la ku na
do not wake my lit - tle son, ly - ing here in his cra - dle.__

Es - tre - lli - tas del cie - lo, Ra - yos de lu - na,
es tɾe yi tas ðel sye lo ɾa yos ðe lu na
Lit - tle stars in the heav - ens, moon soft - ly glow - ing,

A - lum-brad a mi ni - ñi - to, Que es-tá en la__ cu - na.__
a lum bɾað a mi ni nyi to kes taen la ku na
shine up - on my lit - tle son, ly - ing here in his cra - dle.__

¡E - á, e - á, e - á, e - á, e - á, e - á, e - á, e - á!
e a e a e a e a e a e a e a e a
Ay-ah, ay - ah, ay-ah, ay-ah, ay-ah, ay-ah, ay-ah, ay - ah.__

CONCEPT
METER
SKILLS
LISTEN, SING
LINKS
CULTURES

CD-ROM

Use *Orchestral Instruments* **CD-ROM** to learn more about reed instruments.

One of the songs you have sung, "No despiertes a mi niño," includes both $\frac{2}{4}$ and $\frac{3}{4}$ meters. Some music has three or more different meters.

 LISTENING CD 12:18

Dance for Piccolo, Oboe, Bassoon, and Side Drum by Richard Gill

This is a piece of chamber music by Richard Gill, an Australian composer, conductor, and educator. Music written for a small group of performers, originally meant to be played in a smaller room or chamber rather than a church or auditorium, is **chamber music**.

Listen to "Dance for Piccolo, Oboe, Bassoon, and Side Drum" while following the listening map. What meters do you hear in this music?

bassoon, piccolo, oboe, side drum

Listening Map for Dance for Piccolo, Oboe, Bassoon, and Side Drum

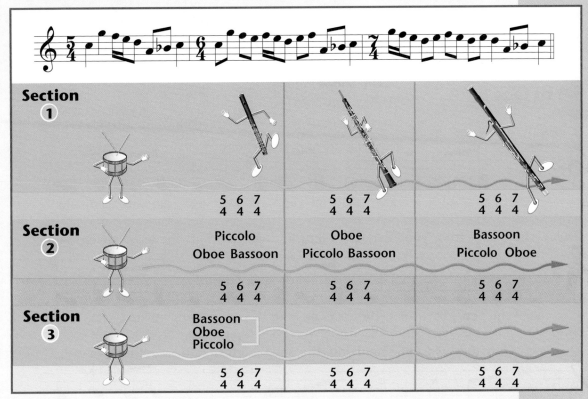

Section 1	$\frac{5}{4}$ $\frac{6}{4}$ $\frac{7}{4}$	$\frac{5}{4}$ $\frac{6}{4}$ $\frac{7}{4}$	$\frac{5}{4}$ $\frac{6}{4}$ $\frac{7}{4}$
Section 2	Piccolo Oboe Bassoon $\frac{5}{4}$ $\frac{6}{4}$ $\frac{7}{4}$	Oboe Piccolo Bassoon $\frac{5}{4}$ $\frac{6}{4}$ $\frac{7}{4}$	Bassoon Piccolo Oboe $\frac{5}{4}$ $\frac{6}{4}$ $\frac{7}{4}$
Section 3	Bassoon Oboe Piccolo $\frac{5}{4}$ $\frac{6}{4}$ $\frac{7}{4}$	$\frac{5}{4}$ $\frac{6}{4}$ $\frac{7}{4}$	$\frac{5}{4}$ $\frac{6}{4}$ $\frac{7}{4}$

One of the meters you just heard was $\frac{7}{4}$. Many folk songs from Eastern Europe are performed in this and other irregular meters. "Bulgarian Folk Melody" is in $\frac{7}{8}$ meter. There are seven beats in the measure and the eighth note receives one beat in $\frac{7}{8}$ **meter**. The accented groupings are usually 2 + 2 + 3 or 3 + 2 + 2.

MAP

HUNGARY
ROMANIA
SERBIA
BULGARIA
GREECE

 LISTENING CD 12:19

Bulgarian Folk Melody, Traditional

This melody from Bulgaria uses a beat grouping in $\frac{7}{8}$ of 3 + 2 + 2. Perform the pattern below with this piece.

Use speech, body percussion, and movement to feel the seven beats in groups of 3 + 2 + 2.

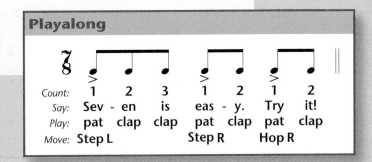

Playalong

Count:	1	2	3	1	2	1	2
Say:	Sev -	en	is	eas -	y.	Try	it!
Play:	pat	clap	clap	pat	clap	pat	clap
Move:	Step L			Step R		Hop R	

Different Groups of Seven

Sing "Shope, Shope" and notice the beat groupings.

SHOPE, SHOPE

Oh, Shope, Shope

CD 12:20

Bulgarian Folk Song
English Words by Linda Worsley

(2+2+3)

do

Bulgarian: Оз до - ле и - дат шо - пи ер - ге - не, ой шо - пе шо - пе
Pronunciation: ɔz dɔ lɛ i dat ʃɔ pi ɛr gɛ nɛ ɔi ʃɔ pe ʃɔ pe
English: They came from yon - der, tra - v'ling in win - ter, hats made of sheep - skin

шо - пи ер - ге - не На гла - ви но - сят ов - чи кал - па - ци,
ʃɔ pi ɛr gɛ nɛ na gla vi nɔ syat ɔv chi kal pa tsi
keep - ing the cold out, hold - ing the shep - herd's staff as they tra - vel,

("eh")
ой шо - пе, шо - пе, ов - яи кал - па - ци О - дят и шаш - кат
ɔi ʃɔ pe ʃɔ pe ɔv chi kal pa tsi ɔ dyat i shash kat
boots made of pig - skin, old, thin, and worn out. March - ing and sing - ing,

с тен - ки кри - ва - ци, ой шо - пе, шо - пе с тен - ки кри - ва - ци
sten ki kɾi va tsi ɔi ʃɔ pe ʃɔ pe sten ki kɾi va tsi
There is noth - ing high - er high - er than Vi - to - sha! There is noth - ing high - er."

Но - зе - те им у свинс - ки о - пин - ци, ой шо - пе, шо - пе свинс - ки о - пин - ци
nɔ zɛ tɛ im u svins ki ɔ pin tsi ɔi ʃɔ pe ʃɔ pe svins ki ɔ pin tsi
March - ing and sing - ing, There is no ri - ver deep as Is - ka - ra, No ri - ver deep - er!

> (clap) > > (clap) >
ой шо - пе, шо - пе ой шо - пе, шо - пе Хей, Хей Хей Хей
ɔi ʃɔ pe ʃɔ pe ɔi ʃɔ pe ʃɔ pe hei hei hei hei

220

Meet the Musician

Béla Bartók (1881–1945) was a Hungarian composer and pianist. He was fascinated with folk music from various countries. He used folk elements in some of his compositions. Bartók wrote piano music (including music for teaching piano to children), orchestral music, concertos, and chamber music. He moved to the United States in 1940.

 LISTENING CD 12:25

Dance No. 2 from *Six Dances in Bulgarian Rhythm* from *Mikrokosmos*, Volume 6, No. 149
by Béla Bartók

Mikrokosmos ("Little World") is a six-book collection of piano teaching pieces. It starts easy and gets progressively harder.

Listen for the way $\frac{7}{8}$ is accented in Dance No. 2. Clapping and counting will help.

 How is Dance No. 2 similar to "Shope, Shope"?

Passing on Traditions

CONCEPT
CULTURAL CONTEXT

SKILLS
LISTEN, SING

LINKS
CULTURES, DANCE

Music continues to be an important part of Native American cultures. For years, Mohawks have learned songs through the **oral tradition**, learning by listening rather than by reading. Many Native American cultures use **vocables**, which are vocal sounds without a specific meaning.

LISTENING CD 12:26

Tekanionton'néha'
Mohawk Social Song and Dance

"Tekanionton'néha'" (Alligator Dance) is a dance performed by the people of the Mohawk nation. This song probably originated among the Seminoles or the Creek Indians in the South, where alligators live. The Mohawks learned this song through cultural exchange in a peace-making process.

Listen to "Tekanionton'néha'."

Notice that "Tekanionton'néha'" does not have a clear sense of meter. This is often a feature of traditional Native American music. To represent this in notation, no meter signature or changing meter signatures are used in this song.

Sing "Tekanionton'néha'." Play a steady drum pulse with it.

A Mohawk performs the Smoke Dance, another Iroquois social dance.

Tekanionton'néha'

Alligator Dance

Mohawk Social Song and Dance

3 times: (1: soloist, 2-3: group)

Vocables: ho   ya   ne   ho   ya   ni   ho   ya   ne - e   ho   ya   ni

3 times (group)

ho ya ne ho ya ni ho ya ne___ho ya ni   ho ya ne ho - e ya he

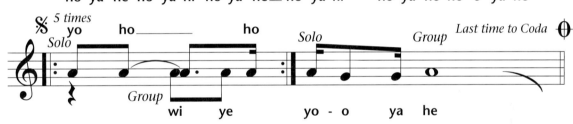

5 times

yo   ho_____   ho

Solo   *Solo*   *Group*   *Last time to Coda*

Group

wi   ye   yo - o   ya he

4 times (1: solo, 2-4: group)   *Group*   *D.S. al Coda*

ha yo wa ni ho ya ni wi ho ya he   ha yo wa ni ho - o ya he

Coda

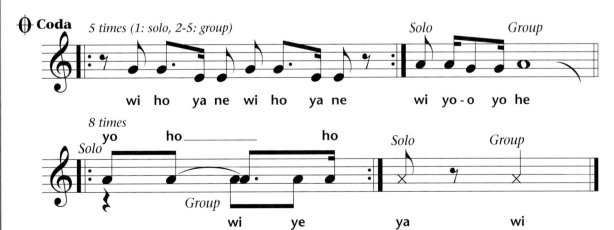

5 times (1: solo, 2-5: group)   *Solo*   *Group*

wi ho   ya ne wi ho   ya ne   wi yo - o   yo he

8 times

yo   ho_____   ho   *Solo*   *Group*

Solo

Group

wi   ye   ya   wi

Navajo Songs

The Navajo song "Jó Ashílá" also comes from the oral tradition.

▲ Marilyn Hood

LISTENING CD 13:1

Jó Ashílá, Navajo Song

"Jó Ashílá" is a social dance, a social part of a Navajo ceremonial meant to get rid of things such as violence and the effects of war; and for gaining peace of mind.

Listen to Marilyn Hood sing "Jó Ashílá." First sing only the sections highlighted in pink.

JÓ ASHÍLÁ

Traveling Together

CD 13:2

Navajo Song

Navajo: Hee yee' yaa' a', hee yee' yaa' a', Jó a-shí-lá,
Pronunciation: heɪ yeɪ ya a heɪ yeɪ ya a jo 'a shɪ la

jó__ a-shí-lá, jó__ a-shí-lá, hee yee' yaa' a',
jo 'a shɪ la jo 'a shɪ la heɪ yeɪ ya a

T'óó-gá ni-zhó-ní-go baa hó-zhó lá, hee ya hee hee yá,
t'o ga' nɪ ʒon nɪ go ba ho ʒo la heɪ ya heɪ heɪ ya

Jó a-shí-lá, jó__ a-shí-lá, jó__ a-shí-lá,
jo 'a shɪ la jo 'a shɪ la jo 'a shɪ la

224

Sing "Jó Ashílá" in three groups. Group 1 sings those sections highlighted in pink, Group 2 sings sections in yellow, and Group 3 sings sections in green. Notice the repetition of these sections.

LISTENING CD 13:6

Ałchíní Yázhí by Sharon Burch

Sharon Burch is a Navajo singer, guitarist, and songwriter. While her music draws upon her Navajo heritage, it also has folk and pop influences.

Listen to the song "Ałchíní Yázhí" sung by Sharon Burch.

A Tone Color for Each Voice

CONCEPT
TONE COLOR
SKILLS
SING, LISTEN
LINKS
THEATER

In the musical *The Wiz*, the Winkies were enslaved by the Wicked Witch of the West. They celebrate their freedom with the song "Everybody Rejoice."

Describe the differences in the voices you hear.

Everybody Rejoice

from the musical *The Wiz*

CD 13:7

Words and Music by Luther Vandross

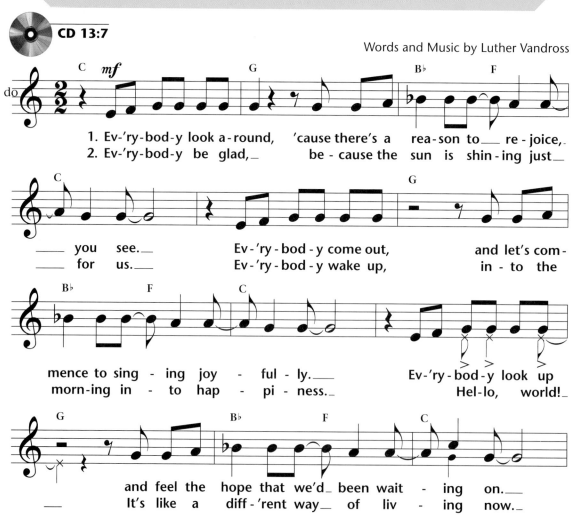

1. Ev-'ry-bod-y look a-round, 'cause there's a rea-son to__ re-joice,__
2. Ev-'ry-bod-y be glad,__ be-cause the sun is shin-ing just__

___ you see.__ Ev-'ry-bod-y come out, and let's com-
___ for us.__ Ev-'ry-bod-y wake up, in-to the

mence to sing-ing joy-ful-ly.__ Ev-'ry-bod-y look up
morn-ing in-to hap-pi-ness.__ Hel-lo, world!__

and feel the hope that we'd__ been wait-ing on.__
___ It's like a diff-'rent way__ of liv-ing now.__

Instrumental Tone Colors

Each instrument has its own tone color or voice. Composers use the special "voices" of instruments to speak in a musical way. Chamber music ensembles often feature different instrument families. This chart gives some common chamber music ensembles. The ensembles are often named by the number of performers.

Chamber Ensemble	Instruments in the Ensemble
String quartet	violin, violin, viola, cello
Woodwind quintet	flute, oboe, clarinet, French horn, bassoon
Brass quintet	trumpet, trumpet, French horn, trombone, tuba
Percussion ensemble	various percussion instruments

 LISTENING CD 13:10

Chamber Ensembles (montage)

You will hear four chamber music ensembles. Match what you hear to the pictures on this page.

Fourth Movement (*Allegro molto*) (excerpt) from String Quartet in C Major, Op. 59, No. 3 by Ludwig van Beethoven for string quartet

Third Movement ("Jongleurs") from *La Cheminée du Roi René*, Op. 205 by Darius Milhaud for woodwind quintet

Allegro (excerpt) by George Frideric Handel for brass quintet

"Third Construction for Percussion Ensemble" (excerpt) by John Cage for percussion ensemble

woodwind quintet

brass quintet

string quartet

percussion ensemble

LISTENING CD 13:11

Use *Orchestral Instruments* **CD-ROM** to learn more about orchestral percussion instruments.

Theme and Percussion Variation from *Young Person's Guide to the Orchestra* (excerpts)
by Benjamin Britten

Benjamin Britten used a range of unique tone colors when he wrote *The Young Person's Guide to the Orchestra*. This piece is a theme and variations followed by a fugue. Britten wrote the variations on a theme by Henry Purcell. The variations are played by each family of orchestral instruments as well as by different instruments or groups of instruments. The percussion variation highlights small groups of percussion instruments.

Listen for the variety of instrumental tone colors as you follow the listening map.

Listening Map for Theme and Percussion Variation

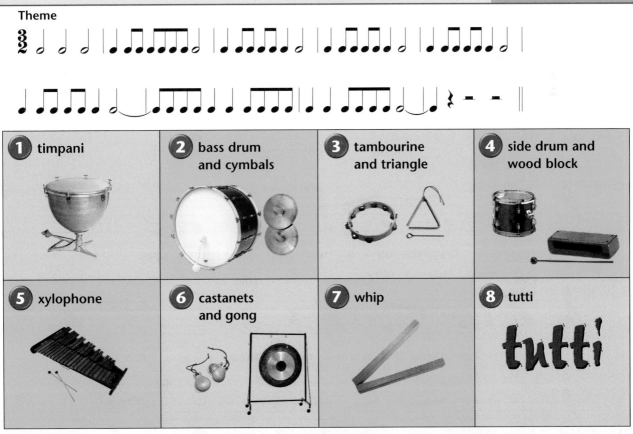

Which instruments could you recognize?

Reach Out with Singing

CONCEPT
MELODY
SKILLS
SING,
EVALUATE
LINKS
CULTURES,
THEATER

Some songs just reach out and invite you in. At concerts you see audiences "into the music," singing and dancing along with the performers. "What the World Needs Now" is such a song.

One way to reach out as you perform is through the way you sit, stand, or move. Good posture for singing involves sitting, standing, or moving relaxed and tall. This gives the best position for making a good singing tone. Free and easy movement also helps the appearance and sound. Stiffness will hinder your sound and appearance.

Sing "What the World Needs Now." Allow yourself to move easily with the music.

What the World Needs Now

CD 13:12

Words by Hal David
Music by Burt Bacharach

Refrain

What the world needs now is love, sweet love. It's the on-ly thing that there's just too lit-tle of. What the world needs now is love, sweet love. No, not just for some, but for ev-'ry-one.

Verse

Dm7
We don't need an - oth - er moun - tain.

Dm7 · Cm9 · F6(9) · B♭maj7
There are moun - tains and hill - sides e - nough to climb;

B♭6 · Cm7 · F6(9) · B♭maj7
There are o - ceans and riv - ers e - nough to cross, e -

Dm7 · G7 · C9 · Cm11
nough to last till the end of time. What the

Coda
A · D7 · B♭6 · B♭
ev - 'ry - one. No, not just for some, oh, but

Am7 · B♭maj7 · C7 · F
just for ev - 'ry - one.

Effective Singing

Diction and breathing are also important to good singing. The way of pronouncing words is **diction**. When you sing, use good diction so the song's message can be understood. All singers in a group need to pronounce the words the same way. In music, most of the length of a note is on the vowel. The consonants at the beginning, middle, or end of a word need to be crisp and clear.

When you breathe for singing, you need to take in enough air to make your breath last for the length of a phrase. You also need to plan where to breathe in the music. Most often this is at the end of a phrase, to help the words make sense. Commas or periods and rests are hints of places where a breath could be taken.

As you listen to others sing, listen carefully for good performance practices.

Evaluate the singers' performances using this chart.

How Did They Do?

Articulation/Diction	words not clear	most words clear	all words very clear
Breathing/ Breath Support	not enough breath to sing entire phrase, low energy	enough breath to sing entire phrase, but low energy	enough breath to sing entire phrase, energy to connect with the audience
Posture/Movement	doesn't allow good breathing or movement	generally good, but somewhat stiff movement	easy carriage for breathing and movement

Learn About Azerbaijan

Azerbaijan is a country in Western Asia. It lies upon the Caucasus Mountains and on the Caspian Sea. The Azeri language is related to Turkish. The Azeri people probably descended from Turkish nomads traveling from Central Asia more than one thousand years ago. The northern region of their neighbor Iran has a large Azeri population. Azerbaijan is roughly the size of Maine.

Global Voices

Bəri Bax! Azerbaijani Folk Song

Young people all over the world can be drawn into music. Some love to perform, which is a way of connecting with others. A group of students perform "Bəri Bax!" (Look at Me!). They are from Azerbaijan, a country that used to be a part of the Soviet Union. The song speaks of courtship and that everyone would approve if the two married.

Pəncərədən daş gəlir, ay bəri bax, bəri bax.
Xumar gözdən yaş gəlir, ay bəri bax, bəri bax.
Səni mənə versələr, ay bəri bax, bəri bax.
Hər görənə xoş gələr, ay bəri bax, bəri bax.

Don't throw stones out of your window,
    Look at me, look at me.
Don't let tears drop out of your charming eyes,
    Look at me, look at me.
If you are allowed to marry me,
    Look at me, look at me.
Everyone around us will approve it!
    Look at me, look at me.

Listen to "Bəri Bax!" for good performance practices.

MAP
RUSSIA
ARMENIA
TURKMENISTAN
AZERBAIJAN
IRAN AFGHANISTAN

Bring Harmony to the World

CONCEPT
HARMONY
SKILLS
DANCE, SING, PLAY
LINKS
CULTURES

You will soon be moving up in school and out into the world. It's a time to discover new places for you and your music, to add to what you already know in ways you haven't anticipated.

You can dance, play, and sing wherever you go. "Dance for the Nations" (page 206) is a three-part canon. Notice how the vocal harmony is created as you sing the song.

Do this dance with "Dance for the Nations."

Formation: three concentric circles, facing inward

Dance Steps
Measures 1–2: In place, circle right in 4 steps.
Measure 3: Join hands with neighbors and raise arms.
Measure 4: Lower arms.
Measures 5–8: Holding hands, circle faces right and takes 7 steps forward (counterclockwise). Reverse body facing on Beat 8.
Measures 9–10: Take 3 steps forward (clockwise) in 3 beats. Reverse body facing on Beat 4.
Measures 11–12: Take 3 steps backward (clockwise) in 3 beats. On Beat 4, face center and drop hands.

Sing the melody of "We Want to Sing" and listen for a harmony part. Notice how the harmony part travels down the scale in the verse and imitates the melody in the refrain.

Sing the song in two-part harmony.

We Want to Sing

CD 13:17

Words and Music by Roger Emerson

Spotlight Your Success!

REVIEW

1 Which beat grouping will work for $\frac{7}{8}$ meter?

    a. 3 + 2 + 2   **b.** 4 + 2 + 3   **c.** 3 + 2

2 Which diagram shows the conducting pattern for $\frac{3}{4}$?

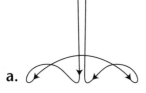

    a.   **b.**   **c.**

3 What is the name of a famous jazz piece in $\frac{5}{4}$ meter?

    a. "Give Me Five"   **b.** "Five by Four"   **c.** "Take Five"

4 What language is used in "El vito"?

    a. Spanish   **b.** Bulgarian   **c.** Navajo

READ AND LISTEN

1 **Read** this melody. Then listen. Which meter do you hear?

    a. changing meter   **b.** $\frac{3}{4}$ **c.** $\frac{5}{8}$

2 **Read** this rhythm. Then listen. Which meter do you hear?

    a. changing meter   **b.** $\frac{4}{4}$ **c.** $\frac{7}{8}$

3 **Read** this rhythm. Then listen. Which meter do you hear?

a. $\frac{2}{4}$ b. $\frac{5}{8}$ c. $\frac{7}{8}$

THINK!

1 What effect do you think good singing posture would have on an audience? Why?

2 If you were a composer, how would you determine what meter to write a song in?

3 Compare the characteristics of traditional Native American music with those of a favorite song.

4 **Write** why you think irregular meters are not common in American music.

CREATE AND PERFORM

1 **Choose** a beat grouping for $\frac{7}{8}$.

2 **Write** a four-measure rhythm.

3 **Play** your rhythm on a pitched or unpitched instrument.

Spotlight on
Music Reading

Spotlight on Music Reading

Spotlight on Music Reading

Sing *Do Re Mi*

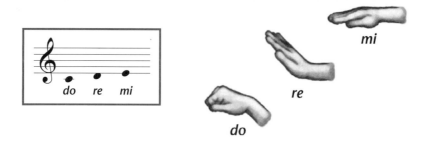

do   re   mi

Learn a *do re mi* countermelody for the first four measures of "In That Great Git'n Up Mornin'."

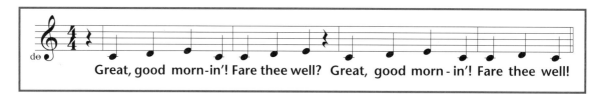

Great, good morn-in'! Fare thee well? Great, good morn-in'! Fare thee well!

Sing the countermelody with the song on page 10.

Practice Basic Rhythms and Pitches

A quarter note ♩ = one sound to a beat.

Two eighth notes ♫ = two sounds to a beat.

A quarter rest 𝄽 = one beat of silence.

A half note ♩ = a sound lasting two beats.

Find the half notes, quarter notes, and eighth-note pairs then sing "Babylon's Fallin'."

CD 13:22

Virginia Folk Song

Sing "Babylon's Fallin'" again and trace the shape of the melody.

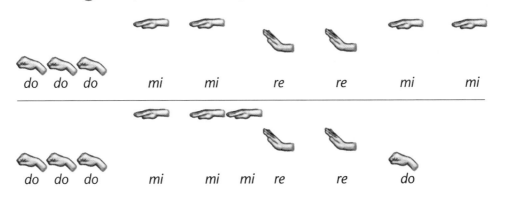

Create with Pitches and Rhythms

Melodies move in three ways: with repeated notes, by steps, and by skips or leaps. **Find** examples of these as you sing the song below.

Words of Wisdom

CD 13:25

Music by Marilyn Copeland Davidson
Words Attributed to Benjamin Franklin

Ear-ly to bed and ear-ly to rise, Makes a man health-y, wealth-y and wise.

What good is a sun-dial in_ the shade? Say-ings like these Ben Frank-lin made.

Benjamin Franklin

"Words of Wisdom" includes a saying from Poor Richard's Almanac.

Create a melody using one of the sayings below.

- When you're finished changing, you're finished.
- He that falls in love with himself will have no rivals.
- Little strokes fell great oaks.
- Drive thy business or it will drive thee.

Listen for repeated notes, steps, and skips or leaps in your classmates' melodies.

UNIT 1 **READING**

CONCEPT
MELODY

SKILLS
READ, SING

Sing with *So*

A fermata ⌢ means to hold that note longer than its value.

Find the fermata in this song.

Sing the song, first with pitch syllables then with the words.

What pitch do you find other than *do re mi*?

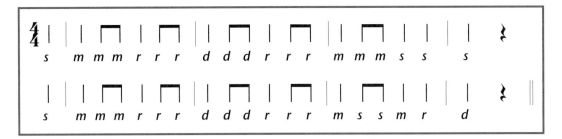

This song begins with an upbeat, a note that comes before the first full measure. Do you know any other songs that begin with an upbeat?

O, I'm Gonna Sing

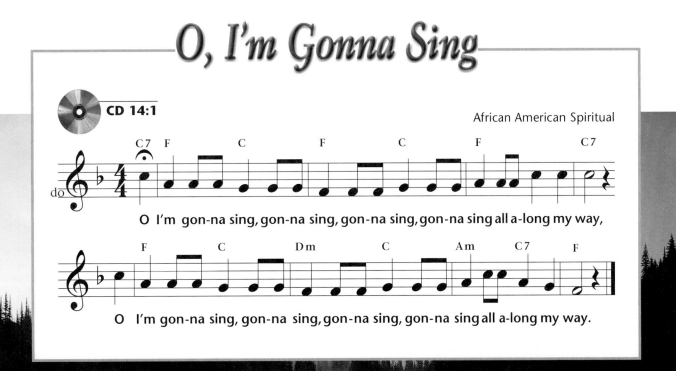

CD 14:1

African American Spiritual

O I'm gon-na sing, gon-na sing, gon-na sing, gon-na sing all a-long my way,

O I'm gon-na sing, gon-na sing, gon-na sing, gon-na sing all a-long my way.

CONCEPT
MELODY

SKILLS
READ, SING

Sing a Pentatonic Song

*S*o and *la* can be added to *do re mi* to complete a pentatonic, or five-tone, scale.

do   re   mi   so   la

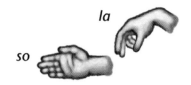

so   la

Sing this five-tone Japanese song.

DETA, DETA

The Moon

CD 14:4

Japanese Children's Song
Collected and Transcribed by
Kathy B. Sorensen

do

F

Japanese: で   た   で   た   つ   き   が
Pronunciation: de   ta   de   ta   tsu   ki   ga
English: Now   the   moon   is   com - ing   out!

F   C

ま — ろ い ま — ろ い ま ん ま ろ い
ma   ru   i   ma   ru   i   ma   n   ma   ru   i
Big and round, so big and round, as round___ as a tray.

F   C   F

ぼ — ん の よ な つ き が
bo   n   no   yo   na   tsu   ki   ga
Big___   and___   round   just   like   a   tray.

2. Now the moon is hiding!
   Gone away, O gone away,
   Behind the clouds.
   Black as ink, behind the clouds.

Compose a Pentatonic Melody

Composers often start with a simple melodic or rhythmic idea called a motive and build a melody on it.
This motive is from a symphony by Haydn.

Identify the pitches and rhythms.

 **LISTENING** CD 14:8

Symphony No. 35, Fourth Movement
by Franz Joseph Haydn

Listen and signal with *do re mi* hand signs each time you hear the motive in the music. Listen again and follow the form chart below.

In which sections do you hear the *do re mi* motive?

Franz Joseph Haydn

Create your own melody using Haydn's motive as a starting point. Choose any pitches from the pentatonic scale to complete your melody.

A Folk Song with Syncopation

You know that these rhythms are equal:

Sing the following pattern with high *do*.

do' do' so la so

How many times can you find the pattern in this pentatonic song?

MAP
MOROCCO
WESTERN SAHARA
MAURITANIA
MALI
GUINEA
NIGERIA

Fun wa ní alaafía

Send Us Your Peace

CD 14:9

Yoruba Welcome Dance

Yoruba:	**Fun**	**wa**	**ni̯a**	**laa - fia,**	**a -**	**se**	**a -**	**se.**
Pronunciation:	fun	wa	nea	la fia	a	she	a	she
English:	**Send**	**us**	**your**	**peace now,**	**oh**	**yes,**	**oh**	**yes.**

	Fun	**wa**	**ni̯a**	**laa - fia,**	**a -**	**se**	**a -**	**se.**
	fun	wa	nea	la fia	a	she	a	she
	Send	**us**	**your**	**peace now,**	**oh**	**yes,**	**oh**	**yes.**

More Rhythm Patterns

Find and read this syncopated rhythm (♪ ♩ ♪) and the dotted quarter-eighth note rhythm (♩. ♪) in this song. Sing the song.

CD 14:13

American Sea Chantey

Verse

1. I heard, I heard the Old Man say,
2. We'll work to - mor-rer, but no work to - day,
3. We're bound a - way for 'Fris - co Bay,
4. A Yan - kee ship wid a Yan - kee crew,
5. Oh, haul a - way, Oh, haul a - way!

John Ka - na - ka, na - ka, Tu - lai - ay!

To - day, to - day is a hol - i - day,____
We'll work to - mor-rer, but no work to - day,____
We're bound a - way at the break of day,____
Oh, we're the buck-os fer to push 'er through.____
Oh, haul a - way, an'____ make your pay.____

John Ka - na - ka, na - ka, Tu - lai - ay.

Refrain

Tu - lai - ay, Oh! Tu - lai - ay,

John Ka - na - ka, na - ka, Tu - lai - ay.

CONCEPT
MELODY

SKILLS
READ, SING

Sing with Low *So* and Low *La*

Find each low *so* and low *la* in the song.

Sing a calypso song with syncopation.

Hill an' Gully

CD 14:16

Jamaican Calypso Music
Words by MMH

Refrain

All F

do

Hill an' gul - ly rid - er, Hill an' gul - ly.

F

Hill an' gul - ly rid - er, Hill an' gul - ly.

Verse

Call F *Response* B♭ F

1. Rode my horse right down - town,⎫ Hill an' gul - ly.
2. And the peo - ple there say,⎭

Call F *Response* B♭ F

Wore a coat of dark brown,⎫ Hill an' gul - ly.
Give your horse some fresh hay,⎭

Call F *Response* B♭ F

And my face had an ug - ly frown,⎫ Hill an' gul - ly,
And then come back here some oth - er day,⎭

Call F *Response* B♭ *D.C. al Fine* F

'Cause he threw me and I tum-bled down,⎫ Hill an' gul - ly.
When a song has chased your frown a - way,⎭

250

Create Your Own Rhythms

Clap these rhythm patterns.

Which of these rhythm patterns is in this song?

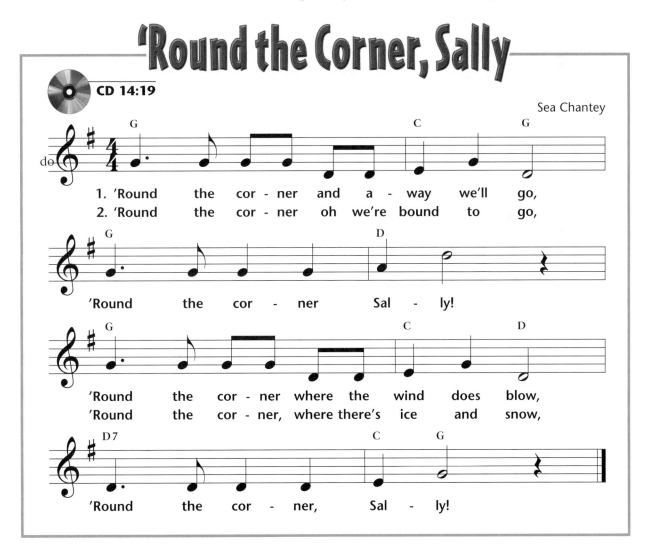

'Round the Corner, Sally

CD 14:19

Sea Chantey

1. 'Round the cor - ner and a - way we'll go,
2. 'Round the cor - ner oh we're bound to go,

'Round the cor - ner Sal - ly!

'Round the cor - ner where the wind does blow,
'Round the cor - ner, where there's ice and snow,

'Round the cor - ner, Sal - ly!

Identify the pitches in the last two measures of the song.

Create your own ostinato using these pitches
and one of the rhythm patterns above.

CONCEPT
RHYTHM

SKILLS
READ, SING

A Spiritual with Syncopation

This song has a dotted pattern (♪ ♩.) and a syncopated pattern (♪ ♩ ♪).

la	D
so	C
mi	A
re	G
do	F
la₁	D₁
so₁	C₁

so₁ so₁ la₁ do do re mi mi re do   mi so la so do mi mi re do

C C D F F G A A G F   A C D C F A A G F

Identify the measures that have the dotted pattern.

Clap and say the words in rhythm.

CD 14:22

African American Spiritual

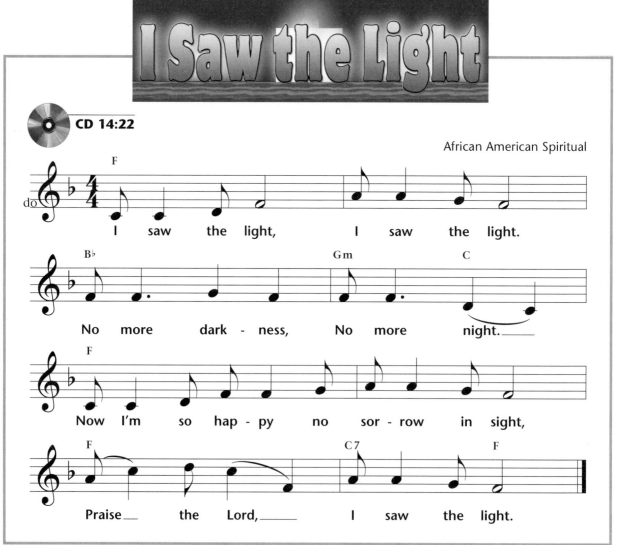

I   saw   the   light,   I   saw   the   light.

No   more   dark - ness,   No   more   night.____

Now   I'm   so   hap - py   no   sor - row   in   sight,

Praise____   the   Lord,____   I   saw   the   light.

CONCEPT
RHYTHM

SKILLS
READ, SING, CREATE

Create a Rhythm Ostinato

Create an ostinato using these three rhythm patterns.

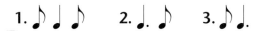

Old Dan Tucker

American Folk Song
Folk Version of Dan Emmett's Minstrel Song

CD 14:25

Verse

1. Old Dan Tuck-er's a fine old man.
2. Old Dan Tuck-er be-gan in ear-ly life, To

Washed his face in a fry-ing pan,
play the ban-jo and the fife. He'd

Combed his head with a wag-on wheel
play the head boys and the gals to sleep,

And died with a tooth-ache in his heel.
And then in-to his bunk he'd creep.

Refrain

Get out the way, Old Dan Tuck-er, You're too late to

get your sup-per. Sup-per's o-ver and din-ner's cook-in'

And Old Dan Tuck-er's just stand-in' look-in'.

Practice with Rhythms and Pitches

Identify the measures where you find low *la*.

Find the ♪♩♪ pattern and sing this spiritual.

Compare Syncopated Rhythms

THINK! Compare and contrast this rhythm ♪ ♩ ♪ with the purple rhythms in the song.

'Way Down Yonder in the Brickyard

CD 15:1

Traditional African
American Game Song
As Performed by the Georgia Sea Island Singers

255

Sing with *Fa*

do   re   mi   fa

fa

When the Saints Go Marching In

CD 15:5

African American Spiritual

1. Oh, when the saints_____ go march-ing in,_____
2. Oh, when the stars_____ re - fuse to shine,_____
3. Oh, when I hear_____ that trum-pet sound,_____

Oh, when the saints go march - ing in,
Oh, when the stars re - fuse to shine,
Oh, when I hear that trum - pet sound,

Oh, Lord, I want to be in that num - ber_____

When the saints go march - ing in.
When the stars re - fuse to shine.
When I hear that trum - pet sound.

Play this bell pattern with the song.

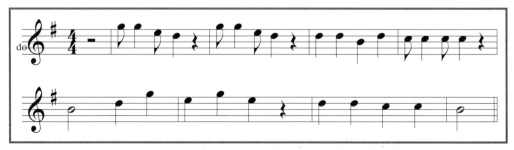

More Practice with *Fa*

Find *fa* in this song about world peace.

MAP
NORWAY
FINLAND
SWEDEN
ESTONIA
LATVIA
RUSSIA

Song of Peace

CD 15:8

Music by Jean Sibelius
Words by Lloyd Stone
Words Adapted by Judy Bond

1. This is my song, a song for all the na-tions,_____
2. My coun-try's skies are blu-er than the o-cean,_____

A song of peace for lands a-far and mine._____
And sun-light beams in clo-ver leaf and pine._____

This is my home, the coun-try where my heart is,_____
But oth-er lands have sun-light, too, and clo-ver,_____

Here are my hopes, my dreams, my ho-ly shrine;_____
And skies are ev-'ry-where as blue as mine,_____

But oth-er hearts in oth-er lands are beat-ing_____
O hear my song, a song for all the na-tions,_____

With hopes and dreams as true and high as mine._____
A song of peace for their land and for mine._____

CONCEPT
MELODY
SKILLS
READ, SING

Sing with *Ti*

mi₁ so₁ la₁ ti₁ do

ti

Find *ti* in this song.
Sing the song.

Aquaqua

CD 15:11

Israeli Children's Game
Collected by Rita Klinger

Vocables: A - qua qua del - la o - mar qua qua qua
Pronunciation: a kwa kwa de la o maɾ kwa kwa kwa

del si - ma tri - co tri - co tri - co tra
del si ma tri ko tri ko tri ko tra

va - lo va - lo va - lo va-lo va-lo va - lo 1 2 3 4 5
va lo va lo va lo va lo va lo va lo

Sing the yellow section of this Puerto Rican folk song, first with pitch syllables then with the words.

la

ti

MAP

BAHAMAS
CUBA
HAITI
DOMINICAN
REPUBLIC
PUERTO
RICO
BRITISH VIRGIN ISLANDS

La paloma se fue

The Dove That Flew Away

CD 15:15

Puerto Rican Folk Song
Arranged by Alejandro Jiménez
English Version by MMH

Gently

p

C

do

Spanish:	¿Se	-	ño	-	res	no han	vis	-	to
Pronunciation:	se		nyo		res	noan	βis		to
English:	**Has**	**an**	-	**y**	-	**one**	**seen**		**him?**

G7   C

la	pa	-	lo	-	ma	que	vo	-	ló	del	pa	-	lo	-	mar?
la	pa		lo		ma	ke	βo		lo	ðel	pa		lo		maɾ
The___	**dove**		**that**		**flew**	**a**	-	**way**	**and**	**left**	**his**		**home.**

f   F   C

Se	fue	la	pa	-	lo	-	ma,	se	fue	la	pa	-	lo	-	ma,
se	fwe	la	pa		lo		ma	se	fwe	la	pa		lo		ma
He's	**gone,**	*la*	*pa*	-	*lo*	-	*ma,*	**he's**	**gone,**	*la*	*pa*	-	*lo*	-	*ma,*

G7   C

se	fue	pa	-	ra	no	vol	-	ver.
se	fwe	pa		ɾa	no	βol		βeɾ
He's	**gone,**	**nev**	-	**er**	**to**	**re**	-	**turn.**

Sing in ¾ Meter

Find *fa* and *ti* in this song.

Conduct in ¾ while singing the song.

Streets of Laredo

CD 15:19

Cowboy Song

1. As I_____ walked out in the streets of La - re - do,
2. "I see by your out - fit that you are a cow - boy,"
3. "Now once in the sad - dle I used to ride hand - some,
4. "Get six jol - ly cow - boys to car - ry my cof - fin,
5. We'll beat the drum slow - ly and play the fife low - ly,

As I_____ walked out in La - re - do one day,
These words he did say as I bold - ly walked by;
'A hand - some young cow - boy' is what they would say.
Get six pret - ty maid - ens to sing me a song;
We'll play the dead march as we bear him a - long.

I spied a young cow - boy all wrapped in white lin - en,
"Come, sit down be - side me and hear my sad sto - ry,
I'd ride in - to town and go down to the card - house,
Take me to the val - ley and throw the clods o'er me,
We'll go to the val - ley and throw the clods o'er him;

All wrapped in white lin - en and cold as the clay.
I'm shot in the chest and I know I must die."
But I'm shot in the chest and I'm dy - ing to - day."
For I'm a young cow - boy and know I've done wrong."
He was a young cow - boy, but he had done wrong.

6. We swung our ropes slowly and rattled our spurs lowly,
   And gave a wild whoop as we bore him along,
   For we all loved our comrade, so brave, young, and handsome.
   We all loved our comrade, although he'd done wrong.

Major Scales

Sing and play this scale.

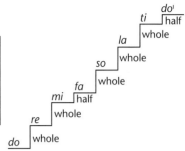

G A B C D E F♯ G
do re mi fa so la ti do'

Listen for the half and whole steps as you sing.

Read the yellow and pink sections of this song then sing each part. Finally, sing the song in two parts.

Da pacem Domine

Give Us Peace

CD 15:22

Words and Music by Melchior Franck
English Words by Linda Worsley

Part 1

do

Latin: Da pa - cem Do - mi - ne, Da pa - cem
Pronunciation: da pa chɛm dɔ mi nɛ da pa chɛm
English: Peace, give us peace, oh, Lord, Oh, give us
do re mi fa fa mi

Part 2

do

Latin: Da pa - cem Do - mi - ne, Da
Pronunciation: da pa chɛm dɔ mi nɛ da
English: Peace, give us peace, oh, Lord, Oh,
so͵ la͵ ti͵ do do ti͵

Do - mi - ne, in di - e - bus Nos - tris.
dɔ mi nɛ in di ɛ bus nɔs tris
peace,___ Lord, for___ all our life - time.

pa - cem Do - mi - ne in di - e - bus___ Nos - tris.
pa chɛm dɔ mi nɛ in di ɛ bus nɔs tris
give us peace, Lord, for all___ our life - time.

261

Sing in ⁶₈ Meter

CONCEPT
MELODY/METER
SKILLS
READ, SING

Clap or play these ⁶₈ rhythm patterns then clap or play them as ostinatos with the song.

Read and sing the highlighted patterns in the song.

Vive l'amour

CD 16:1

American College Song

1. Let's all come to-geth-er and raise a loud cheer, } Vi-ve la com-pag-nie,
2. All join in a song and our voi-ces will blend, }

To all of the friends who are gath-er-ing here, } Vi-ve la com-pag-nie.
We sing to the friend-ship that nev-er will end, }

Refrain

Vi-ve la, vi-ve la, vi-ve l'a-mour,   Vi-ve la, vi-ve la, vi-ve l'a-mour,

Vi-ve l'a-mour,   vi-ve l'a-mour,   Vi-ve la com-pag-nie!

More $\frac{6}{8}$ Rhythms

This song from Newfoundland contains all the pitches in a diatonic scale.

MAP

CANADA

NEWFOUNDLAND

Lots o' Fish in Bonavist' Harbor

CD 16:4

Newfoundland Folk Song

Verse

A7   D

do

1. There's lots o' fish in Bon - a - vist' Har - bor,
2. Oh, Sal - ly went to church ev - 'ry Sun - day,

G   A7

Lots   o'   fish   right   in   a - round   here.
Not for   to   sing   nor   for_____   to   hear.

D

Boys   and   girls   are   fish - in'   to - geth - er,
But   to   see   the   fel - ler   from   For - tune

G   D   A7   D

For - ty - five   from   Car - bon - ear.
What   was   down   here   fish - in'   last   year.

Refrain

A7   D

Oh,   catch - a - hold   this   one,   catch - a - hold   that   one,
Dance a - round this   one,   dance a - round   that   one,

1. G   A7   2. G   D   A7   D

Swing a-round this one, swing a-round she; Did-dle dum dee dum, did-dle dum dee.

263

Sixteenth Notes

In $\frac{2}{4}$ these combinations of rhythms equal one beat.

Find these rhythm patterns in this song.

Old Turkey Buzzard

CD 16:7

North Carolina Folk Song

Old tur - key buz - zard, lend me your wings

To fly a - cross the riv - er to see Sal - ly King.

264

More Sixteenth-Note Rhythms

CONCEPT
RHYTHM
SKILLS
READ, SING

Clap, say, or play this rhythm as an ostinato with the song.

Get a - long home, Cin - dy, Cin - dy.

CD 16:10   Appalachian Folk Song

Verse   F   C 7

1. I wish I was an ap - ple a - hang - ing on a tree,
2. She told me that she loved me, She called me "su - gar plum,"
3. I wish I had a nee - dle as fine as I could sew,

And ev - 'ry time my Cin - dy passed, she'd take a bite of me!
She threw her arms a - round me, and I thought my time had come.
I'd sew that gal to my coat - tail and down the road I'd go.

Refrain
Descant

Get a-long home!   Get a-long home!

Melody   B♭   F

Get a-long home, Cin - dy, Cin - dy, Get a-long home, Cin - dy, Cin-dy.

Get a-long home!   I'll mar - ry you some-day.

B♭   F   B♭   F

Get a-long home, Cin - dy, Cin - dy, I'll mar - ry you__ some-day.

Use What You Know

Identify the sixteenth-note rhythms in the song below.

Practice patting or saying these rhythm patterns then sing the song.

Oh, I went to the rock to hide my face, The rock cried out, "No hid - in' place!"

Oh, the rock cried out, "I'm burn-in' too, I want to go to heav-en as well as you."

There's No Hidin' Place

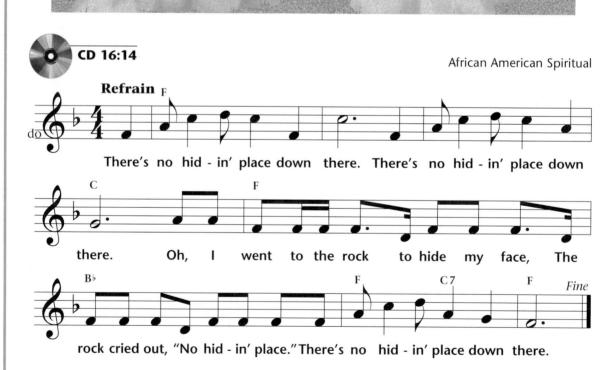

CD 16:14

African American Spiritual

Refrain F

There's no hid - in' place down there. There's no hid - in' place down

there. Oh, I went to the rock to hide my face, The

rock cried out, "No hid - in' place." There's no hid - in' place down there.

Pat or play this pattern with the song.

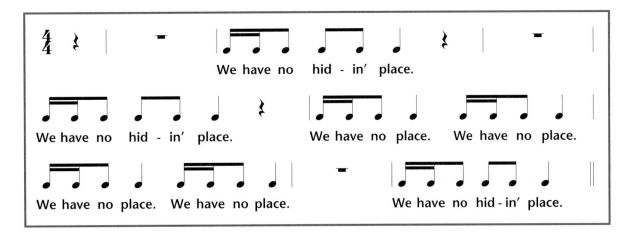

We have no hid - in' place.
We have no hid - in' place.
We have no place. We have no place.
We have no place. We have no place.
We have no hid - in' place.

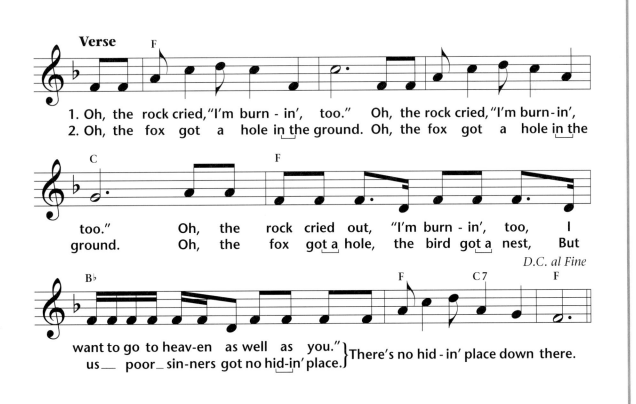

Verse

1. Oh, the rock cried, "I'm burn - in', too." Oh, the rock cried, "I'm burn-in',
2. Oh, the fox got a hole in the ground. Oh, the fox got a hole in the

too." Oh, the rock cried out, "I'm burn - in', too, I
ground. Oh, the fox got a hole, the bird got a nest, But

D.C. al Fine

want to go to heav-en as well as you." } There's no hid - in' place down there.
us poor sin-ners got no hid-in' place. }

More Syncopated Rhythms

Find the ♪♪ rhythm in this song from Peru.

MAP
COLOMBIA
PERÚ   BRAZIL
BOLIVIA
CHILE

Los maizales

The Cornfields

CD 16:17

Peruvian Folk Song
English Words by Linda Worsley

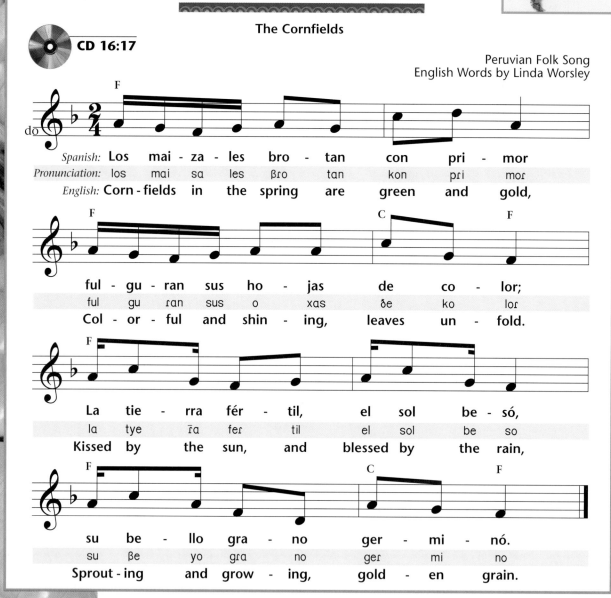

Spanish: Los mai - za - les bro - tan con pri - mor
Pronunciation: los mai sa les βɾo tan kon pɾi moɾ
English: **Corn - fields in the spring are green and gold,**

ful - gu - ran sus ho - jas de co - lor;
ful gu ɾan sus o xas ðe ko loɾ
Col - or - ful and shin - ing, leaves un - fold.

La tie - rra fér - til, el sol be - só,
la tye ɾa feɾ til el sol be so
Kissed by the sun, and blessed by the rain,

su be - llo gra - no ger - mi - nó.
su βe yo gɾa no geɾ mi no
Sprout - ing and grow - ing, gold - en grain.

 LISTENING CD 16:21

Let's Run Across the Hill by Heitor Villa-Lobos

Listen and raise a hand when you hear ♪♪ in this piece by a Brazilian composer.

CONCEPT
TONALITY
SKILLS
READ, SING, PLAY

A Song in a Minor Key

Sing and play these scales. **Name** the scale for this song.

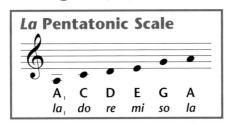

La **Pentatonic Scale**

A, C D E G A
la, do re mi so la

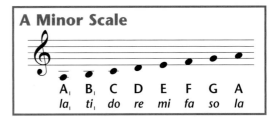

A Minor Scale

A, B, C D E F G A
la, ti, do re mi fa so la

MAP

BRAZIL
PARAGUAY
BOLIVIA
CHILE   URUGUAY
ARGENTINA

De allacito carnavalito

CD 16:22

The Carnival Is Coming

Argentine Folk Song
English Version by MMH

Am   Em

do

Spanish: De a-lla - ci - to, de a-lla - ci - to,   ya vie-ne el car - na - va - li - to;
Pronunciation: ðea ya si to ðea ya si to   ya βye nel kar na βa li to
English: Ev - 'ry-one there is___ com-ing down to the *car - na - va - li - to.*

Em   Am

To-dos ba - jan   en pa - re - ja,   yo voy ba-jan - do so - li - to.
to ðos βa xan en pa ɾe xa   yo βoi βa xan do so li to
Ev - 'ry - one comes down in cou-ples, I am a lone - ly___ so-lo.

Say or play this accompaniment with the song.

Playalong

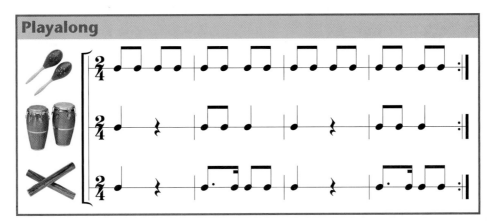

A Canon in a Minor Key

Describe what makes these songs minor.

How do they sound different from other songs you know?

By the Singing Water

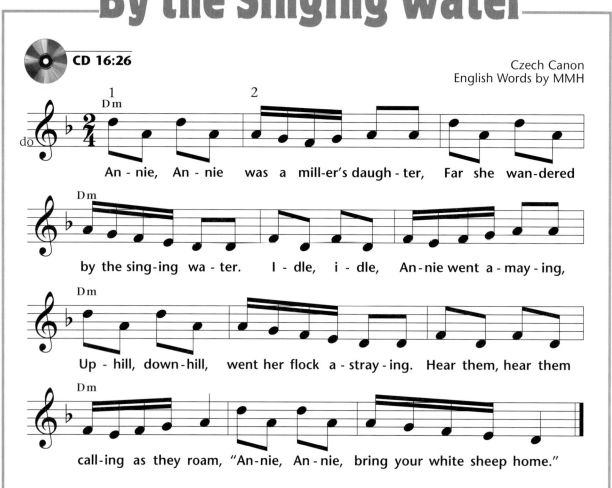

CD 16:26

Czech Canon
English Words by MMH

An - nie, An - nie was a mill-er's daugh - ter, Far she wan-dered

by the sing-ing wa - ter. I - dle, i - dle, An-nie went a-may-ing,

Up - hill, down-hill, went her flock a-stray-ing. Hear them, hear them

call-ing as they roam, "An-nie, An - nie, bring your white sheep home."

Listen for Minor

Bedřich Smetana wrote a piece for orchestra called "The Moldau." It was inspired by a great river in his country.

This melody is the main theme from "The Moldau."
Sing or play the melody, which is in a minor key.

LISTENING CD 16:29

The Moldau from *Má Vlast (My Country)*
by Bedřich Smetana

Listen for the theme of "The Moldau," which is in minor. Raise your hand when you hear the theme change to major.

Listening Map for The Moldau

Sing Chord Roots

Each chord in music has a root.

Find the roots for the I and V chords below.

Name the pitch syllable for each root.

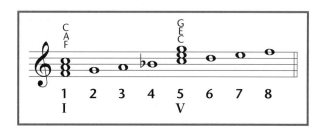

Play the I and V chords on resonator bells.

C   G

A   E

F   C

Mi gallo

My Rooster

Three-Part Round
English Words by MMH

CD 16:30

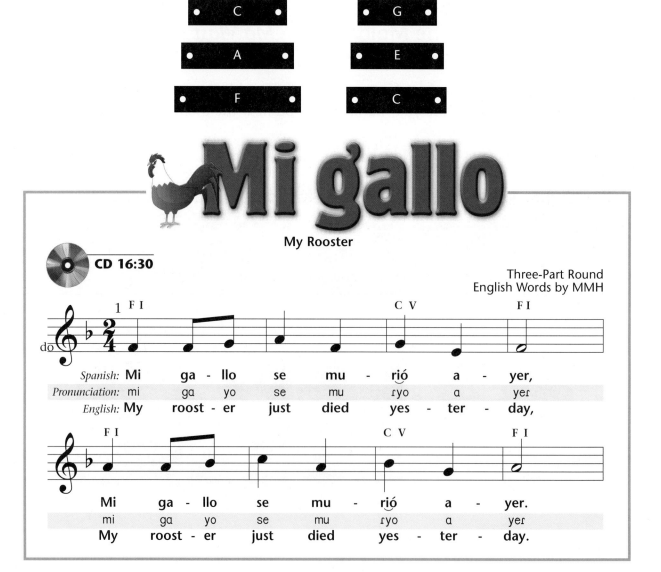

Spanish: Mi ga - llo se mu - rió a - yer,
Pronunciation: mi ga yo se mu ɾyo a yeɾ
English: My roost - er just died yes - ter - day,

Mi ga - llo se mu - rió a - yer.
mi ga yo se mu ɾyo a yeɾ
My roost - er just died yes - ter - day.

2

Ya no can - ta - rá co - co - rí, co - co - rá,
ya no can ta ɾa ko ko ɾi ko ko ɾa
He will nev - er sing co - co - rí, co - co - rá,

Ya no can - ta - rá co - co - rí, co - co - rá.
ya no can ta ɾa ko ko ɾi ko ko ɾa
He will nev - er sing co - co - rí, co - co - rá.

3

Co - co - rí, co - rí, co - rá,_____
ko ko ɾi ko ɾi ko ɾa
Co - co - rí, co - rí, co - rá,_____

Co - co - rí, co - rí, co - rá._____
ko ko ɾi ko ɾi ko ɾa
Co - co - rí, co - rí, co - rá._____

Sing this chord root ostinato with the song.

do_____ so do

CONCEPT
HARMONY
SKILLS
READ, SING, LISTEN

Practice Harmony and Rhythm

Identify the root of each chord in the song.
Read and sing this chord root accompaniment with the song.

Where, oh, where is John?

CD 17:1

Czechoslovakian Folk Song

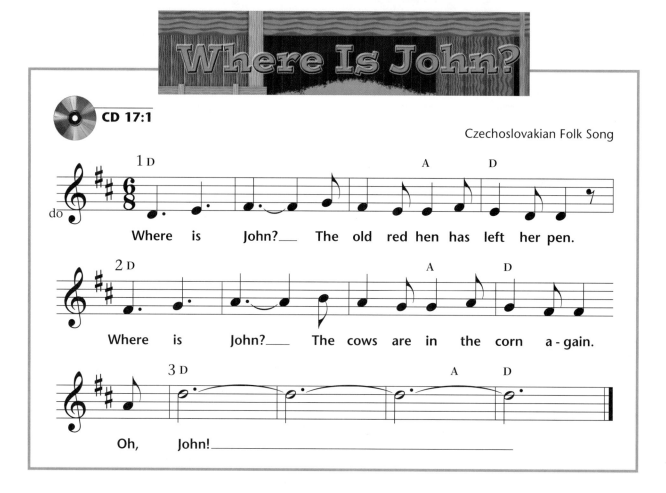

1 D   A   D
Where   is   John?___ The old red hen has left her pen.

2 D   A   D
Where   is   John?___ The cows are in the corn a-gain.

3 D   A   D
Oh,   John!_____

LISTENING CD 17:6

Chorus of Villagers from *The Bartered Bride*
by Bedřich Smetana

Bedřich Smetana used the folk melody from "Where Is John?"
in his opera *The Bartered Bride*.

Listen to a professional opera chorus and orchestra perform
"Chorus of Villagers" in Czech.

Sing this version from the opera.

Chorus of Villagers

from the opera *The Bartered Bride*

Music by Bedřich Smetana
Words by Karel Sabina
English Words by MMH

CD 17:7

Czech: Proč by - chom se ne - tě - ši - li,____
Pronunciation: proch bi xom sɛ nɛ tye shi li
English: We're to - geth - er, laugh-ing, sing-ing, cel - e - brat-ing,

proč by - chom se ne - tě - ši - li,____
proch bi xom sɛ nɛ tye shi li
In our vil - lage, laugh-ing, sing-ing, cel - e - brat-ing.

když nám pán bůh zdra - ví dá,____ zdra - ví dá,
gdiʒ nam pan bux zdra vi da zdra vi da
For we have the best of life, the best of life,

když nám pán bůh zdra - ví dá, zdra - ví dá,
gdiʒ nam pan bux zdra vi da zdra vi da
For we have the best of life, best of life,

když nám pán bůh zdra - ví dá,____ zdra - ví dá?
gdiʒ nam pan bux zdra vi da zdra vi da
For we have the best of life, the best of life.

I-V7 Harmony in C and F

This Hawaiian song is about beautiful pandanus trees swaying by the sea.

Remember that an eighth rest lasts as long as an eighth note. In $\frac{2}{4}$ meter, an eighth rest represents a silence lasting half a beat.

Find the eighth rests (꞉) in this song.

Pandanus tree

Nani Wale Na Hala

The Swaying Pandanus Trees

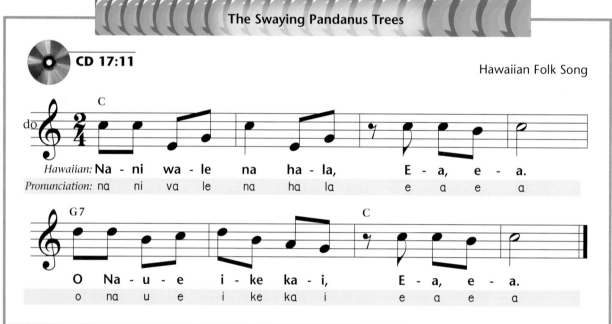

CD 17:11

Hawaiian Folk Song

do

C

Hawaiian: Na - ni   wa - le   na   ha - la,   E - a,   e - a.
Pronunciation: na   ni   va   le   na   ha   la   e   a   e   a

G 7   C

O   Na - u - e   i - ke   ka - i,   E - a,   e - a.
o   na   u   e   i   ke   ka   i   e   a   e   a

Hawaiian puili sticks are made from split bamboo and are used in traditional Hawaiian music.

Identify the root of the I chord and the V7 chord in this song and sing them as you listen to the song.

Play this puili stick pattern on the beat with the song. Tap the floor, tap the stick ends together, or tap your shoulder with the beat.

Line 1: Floor, floor, ends, ends, floor, floor, ends, ends.

Line 2: Floor, R shoulder, floor, L shoulder, ends, ends, floor, rest.

Read and sing this song from West Africa.

Create and perform an accompaniment using the I and V7 chords indicated.

Many people in West Africa work during the week and visit the city on Saturday night.

Sing the Blues with I, IV, and V

The standard blues progression is 12 measures long and easy to remember.

Play I, IV, and V chords as you listen to City Blues.

Sing the song and play the blues chord progression.

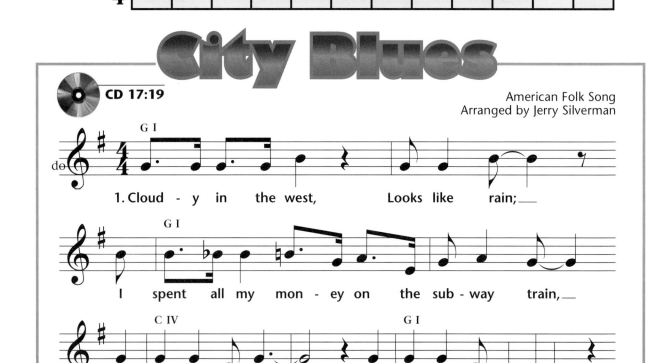

City Blues

CD 17:19

American Folk Song
Arranged by Jerry Silverman

1. Cloud - y in the west, Looks like rain;
I spent all my mon - ey on the sub - way train,
In New York Cit - y, In New York Cit - y,
In New York Cit - y, you real - ly got to know your way.

2. Went to Detroit, it was fine;
I watched the cars movin' off th' assembly line,
In Detroit City, In Detroit City,
In Detroit City, you really got to know your way.

3. I looped the loop, I rocked and reeled;
I thought the Cubs played ball in Marshall Field,
In the Windy City, In the Windy City,
In the Windy City, you really got to know your way.

Some large cities have subways for public transportation.

278

I and V7 Harmony in an Opera Duet

Sing this melody and use the F and C chord symbols to play an accompaniment for the song.

Sound the Trumpet

CD 17:22

Music by Vincenzo Bellini
English Words by MMH

Sound, sound the trum-pet loud - ly, brave-ly we soon will join the bat-tle.

'Tis sweet to face such dan - ger, with pride_ of love and home.

Hail to the con-q'ring vic - tor; Bring to us e - ter - nal fame!

Morn-ing will rise on na - tions whose on - ly dreams are faith and free-dom.

Earth's ty-rants who op - pose___ us will sink___ in end-less shame!

LISTENING CD 17:25

Sound the Trumpet from *I Puritani*
by Vincenzo Bellini

Bellini wrote his opera *I Puritani (The Puritans)* in 1834. At this point in the plot, two friends encourage each other before going to war.

Listen to an opera performance of "Sound the Trumpet."

Music Reading 279

Music in $\frac{5}{4}$ Meter

An accent is a stress on a note or chord. In $\frac{5}{4}$ meter, the accents are usually on beats one and three or beats one and four. This gives a grouping of 2 + 3 or 3 + 2.

Read and clap each example. Clap the accented beats more strongly. Describe the differences among them.

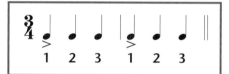

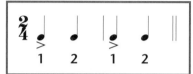

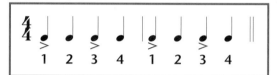

Read and clap these patterns in $\frac{5}{4}$ meter.

Both of these orchestral themes are in $\frac{5}{4}$ meter. Each measure has a grouping of 2 + 3.

Read and sing each theme.

Theme from "Hopscotch" by Sir William Walton

Theme from Symphony No. 6, Second Movement by Piotr Ilyich Tchaikovsky

 LISTENING **CD 17:26, 27**

Leggiero (Hopscotch) from *Music for Children*   by Sir William Walton

Symphony No. 6 ("Pathetique"), Second Movement   by Piotr Ilyich Tchaikovsky

Listen to these two selections in $\frac{5}{4}$ meter.

Move to show the meter while listening.

Compare the two selections.

Sir William Walton

Piotr Ilyich Tchaikovsky

Changing Meters

Identify the meter of the song.

Read and sing the song.

Is That Mister Reilly?

CD 17:28

Words and Music by Pat Rooney

Is that Mis - ter Reil - ly, can an - y - one tell?

Is that Mis - ter Reil - ly that owns the ho - tel?

Well, if that's Mis - ter Reil - ly, they speak of you high - ly.

Well up - on my soul Reil - ly, you're do - ing quite well.

Charles Ives was an American composer. He enjoyed using rhythm and meters to treat well-known melodies in unique and sometimes amusing ways. Ives used the melody of "Is That Mister Reilly?" and changing meters to create his song, "The Side Show."

Identify the meter changes in this version of the song.

Clap the rhythm of the song while counting the beats and accenting the first beat in each measure.

**LISTENING** CD 17:31

The Side Show by Charles Ives

"Is___ that Mis-ter Ri-ley, who___ keeps the ho-

tel?" is the tune that ac-comp-'nies the trot-ting track bell; An

old horse un - sound,_ turns the mer-ry-go-round, mak-ing

poor Mis-ter Ri-ley look a bit like a Rus - sian dance,_

_ Some speak___ of so high-ly, as___ they do of Ri - ley!___

Listen to "The Side Show," clapping the rhythm and counting with the beats.

⁷⁄₈ Meter

Clap this rhythm pattern. Put more emphasis on the accented notes.

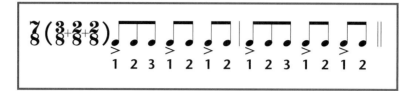

Listen to "Samiotissa" and pat the rhythm.

Sing the song.

MAP

BULGARIA
ALBANIA
GREECE
TURKEY

SAMIOTISSA

CD 18:1

Greek Folk Song from Samos
English Words by Linda Worsley

Νά στρώ - σω ρό - δα στό για - λό Σα - μιώ - τισ - σα Τριαν -
na stro so ro δa sto ya lo sa myo tis sa tryan
I will spread ro - ses on the shore, *Sa - mio - tis - sa*, And

τά - φνλ - λα στήν άμ - μο_____ μο_____
da fil la stin am mo mo
bright car - na - tions on the sand._____ sand._____

Sing in $\frac{3}{2}$ Meter

Pat this rhythm in $\frac{3}{4}$ meter.

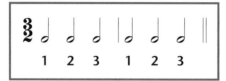

1 2 3   1 2 3

Pat this rhythm pattern in $\frac{3}{2}$ meter.

1 2 3   1 2 3

What kind of note gets one beat in the second rhythm pattern?

How is the first pattern different from the second pattern? How are they the same?

Pete Seeger, Arlo Guthrie, and friends sing at a concert in Cleveland, Ohio.

Find lines in the song with the same rhythm.

Sing this traditional American song in $\frac{3}{2}$ meter.

How Can I Keep from Singing?

 CD 18:5

Music by Rev. R. Lowry
Words by Anne Warner
Arranged by Pete Seeger

My life flows on in end-less song, A-bove Earth's la-men-ta-tion.

I hear the real, though far-off hymn, that hails a new cre-a-tion.

Through all the tu-mult, and the strife, I hear that mu-sic ring-ing.

It sounds an ech-o__ in my soul, How can I keep from sing-ing?___

 LISTENING CD 18:8

How Can I Keep from Singing?
traditional American song sung by Pete Seeger

Listen to Pete Seeger sing "How Can I Keep from Singing?" Listen for ways Seeger changes the rhythms and makes the song his own in this performance.

Music Reading 287

Spotlight on Performance

Spotlight on Performance

Broadway For Kids

MTI's BROADWAY junior

Mini musicals specifically designed for classroom study and presentation, featuring scenes and songs from the musical The Music Man Junior.

MEREDITH WILLSON'S
THE MUSIC MAN JUNIOR

**Book, Music, and Lyrics by Meredith Willson
Story by Meredith Willson and Frank Lacey**

Musical Numbers

Rock Island

Iowa Stubborn

76 Trombones

Pick-A-Little/ Goodnight, Ladies

The Wells Fargo Wagon

The Music Man Junior, Palo Alto Children's Theatre, Palo Alto, CA

Scene 1: A train on the way to River City, Iowa

Rock Island

CD 18:9

Words and Music by Meredith Willson

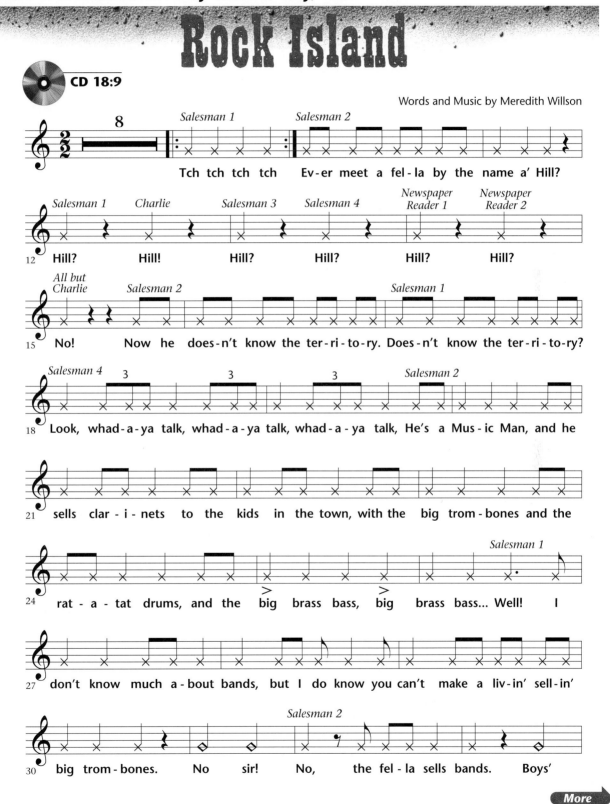

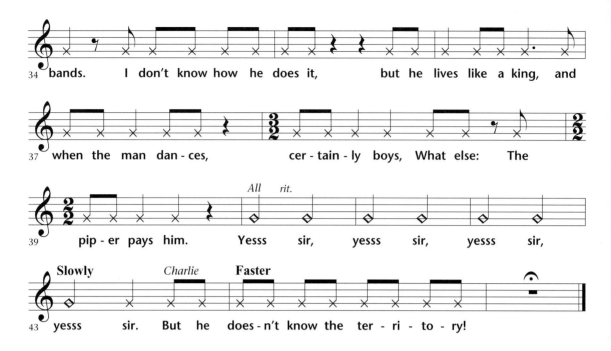

34 bands.   I don't know how he does it,   but he lives like a king, and

37 when the man dan - ces,   cer - tain - ly boys, What else: The

All   *rit.*

39 pip - er pays him. Yesss   sir,   yesss   sir,   yesss   sir,

Slowly   *Charlie*   **Faster**

43 yesss   sir. But   he   does - n't know the ter - ri - to - ry!

CONDUCTOR: River City, Iowa!

STRANGER (HAROLD HILL): Gentleman, you intrigue me. I think I'll have to give Iowa a try.

CHARLIE COWELL: Don't believe I caught your name.

HAROLD: Don't believe I dropped it.

(HAROLD turns his suitcase towards the audience, which says "PROF. HAROLD HILL," and EXITS the train.)

SALESMAN 1: So, Harold Hill ventured into the small town of River City, Iowa, to try his luck.

About the Script

CHARACTER NAMES are colored **RED**

DIALOGUE is colored **BLUE**

STAGE DIRECTIONS are colored *GREEN*

Words and Music by Meredith Willson

Oh,___ there's noth - in' half - way___ a-bout the I - o - wa way to treat you, when we treat you, which we may not do at all. There's an I - o - wa kind - a spe - cial chip - on - the - shoul - der at - ti - tude we've nev - er been with - out that we re - call. We can be cold as our fall - ing ther - mo - me - ters in De - cem - ber if you ask a - bout our weath - er in Ju - ly. And we're so by gad stub - born, we can stand touch - in' nos - es for a week at a time and nev - er see eye - to -

More

eye. But what the heck! You're wel - come,

join us at the pic - nic. You___ can have your fill of all the

food you bring your - self. You real - ly ought to give I - o - wa___

Hawk - eye, I - o - wa,___ Du - buque, Des Moines, Dav - en - port, Mar - shall - town,

Ma - son Cit - y, Ke - o - kuk, Ames, Clear Lake, ought to give I - o - wa___ a

try.___

(As the TOWNSPEOPLE go about their business, MARCELLUS spies HAROLD.)

SALESMAN 2: Harold Hill was surprised to run into his old buddy Marcellus Washburn.

MARCELLUS: What are you doing here? *(HAROLD pantomimes conducting.)* You're not back in the band business!

HAROLD: Yup!

MARCELLUS: But you don't know anything about music.

HAROLD: Marcellus, stop worrying.

MARCELLUS: We got a lady music teacher here who'll expose you before you get your bags unpacked.

HAROLD: If she passes by, point her out to me.

MARCELLUS: I will.

(HAROLD puts down his suitcase and speaks loudly to MARCELLUS, drawing a crowd.)

Meet the Musician

Meredith Willson was born in 1902 in Mason City, Iowa. He learned to play the flute as a child. He became good enough to play professionally while he was still in high school. After high school, he left Iowa to study at the Damrosch Institute of Musical Art, which later became the Juilliard School. While he was at the Institute, he also played flute and piccolo in the John Philip Sousa Band. He later joined the New York Philharmonic Orchestra, where he was first flutist. Willson was the musical director for various radio programs; he also composed many music scores, band compositions, and choral works. Willson wrote three Broadway musicals: *The Music Man, The Unsinkable Molly Brown,* and *Here's Love.* He has also written two autobiographies and a novel.

76 Trombones

CD 18:11

Bright Two (♩ = ca. 112)

Harold (spoken freely)

Words and Music by Meredith Willson

May I have your at-ten-tion, please? At-

ten-tion, please! I can deal with this trou-ble,

friends, with a wave of my hand, this ver-y hand! Please ob-

serve me if you will. I'm Pro-fes-sor Har-old

Hill, and I'm here to or-gan-ize the Riv-er Cit-y Boys'

Band! Prrrrr!___ Oh, a band-'ll do it, my

friends, oh, yes! I mean a boys' band, do you hear me? I say,

Riv-er Cit-y's got-ta have a boys' band, and I mean she needs it to-

day. Well, Pro-fes-sor Har-old Hill's___ on hand and

River City's gon-na have her boys' band! And that band's gon-na be in un-i-form!

Townspeople

Sev-en-ty-six trom-bones led the big pa-rade, with a hun-dred and ten cor-nets close at hand. They were fol-lowed by rows and rows of the fin-est vir-tu-o-sos, the cream of ev-'ry fa-mous band.

Sev-en-ty-six trom-bones caught the morn-ing sun, with a hun-dred and ten cor-nets right be-hind. There were more than a thou-sand reeds spring-ing up like weeds. There were horns of ev-'ry shape and kind. There were fif-ty mount-ed can-non in the bat-ter-y, thun-der-ing, thun-der-ing, loud-er than be-fore.

More →

Clar - i - nets of ev -'ry size and trum - pet - ers who'd im - pro - vise a full oc - tave

mf

cresc.

high - er than the score. Sev - en - ty - six trom - bones hit the

ƒ

coun - ter - point, while a hun - dred and ten cor - nets blazed a - way.

(shouted)

To the rhy - thm of Harch! Harch! Harch! All the kids be - gan to

march, and they're march - ing still_____ right to -

day!_____ March - ing still right to - day!

2

(There is a commotion of excitement from the TOWNSPEOPLE as most of them EXIT. MAYOR SHINN steps forward to talk to EWART, OLIN, OLIVER, and JACY of the School Board.)

SALESMAN 3: The mayor wasn't buying Harold Hill's remedy for the town's troubles.

SHINN: Gentlemen of the School Board, this calls for emergency action. That man is a spellbinder. Find out if he ever got his college music degree!

(SHINN EXITS. The SCHOOL BOARD approaches HAROLD as a few LADIES stay to listen in.)

SALESMAN 4: Harold Hill evaded the School Board's request for his degree by teaching them the joy of singing in harmony.

SALESMAN 5: But, some of the ladies were suspicious, too.

Pick-A-Little / Goodnight, Ladies

Words and Music by Meredith Willson

CD 18:12

(♩ = ca. 126)

The Ladies - all three times

1.-3. Pick a lit-tle, talk a lit-tle, pick a lit-tle, talk a lit-tle,

School Board - 2nd and 3rd times

2. Good - night,
3. Fare - well,

cheep, cheep, cheep, talk a lot, pick a lit-tle more.

lad - ies, _____
lad - ies, _____

Pick a lit-tle, talk a lit-tle, pick a lit-tle, talk a lit-tle,

Good - night,
Fare - well,

cheep, cheep, cheep, talk a lot, pick a lit-tle more.

lad - ies, _____
lad - ies, _____

Pick a lit-tle, talk a lit-tle, pick a lit-tle, talk a lit-tle,

Good - night,
Fare - well,

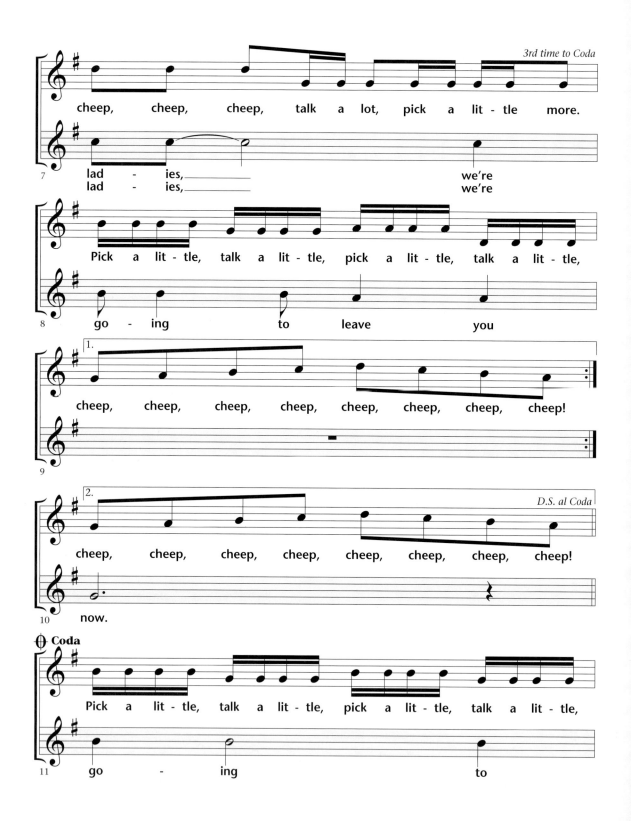

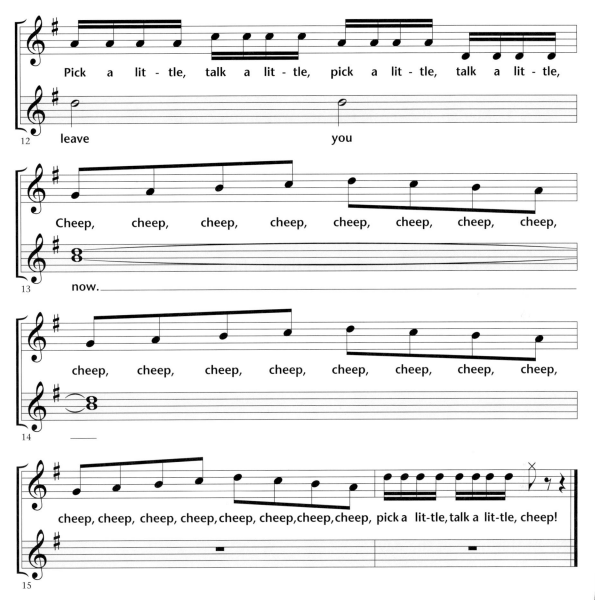

Pick a lit - tle, talk a lit - tle, pick a lit - tle, talk a lit - tle,

leave you

Cheep, cheep, cheep, cheep, cheep, cheep, cheep, cheep,

now.

cheep, cheep, cheep, cheep, cheep, cheep, cheep, cheep,

cheep, cheep, cheep, cheep, cheep, cheep, cheep, cheep, pick a lit - tle, talk a lit - tle, cheep!

The Music Man Junior,
Palo Alto Children's
Theatre, Palo Alto, CA

Scene 3: Town Square

SALESMAN 5: Harold Hill continued to sell instruments to all the boys in town.

SALESMAN 1: And he kept escaping the School Board's requests for his credentials.

SALESMAN 2: Marian, the music teacher, was suspicious of Harold Hill, too.

MRS. PAROO: Marian, now what are you up to?

MARIAN: I have a feeling the *Indiana Journal* may help me poke some holes in the Professor's claims.

SALESMAN 3: Marian found some interesting information about Harold Hill's background at the library.

SALESMAN 4: He couldn't have graduated from college in Gary, Indiana, in aught 5 …

SALESMAN 5: … because the town wasn't even built until aught 6.

SALESMAN 1: Before Marian could take her evidence to the Mayor for inspection, an amazing thing happened.

MRS. PAROO: The Wells Fargo wagon is just comin' up from the depot!

SHINN: At this hour of the day?

WINTHROP: It could be the band instruments!

SHINN: The band instruments! I want that man's credentials!

(The whole town is excited and comes on to welcome the arrival of the Wells Fargo wagon.)

The Music Man Junior,
Palo Alto Children's
Theatre, Palo Alto, CA

The Wells Fargo Wagon

CD 18:13

Words and Music by Meredith Willson

Townspeople
O - ho, the Wells Far - go Wa - gon is a -

com - in' down the street. Oh, please, let it be for me. O - ho, the

Wells Far - go Wag - on is a - com - in' down the street. I

1st voice
wish, I wish I knew what it could be. I got a box of ma - ple su - gar on my

2nd voice birth - day. In March, I got a grey mack - i - naw. *3rd voice* And

once, I got some grape - fruit from Tam - pa... *4th voice* Mont - gom - 'ry

Townspeople
Ward sent me a bath - tub and a cross - cut saw. O - ho, the

Wells Far - go Wag - on is a - com - in' now. Is it a

More

303

pre - paid sur - prise or C. O. D.? It could be

6th voice

cur - tains, or dish - es, or a dou - ble boil - er, or it

Townspeople

6th voice

could be, Yes, it could be, Yes, you're right, it sure - ly could be, Some-thin'

Townspeople

6th voice

spe - cial, some-thin' ver - y ver - y spe - cial now, just for me.

Townspeople **f**

O - ho, you Wells Far - go Wag - on keep a -

com-in', O - ho, you Wells Far - go Wag - on keep a - com-in', O - ho, you

Wells Far - go Wag - on, don't you dare to make___ a stop,

2

un - til you stop for me.___

(MARIAN pushes her way through the CROWD to crush WINTHROP in an embrace.)

TOWNSPEOPLE: Hurray!

HAROLD: *(Handing WINTHROP the cornet.)* Here you are, Winthrop.

WINTHROP: My cornet! Gee thanks, Professor!

SHINN: Round one for you, Mister Hill, but I better hear some tootin' out'a them horns in pretty short order.

SALESMAN 1: Marian could see how happy Winthrop was— and all because of Harold Hill's band.

SALESMAN 2: In fact, the spirits of every person in town had been lifted.

SALESMAN 3: Harold Hill might have come to River City to sell people something they didn't need …

SALESMAN 4: … but what he gave them was something that changed their lives: the inspiring gift of music.

(SING LAST VERSE OF "76 TROMBONES" ON PAGE 298.)

CURTAIN CALL

The Music Man Junior,
Palo Alto Children's Theatre,
Palo Alto, CA

Forever Rock and Roll

Rock and roll has changed a lot through the years. However, one thing has always stayed the same: Put together cool guitar licks, pounding drum beats, solid bass lines, and a great lead singer and you have an excellent rock and roll mix. Take a journey back in time to sing some great rock and roll songs.

Brian Wilson of the
Beach Boys.

CD 19:1

Surfin' U.S.A.

Music by Chuck Berry
Words by Brian Wilson

If ev'-ry-bod-y had an o - cean a-cross the U. S. A.___ Then ev'-ry-bod-y'd be surf - in'___ like Cal-i-for-ni-a.___ You'd see them wear-in' their bag-gies,___ huar-a-chi san-dals, too.___ A bush-y bush-y blonde hair - do,___ surf-in' U. S. A.___ You'll catch 'em surf-in' at

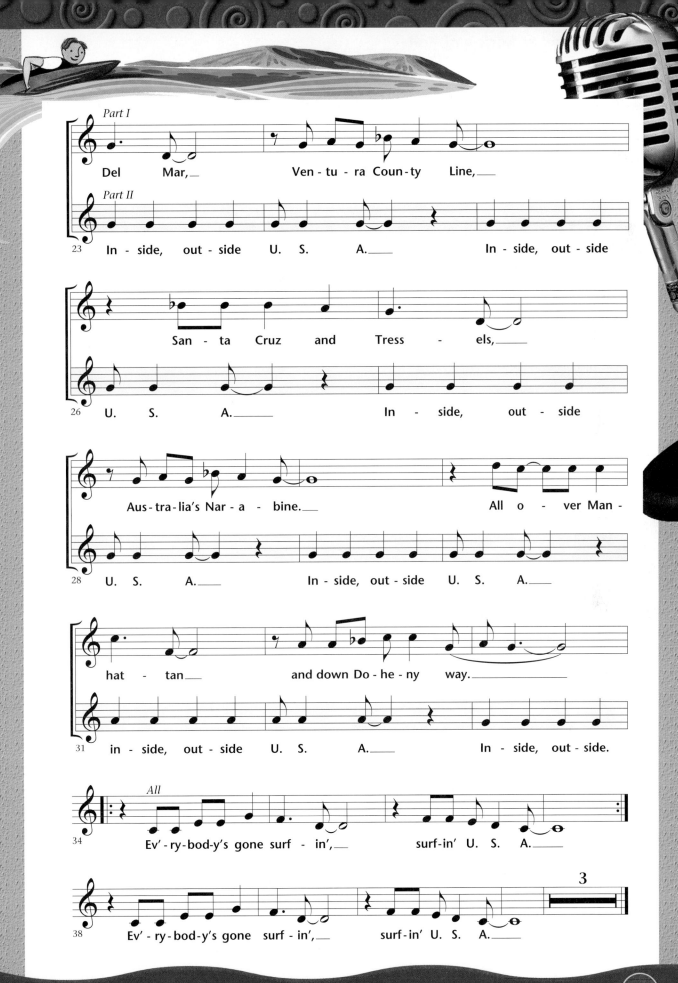

CONCEPT
MELODY
SKILLS
SING, READ

Do you like doing chores? Probably not! Even back in the 1950s, no one liked to do chores. In 1958, the Coasters had a number one hit with this hilarious song about chores around the house. When you sing "Yakety Yak," it almost feels like you are getting in trouble!

SKILL BUILDER: Melodic Contour

The shape of a melody can tell you a lot about a song even before you sing it. The word used to describe the shape of a melody is **contour**. Melodic contours can go up, go down, stay the same, or be a combination of all three.

Describe the melodic contour of "Yakety Yak." Does it look difficult or easy to sing? Why?

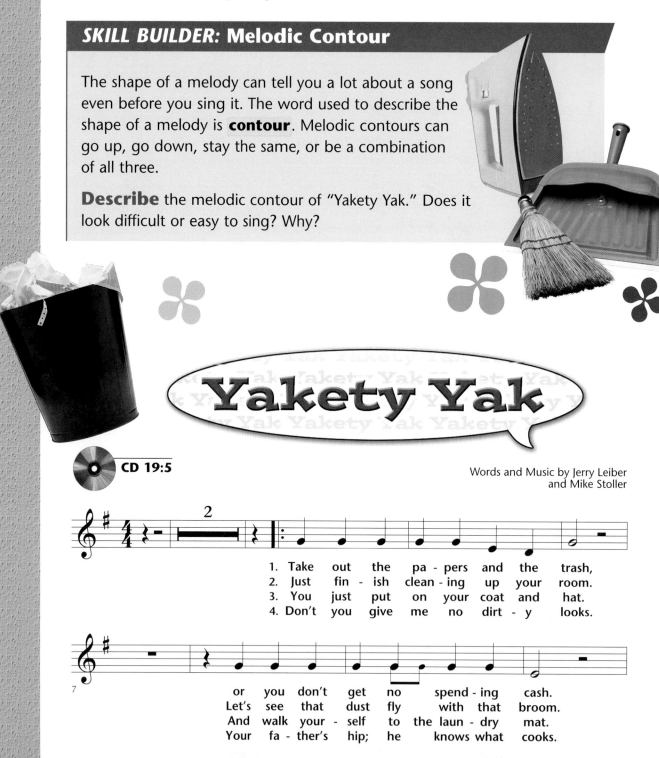

Yakety Yak

CD 19:5

Words and Music by Jerry Leiber
and Mike Stoller

1. Take out the pa - pers and the trash,
2. Just fin - ish clean - ing up your room.
3. You just put on your coat and hat.
4. Don't you give me no dirt - y looks.

or you don't get no spend - ing cash.
Let's see that dust fly with that broom.
And walk your - self to the laun - dry mat.
Your fa - ther's hip; he knows what cooks.

If you don't scrub that kitch - en floor,
Get all that gar - bage out of sight,
And when you fin - ish do - ing that,
Just tell your hood - lum friend out - side,

You ain't gon - na rock 'n' roll no
Or you don't__ go out Fri - day
Bring in the__ dog and put out the
You ain't got__ time to take a

1. 2. 3.

more.   Yak - et - y   yak!   Don't talk back.
night.   Yak - et - y   yak!   Don't talk back.
cat.   Yak - et - y   yak!   Don't talk back.
ride.   Yak - et - y

4.

yak!   Don't talk back,   yak - et - y

yak,   yak - et - y   yak!

Yak - et - y   yak,   yak - et - y   yak!

The Coasters

Music creates a mood that gives listeners a special feeling. With this in mind, songwriters often use descriptive words to help listeners imagine a certain place and time. In "Southern Nights," the songwriter describes a place he knows and loves. What favorite place would you write a song about? How would you describe it to help others picture it?

SKILL BUILDER: Singing Syncopation

Syncopation is a type of rhythm pattern in which stressed sounds occur between beats instead of on the beats. Tied notes are often good clues that a rhythm may be syncopated. In "Southern Nights," there are many examples of syncopation.

Find this syncopated rhythm pattern in the song. How many times does it occur?

Southern Nights

CD 19:8

Words and Music by
Allen Toussaint

South - ern nights, have you ev - er felt a

7 south - ern night? Free as a breeze, not to

10 men-tion the trees, whis-tling tunes that you know and love so.

13 South - ern nights, just as good e - ven when closed your eyes,

CONCEPT
MELODY
SKILLS
SING: VOCAL QUALITY

Heroes are not just made-up characters in the movies or on television. Every person is a hero each and every day because of every smile, every hello, and every nice thing they do. Stand tall and sing "Hero" with a confident voice, because you are a hero, too.

VOICE BUILDER: Shaping Vowels

In singing, vowel sounds create and sustain the vocal tone. The five basic vowel sounds for singing are: *ee, eh, ah, oh, oo.*

Sing the lyrics below with good vowel sounds. Remember to sing with a relaxed jaw, a vertical and round mouth shape, and an open space inside your mouth.

There's a hero (oh)
if you look inside your heart. (ah)
You don't have be afraid of what you are. (ah)
There's an answer if you reach into your soul (oh)
and the sorrow that you know will melt away. (eh)

Find and practice the other important vowel sounds that come at the end of phrases. As you sing, listen and adjust to other singers around you to blend your sound with theirs.

HERO

CD 19:11

Words and Music by Mariah Carey
and Walter Afanasieff

There's a   he - ro   if   you
long   road   when   you

look in - side__ your heart.   You don't have to be__ a-fraid   of what you
face the world_ a - lone.   No one reach-es out__ a hand   for you to

are.___ There's an an - swer if you reach in - to___ your soul___ and the
hold.___ You can find love if you search with - in___ your - self___ and the

sor - row that___ you know will melt a - way.
emp - ti - ness___ you felt will dis - ap - pear.

And then a he - ro comes___ a - long___ with the strength to car - ry on___

___ and you cast your fears___ a - side___ and you know you can___ sur - vive.___

___ So, when you feel like hope___ is gone___ look in - side you and___ be strong___

___ and you'll fin - 'ly see___ the truth___ that a he - ro lies___ in

1.
you.   It's a

2.
you.

That a he - ro lies in you,___

that a he - ro lies in you.

CONCEPT
MELODY

SKILLS
SING: BREATHING

Rock and roll does not always have to be fast and furious. It can also be soft, slow, and thoughtful. "Change the World" is both a mellow and powerful song that inspires people to make a difference in the world. What can you do to change the world and make it a better place?

VOICE BUILDER: Breathing

Singing requires breath, and breath requires support. In order to have good **breath support** while singing, stand tall with your shoulders down. As you breathe, imagine your ribs expanding as your lungs take in air. **Practice** good breath support in the exercise below. Remember to sing with a relaxed jaw, a vertical mouth shape, and an open space inside your mouth to help produce the best sound.

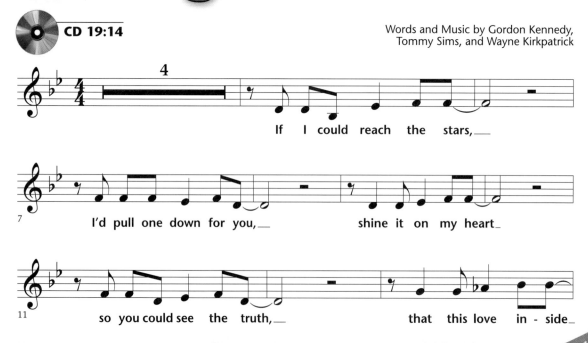

CD 19:14

Words and Music by Gordon Kennedy,
Tommy Sims, and Wayne Kirkpatrick

If I could reach the stars, ___

I'd pull one down for you, ___ shine it on my heart ___

so you could see the truth, ___ that this love in - side ___

CONCEPT
HARMONY
SKILLS
SING

When the group Danny and the Juniors released "Rock and Roll Is Here to Stay" in 1958, they could not have known how true their song's title would be. Decades later, rock music is as popular as ever. Help keep the rock rolling by singing this song with extra energy.

VOICE BUILDER: Chords

Rock and roll musicians perform chords when they play and sing together. Break into three groups and **practice** singing these chords making sure they are in tune.

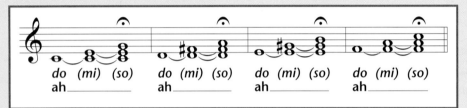

do (mi) (so)   do (mi) (so)   do (mi) (so)   do (mi) (so)
ah_____   ah_____   ah_____   ah_____

Rock and Roll Is Here to Stay

 CD 19:17

Words and Music by
David White

Rock,   oh, ba - by rock,   oh, ba - by

rock,   oh, ba - by rock,   oh, ba - by!

1. Rock and roll is here to stay,___   it will ne - ver die.___
2. Rock and roll will al - ways be,___ I dig it to the end.___

With One Dream

Everyone has hopes and dreams for their lives and for the world. Musicians and composers often express their dreams in their music. How can music express a person's dreams differently than a story or a poem? What dreams do you have that you would share with music?

As you sing the songs in this theme, notice how each composer uses music to share their message.

VOICE BUILDER: Posture Makes Perfect

Before you sing, always go through these steps to check your posture:

1. Feet apart to balance your weight
2. Knees relaxed
3. Back straight
4. Head erect and straight
5. Shoulders down and chest up
6. Hands and arms relaxed and at your sides

If you follow these steps, your voice should feel stronger and singing should be easier. Now you are ready to sing!

Rounds are a great way for singers to warm up their voices. When performing a round, different groups sing the same melody but start at different times. "Lift Up Your Voices" and "Sweet Music" are both three-part rounds, meaning they are created for three groups of singers.

Lift Up Your Voices

CD 19:20

Alsatian Round

1 *f*
Lift up your voi - ces and sing a loud song.

2 *p*
Soft - ly and smooth - ly as we sing a - long.

3 *f*
Join your voi - ces, sing a loud song.

Sweet Music

CD 19:23

Traditional Round

Andante

1
Oh,___ mu - sic, sweet_ mu - sic, thy_ prais - es we sing, We'll_

tell of the___ pleas - ure and___ joy that you bring,

3
Mu - sic, mu - sic, joy that you bring.

CONCEPT
MELODY

SKILLS
SING, READ

In the 1950s and 1960s, many people in the United States marched and sang to demand equal rights for people of every color. Sometimes, tens of thousands of people participated in the marches, winding their way through the countryside or down city blocks. Read the words to "Like a Mighty Stream." Why do you think the composer gave his song this title?

VOICE BUILDER: Large Leaps

The melody of "Like a Mighty Stream" has some large melodic leaps. **Find** these leaps in the music and practice them by singing the exercise below. Pay attention to the way you connect the notes. Avoid "scooping," or sliding your voice up and down between pitches. You can expand your range by repeating the exercise with higher pitches.

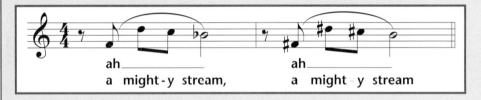

ah_____   ah_____
a might-y stream,   a might-y stream

Like a Mighty Stream

CD 19:26

Words and Music by
Moses Hogan and John Jacobson

With conviction, Moderato

All - Unison

Lift   ev - 'ry voice___
Oh,   ev - 'ry trial___

and   let us___ sing!___   In   ev - 'ry song___
we'll   o - ver - come,___   when   ev - 'ry child___

Dr. Martin Luther King, Jr.

CONCEPT ▶
MELODY

SKILLS
SING: VOCAL TONE

The words to "I Am But a Small Voice" were written by a 13-year-old girl from the Philippines named Odina Batnag. She entered her lyrics in a contest with a million other children from 57 countries, and her lyrics won. As you sing this song, pay attention to the message Odina shares.

VOICE BUILDER: Vocal Tone

Practicing vowel sounds is very important for every singer. "I Am But a Small Voice" contains all five basic vowel sounds: *ee, eh, ah, oh, oo*. **Sing** the exercise below to help prepare you for vowels in "I Am But a Small Voice." The word "one" should use the *ah* vowel sound.

We are one. We are one. We are one.
(ah)   (ah)   (ah)

I Am But a Small Voice

Music by Roger Whittaker
Original words by Odina E. Batnag
English words by Roger Whittaker
Arranged by John Coates, Jr.

CD 19:30

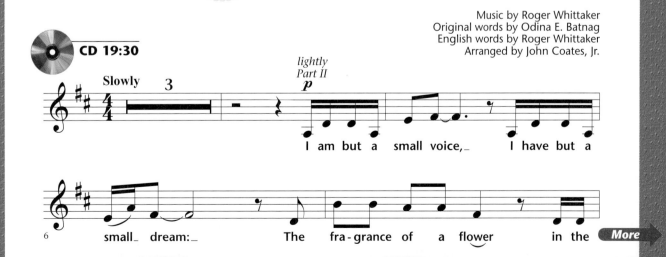

Slowly

I am but a small voice,— I have but a small dream:— The fra-grance of a flower in the

More ▶

LISTENING CD 20:1

One Voice by Barry Manilow

Listen to the Vocal Majority Chorus sing "One Voice." The Vocal Majority Chorus began as a small 12-member all-male choir in 1971 in Dallas, Texas. It has now grown to over 160 singers.

The group is able to blend their voices expressively and change their dynamics smoothly by listening closely to those around them and carefully watching the conductor. When you sing with your choir, always remember to follow these important points.

The Mormon Tabernacle Choir is one of the most well-known choirs in the United States. They have performed with many other groups, including the Vocal Majority Chorus.

CONCEPT
HARMONY

SKILLS
SING: ARTICULATION

Composers and musicians are often inspired by pieces of music they hear. In "I Hear America Singing," the composer André J. Thomas decided to use part of a melody from a spiritual titled "Walk Together, Children."

Read through the music and locate the lyrics of the spiritual.

VOICE BUILDER: Articulation

Singers use crisp consonants to help listeners understand the words in a song. This is called articulation. When you sing, you use the lips, teeth, and tongue to **articulate** the consonants. **Practice** the following phrases quickly and precisely, and concentrate on clean and clear articulation.

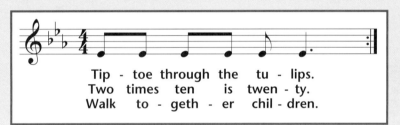

Tip - toe through the tu - lips.
Two times ten is twen - ty.
Walk to - geth - er chil - dren.

I Hear America Singing

CD 20:2

Words and Music by André J. Thomas
Quoting the Spiritual, "Walk Together, Children"

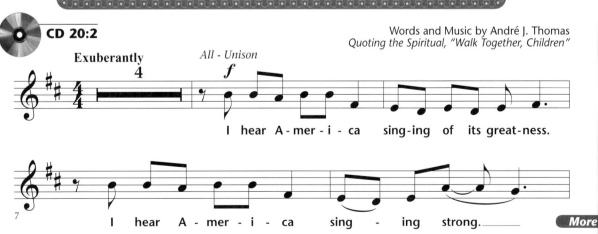

I hear A - mer - i - ca sing-ing of its great-ness.

I hear A - mer - i - ca sing - ing strong._____

More

25 Shout to-geth - er, chil - dren. Don't you get wea - ry. There's a

27 great camp meet - ing in the Prom-ised Land.

Descant
Great camp meet - ing,

29 Great camp meet - ing, A - mer-i-ca's sing - ing, A -

31 We're go-ing to

mer - i - ca's sing - ing. Sing! A -

33 sing of truth and

mer-i-ca's sing - ing, A - mer - i - ca's sing - ing, A -

More

sing and nev - er tire._____ There's a

great camp meet - ing, great camp meet - ing.

And A - mer - i - ca's sing - ing! Great camp meet - ing,

great camp meet - ing in the Prom - ised

great camp meet - ing in the Prom - ised,

Land!_____

great camp meet - ing, A - mer - i - ca's sing - ing,

Prom - ised Land!

great camp meet - ing, Prom - ised Land!

Rhythms of Life

Our days and lives are full of cycles, routines, and patterns. You wake up, brush your teeth, go to school, sing in music class, go home, eat dinner, do homework, and go to sleep. These cycles and patterns are the rhythms of your life. What are some ways they are similar to rhythms in music?

As you will hear in the songs of this theme, the rhythms of life are everywhere. Whether it's an orchestra's pulse, the ocean's currents, a nighttime lullaby, or a slow and steady river, rhythm truly can be found in every part of life.

SKILL BUILDER: Staccato

In "Orchestra Song" you will imitate the sounds of several instruments of the orchestra. When you sing the part of the trumpet, **sing** the words "ta ta ta" with **staccato**, which means short and separate.

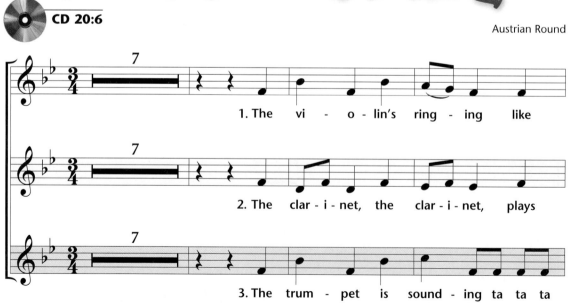

Orchestra Song

CD 20:6

Austrian Round

1. The vi - o - lin's ring - ing like

2. The clar - i - net, the clar - i - net, plays

3. The trum - pet is sound - ing ta ta ta

love - ly___ sing - ing, The vi - o - lin's

doo - dle, doo - dle, doo - dle, doo - dle det, The clar - i - net, the

ta ta ta ta ta ta ta ta ta ta ta, The trum - pet is

ring - ing like love - ly___ song.

clar - i - net plays doo - dle, doo - dle, doo - dle det.

sound - ing ta ta ta ta ta ta ta ta ta ta.

Add these parts to the first three.

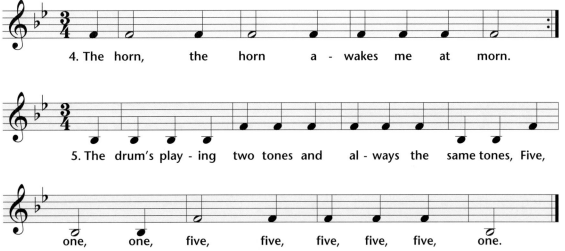

4. The horn, the horn a - wakes me at morn.

5. The drum's play - ing two tones and al - ways the same tones, Five,

one, one, five, five, five, five, five, one.

CONCEPT
MELODY
SKILLS
SING

"**A** Great Big Sea" is a song that was often sung by sailors from the island of Newfoundland in Canada. Sea songs like this helped sailors to take their minds off the long days on the ocean. The lyrics to this song do not make much sense, but they are very fun to sing!

VOICE BUILDER: Diction and Range

This song requires crisp, clean **diction** and energetic rhythm. Diction is how clearly a person pronounces words. **Articulate** the consonants in the phrase below to practice diction. Repeat the exercise several times, starting each time on the next higher pitch.

Repeat at higher pitch levels

Ta - dee - did - dle I - do, ta - dee - did - dle I - do.

A Great Big Sea

MAP

CANADA

NEWFOUNDLAND

CD 20:9

Newfoundland Folk Song
Arranged by Lori-Anne Dolloff

With rollicking fun

A great big sea hove in Long Beach

11 Right fol - or - al Ta - dee - did - dle I - do.____ A

right fol - did-dy fol - dee.
Me

boot is broke, me frock is tore, Right fol - or - al

Ta - dee - did - dle I - do._____ Me boot is broke, me

frock is tore, But Georg - ie Snooks I do a - dore to me

right fol - did-dy fol - dee.
Oh

fish is low and flour is high, Right fol - or - al

Ta - dee - did - dle I - do._____ Oh fish is low and

flour is high, So Georg - ie Snooks he can't have I, To me

right fol - did-dy fol - dee. Dee dee did-dy fol - dee

Boldly
did-dle did-dle dee, did-dle did-dle did-dle dee. But he will meet me

in the fall, Right fol - or - al Ta-dee-did-dle I - do.____

Slower, deliberately *allargando*
If he don't I'll hoist my sail and say good - bye to

a tempo *sempre cresc. ed accel.*
p *mf*
old Can - naille. To me right fol - did-dy did-dy, right fol - did-dy did-dy

f *ff*
Ta - dee - did - dle did - dy fol - dee.

CONCEPT
RHYTHM

SKILLS
SING, READ

Carnaval is a huge celebration held every year in February or March in Brazil. "A Zing-A Za" is one of the many songs people sing at carnaval.

SKILL BUILDER: Steady Rhythm

Performing rhythms accurately as a group is important in every song. Beginning slowly, **clap** the following rhythm patterns one at a time and gradually increase speed. **Find** these rhythms in "A Zing-A Za."

MAP

BRAZIL

SOUTH AMERICA

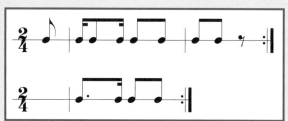

CD 20:12

Brazilian Rural Samba
Arranged by Mary Goetze

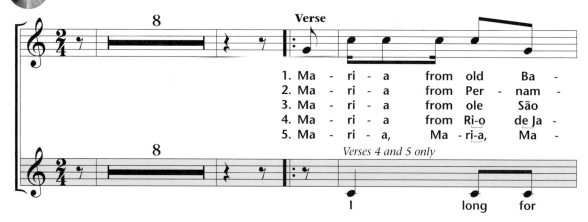

Verse

1. Ma - ri - a from old Ba -
2. Ma - ri - a from Per - nam -
3. Ma - ri - a from ole São
4. Ma - ri - a from Ri-o de Ja -
5. Ma - ri - a, Ma - ri-a, Ma -

Verses 4 and 5 only

I long for

hi - a, Though we nev - er can a -
bu - co, I'll fol - low where - ev - er
Paul - o Who cares if you shriek or
nei - ro With cab - bage leaves in your
ri - a, From you I can nev-er be

Ri - o de Ja - nei - ro, I long for

338

CONCEPT
HARMONY
SKILLS
SING: INTONATION

"Ēinīnī" is a lullaby from Ireland that adults sing to help young children go to sleep. The words are in Gaelic, a language spoken mainly in Scotland and Ireland. When you were younger, you may have heard lullabies before bedtime. What did the lullabies sound like?

SKILL BUILDER: Harmony

"Ēinīnī" is written in two-part harmony. **Practice** harmony with good **intonation** by singing the pitch syllables in the exercise below. Singers who can maintain a steady pitch have good intonation. **Sing** softly so you can hear the other part and blend your voices together.

so   fa   mi   re   do

so fa mi   fa mi re   mi re do   re do ti,   do

MAP

SCOTLAND

IRELAND   ENGLAND

WALES

Ēinīnī
Little Birds Sleep

CD 20:16

Gaelic Folk Song
Arranged by Cyndee Giebler

1st time unison, 2nd time parts
mf

All
Unison

Andante

Gaelic: Ēin - īn - ī,   ēin - īn - ī,   cod - al -
Pronunciation: e   ni   ni   e   ni   ni   ko

aī - gī,   cod - al - aī - gī,   ēin - īn - ī,   ēin -
dle   gi   ko   dle   gi   e   ni   ni   e

CONCEPT
MELODY

SKILLS
SING: BREATHING

Like a slowly rolling river, the rhythm of "A Gentle River Runs" steadily moves the melody and lyrics along through the piece. The lyrics share a message of hope and courage for all people. As you sing, let the calm rhythm of the song fill your voice with energy and strength.

VOICE BUILDER: Long Phrases

Singing long phrases requires good breath management. Try this exercise to expand and manage your breath:

Imagine you have a milkshake as large as the room. Hold the milkshake in front of you and "drink" the air through a giant straw.

Sing the phrase in the exercise below after you take this kind of breath.

A - rise, a - rise, a - rise, a-rise, a - rise.

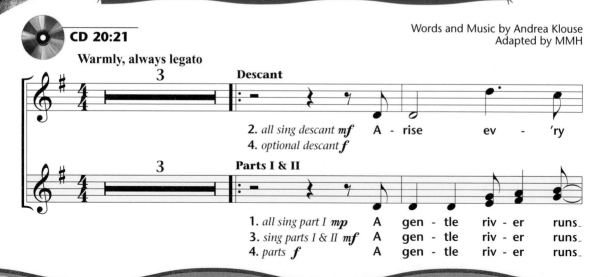

A Gentle River Runs

CD 20:21

Words and Music by Andrea Klouse
Adapted by MMH

Warmly, always legato

Descant

2. *all sing descant* **mf**   A - rise   ev -   'ry
4. *optional descant* **f**

Parts I & II

1. *all sing part I* **mp**   A   gen - tle   riv - er   runs
3. *sing parts I & II* **mf**   A   gen - tle   riv - er   runs
4. *parts* **f**   A   gen - tle   riv - er   runs

Sometimes a composer puts two songs together so they can be performed at the same time. These songs are called partner songs. **Read** the lyrics and locate the two pieces that created "Hallelujah, Get On Board."

VOICE BUILDER: Breathing and Posture

Place your fingertips on the top of your head with your elbows out. Notice how your ribs lift up. Slowly lift your hands from your head and bring your arms up and then down in an arc until they rest at your sides. Repeat this motion while you take a breath and then **sing** this pattern.

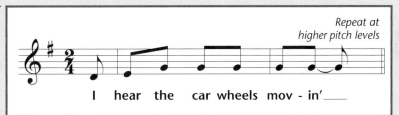

Repeat at higher pitch levels

I hear the car wheels mov - in'____

CD 21:1

Traditional Spirituals
Arranged by Rollo A. Dilworth

With spirit

mf

The gos - pel train's a -
The fare is cheap, and

com - in',____ I hear it just at hand;____ I hear the car wheels
all can go, the rich and poor are there;____ No sec - ond class a -

mov - in',____ and rumb - lin' through the land.⎫ Oh, get on
board this train, no dif - f'rence in the fare.⎭

More

 LISTENING CD 21:5

Get On Board, Children African American Freedom Song

Listen to the SNCC Freedom Singers perform "Get On Board, Children." This version comes from the Civil Rights movement in the United States in the 1950s and 1960s.

Tour of the Americas

The Americas stretch from Canada's northern shore along the Arctic Ocean all the way south past the equator to the tip of Argentina in South America. Within this massive land area, there is a huge variety of incredible music styles. In "Tour of the Americas," you have the chance to sing songs that come from different places in North and South America.

Relax, stand up straight, take a deep breath, and get ready to take a musical trip around the Americas!

VOICE BUILDER: More Than Vocal Cords

The lips, the teeth, and the tongue are used to produce clear diction when singing. Singers combine clear diction with open vowels to produce a quality sound. **Sing** this exercise in unison or in two or three parts to practice this technique.

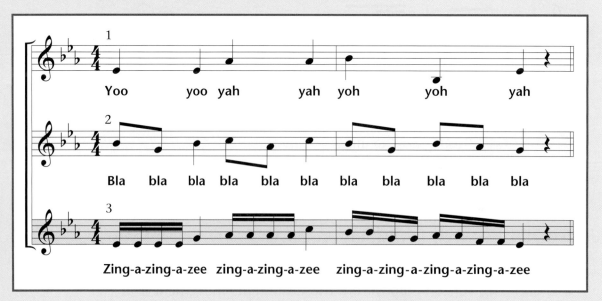

1. Yoo   yoo yah   yah yoh   yoh   yah

2. Bla   bla   bla   bla   bla   bla   bla   bla   bla   bla   bla

3. Zing-a-zing-a-zee zing-a-zing-a-zee   zing-a-zing-a-zing-a-zing-a-zee

"Un lorito de Verapaz" is a folk song from northern Guatemala, a country in Central America just south of Mexico. Guatemala has tropical jungles, volcanoes, and ancient ruins as well as brass bands, marimba music, and beautiful folk songs. The words of this song tell the story of a boy parrot who falls in love with a girl parakeet.

MAP
UNITED STATES
MEXICO
GUATEMALA

CD 21:6

The Parrot of Verapaz

Guatemalan Folk Song
Arranged by Emily Crocker

Buoyantly

All - Unison

Spanish: Un lo - ri - to de Ve - ra -
Pronunciation: un lo ɾi to ðe βe ɾa

paz un buen di - a se_e-na-mo - ró de_u-na lin - da co - to-
pas un bwen di a se na mo ɾo deu na lin da ko to

1.
rri - ta y la po - bre se des-ma - yó.
ɾi ta i la po βɾe se ðes ma yo

2.
(Pt. II)
Un lo yó. Ay lo - ri - ta de
un lo yo ai lo ɾi ta ðe

More

ya ve-rás ya ve-rás sí te vas con o - tro___
ya βe ɾas ya βe ɾas si te βas kon o tro

Ah_____ Ah____

|1.

___ya ve-rás, ya ve-rás. del-ga-di-to me rás.
ya βe ɾas ya βe ɾas del ga ði to me ɾas

|2.

ya ve-rás, ya ve-rás. del-ga-di-to me rás.___
ya βe ɾas ya βe ɾas del ga ði to me ɾas

CONCEPT
HARMONY

SKILLS
SING

Texas has the song "The Yellow Rose of Texas" and New York has "New York, New York," but in Tennessee it's "Rocky Top" all the way. In fact, the state made it an official state song in 1982.

Tennessee state flag

VOICE BUILDER: "Locking In" Chords

Country music singers often describe good vocal harmony as "locking in the chords." **Listen** closely to others' voices while you sing the chords to blend your voice with theirs until the tuning "locks in."

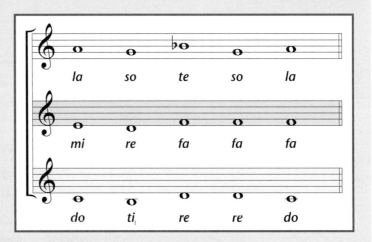

la   so   te   so   la

mi   re   fa   fa   fa

do   ti   re   re   do

Rocky Top

CD 21:11

Words and Music by
Boudleaux Bryant and Felice Bryant

(4 measure introduction)

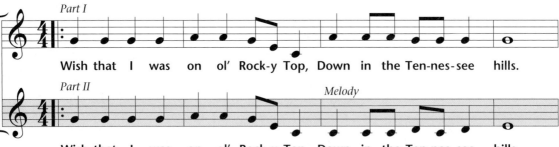

Part I

Wish that I was on ol' Rock-y Top, Down in the Ten-nes-see hills.

Part II   *Melody*

Wish that I was on ol' Rock-y Top, Down in the Ten-nes-see hills.

Ain't no smog-gy smoke on Rock-y Top, Ain't no tel-e-phone bills.

Ain't no smog-gy smoke on Rock-y Top, Ain't no tel-e-phone bills.

Baseball is a very popular sport in many parts of the world, including Asia, Central and South America, and the Caribbean. In the United States, baseball is so popular that many composers have written songs to celebrate the sport. In this song, you will learn two new parts that fit perfectly with the most famous baseball song of all, "Take Me Out to the Ball Game." Put them all together and you will feel like you have hit a home run!

VOICE BUILDER: Have a Ball

Here's a vocal exercise that will keep you "on the ball." Along with the smell of popcorn and the crack of the bat, this melody is sure to remind you of being at a baseball game. **Sing** with pitch syllables first to practice reading notes. Then sing the lyrics. Move the pattern up by half steps and gradually get faster.

do so, la, ti, do so, la, ti, do so, la, ti, do **Charge!**
Go, go, rah, team, go, go, rah, team, go, go, rah, team, go! Charge!

Triple Play

CD 21:15

Words and Music by
John Jacobson and John Higgins
Take Me Out to the Ball Game
Words and Music by Jack Norworth

CONCEPT
HARMONY

SKILLS
SING

For the next stop on the "Tour of the Americas," we are staying in the United States to sing some gospel music. Gospel music started in the early 1900s when African American composers like Thomas Dorsey decided to mix together hymns and spirituals with the music of blues and jazz.

SKILL BUILDER: Singing Harmony

Gospel music often uses harmony. **Sing** the exercise below to practice singing in two parts. Begin singing with pitch syllables and then add the words and the special articulations marked in the music.

do do do____
I feel good!_

do do do____
I feel good!_

do do do____
I feel good!_

fa fa mi____
I feel good!_

fa fa mi____
I feel good!_

fa fa mi____
I feel good!_

Feel Good

CD 21:20

Words and Music by
L. Craig Tyson and Leonard Scott
Arranged by
Barbara Baker and David J. Elliott

Not too fast

Clap

All - Unison
mf

Feel-in' good,_

9

Feel-in' good._____ I got

13

love in my heart and my soul____ And I feel good.____

CONCEPT
RHYTHM
SKILLS
SING

Composing is not always a solo project. Sometimes people prefer to work together to create a piece of music. "On the Sunny Side of the Street" was written in 1930 by the songwriting duo Jimmy McHugh and Dorothy Fields. Jimmy wrote the music and Dorothy wrote the lyrics.

"On the Sunny Side of the Street" is an example of a jazz song. Look for **chromatic** notes in the score before you sing. These are notes that have a flat, sharp, or natural symbol in front of them. Chromatic notes help give the melody a flavor of jazz.

SKILL BUILDER: Swing Rhythm

An important characteristic of many jazz rhythms is swing. Instead of dividing two eighth notes evenly, swing rhythm gives the first eighth note twice as much time as the second. This is often notated as two eighth notes equaling a triplet as in the figure to the right.

Practice swing rhythm by singing these **scat** syllables. Jazz singers use these nonsense syllables to improvise. When you sing scat, imagine your voice is a jazz instrument like a trumpet, saxophone, or trombone.

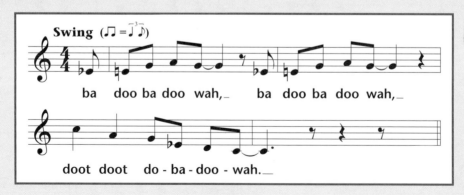

On the Sunny Side of the Street

CD 21:24

Music by Jimmy McHugh
Words by Dorothy Fields
Arranged by Steve Zegree

Moderato Swing

All - Unison

Dah____ dah dah da da dat

ya dat da dat dat dat. Grab your coat, and get your hat,

leave your wor - ry on the door - step.

Just di - rect your feet____ to the sun - ny side____ of the

street. Can't you hear a pit - ter pat? And that

hap - py tune is your____ step. Life can be so

sweet, on____ the sun - ny, sun - ny side of the street.

More

dah dah dah da ba dah dah da ba da ba da ba da ba

(Opt. Solo 3)
da ba da ba da da ba dat dat dat da ba da ba dat da ba da ba

(Opt. Solo 4)
doo ba doo ba doo ba doo ba doo ba doo dat yat da da ba doo dah

Part I
ba doo ba da ba da ba da ba doo dat. I used to

Coda
Gold dust at my feet, on the sun-ny side of the street,

cresc.
on the sun-ny, on the sun-ny, on the

sun - ny side of the street.

Sun - ny day!

LISTENING CD 21:27

Jersey Bounce

Listen to Ella Fitzgerald (1917–1996) improvise scat singing in "Jersey Bounce." What instrument does her voice remind you of?

CONCEPT
RHYTHM

SKILLS
SING

"Uno, dos y tres" is a song that comes from the island of Cuba in the Caribbean Sea. You might hear this song performed during Cuban *carnaval*, a time when Cubans celebrate with parades, music, and dancing. This song is called a *conga*. To dance a *conga*, people form a line and hold on to waist of the person in front. One, two, three, kick!

SKILL BUILDER: Rhythm

This exercise will help you develop your rhythm skills. Using the rhythm below, **perform** this hand jive pattern: *Pat Left, Pat Right, Pat Left, Pat Right, Snap, Snap.* Next, add the vocal part. When you are able to perform both together, try to add some instruments, like conga drums, bongo drums, and claves.

One, two and three

CD 22:1

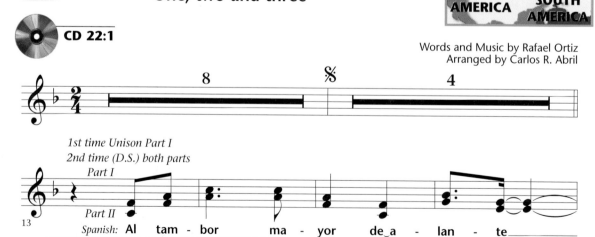

Words and Music by Rafael Ortiz
Arranged by Carlos R. Abril

1st time Unison Part I
2nd time (D.S.) both parts

Part I

13   Part II

Spanish: **Al tam - bor ma - yor de_a - lan - te**

Pronunciation: al tam boɾ ma yor ðea lan te

17 — no hay quien lo pue da_i gua lar_____
noai kyen lo pwe ðai gwa laɾ

21 — con su rit - mo fas - ci - nán - te_____
kon su ɾit mo fas si nan te

25 — de mi Cu - ba tro - pi - cal.
ðe mi ku βa tɾo pi kal

29 Cuen - ten los pa - sos___ que_a - qui lle - ga - mos___
kwen ten los pa sos kea ki lye ga mos

33 U - no dos y tres que pa - so mas ché - ve - re_____ que
u no ðos i tres ke pa so mas che βe ɾe ke

(last time) to Coda
(last time)

37 pa - so mas ché - ve - re_____ el de mi con - ga es el
pa so mas che βe ɾe el ðe mi kong ga es el

D.S. (m. 9) al Coda

41 U - no! Dos! Tres! U - no! Dos! Tres!
u no dos tres u no dos tres

(3 times)
dim. on each repeat
CODA
f

45 de mi con - ga es el de mi con - ga es
ðe mi kong ga es el ðe mi kong ga es

Earth, Sky, and Spirit

Nature is often a powerful inspiration for musicians. Majestic mountains, sparkling stars, the luminous moon, and the songs of insects at night are just some of the millions of things from nature that compel musicians to create music.

This theme features many beautiful examples of music inspired by nature. Some pieces come from the United States and others come from other parts of the world. You will see they all share a respect for Earth and all of the creatures that share it.

VOICE BUILDER: Range

This exercise starts in the middle of your voice, moves to the low part of your voice, and then moves to the high part of your voice. Remember to **sing** the exercise below with a vertical mouth shape, good breath support, and a relaxed and dropped jaw. To expand your vocal range, repeat the exercise at higher and lower pitch levels.

do   so,   do re   mi fa so fa mi re   do
How   I   love   to   sing, la la la la.

Star Canon

CD 22:6

Music by Mary Goetze
Words from *Firefly* by Li Po

I think, if you flew up to the

sky be - side _ the _ moon, _ you would spar - kle like a

1.-4. *(to canon)*

5.

star. Oh, _ star.

CONCEPT
MELODY

SKILLS
SING

The words of "The Path to the Moon" are filled with stunning descriptions of a nighttime trip across the sea. What are some of the words in this song that paint pictures in your mind?

As you sing the song, think about how the melody and the rhythm of the piece match the words you are singing.

VOICE BUILDER: Octaves

The melody of "The Path to the Moon" begins with the leap of an octave. Besides good breath support, a vertical mouth shape, and a relaxed jaw, singing this wide leap requires space inside the mouth for the vowel sound *ah*. Drop your jaw and separate your teeth as you **sing** the high note in this exercise.

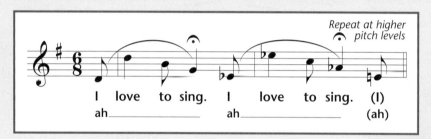

Repeat at higher pitch levels

I love to sing. I love to sing. (I)
ah_____ ah_____ (ah)

The Path to the MOON

CD 22:9

Music by Eric H. Thiman
Words by Madeline C. Thomas

1. I long to sail the
2. So will I sail on a

path to the moon On a deep___ blue night, when the
star - ry night On the path to the moon___ a

CONCEPT
MELODY

SKILLS
SING: VOCAL QUALITY

"**W**ie schön leuchtet der Morgenstern" is a chorale arranged by Johann Sebastian Bach, one of the most famous and important composers of all time. Bach wrote many different types of music, including hundreds of chorales like this for choirs to perform. This arrangement is in **unison**, meaning it is for one part. Chorales usually have four different vocal parts, one each for sopranos, altos, tenors, and basses.

VOICE BUILDER: Putting It Together

Singing well often requires working on several techniques at once. For this exercise, articulate the sound of the "t" precisely while you sing a smooth, legato phrase.

Repeat at higher pitch levels

| do | so | mi | do | do | so | mi | do | do | so | mi | do |
| Stars | bright - ly | shine. | Stars | bright - ly | shine. | Stars | bright - ly | shine. |

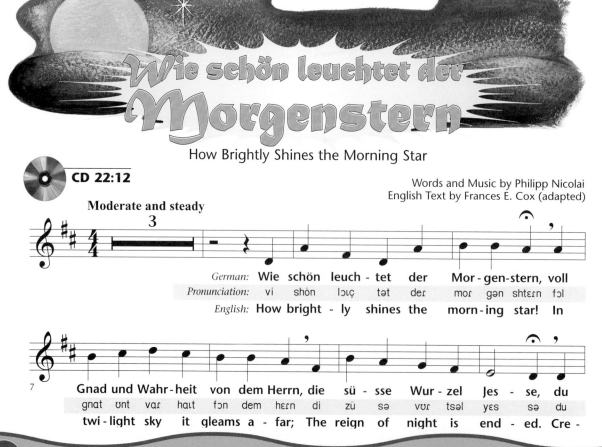

Wie schön leuchtet der Morgenstern
How Brightly Shines the Morning Star

CD 22:12

Words and Music by Philipp Nicolai
English Text by Frances E. Cox (adapted)

Moderate and steady

German: Wie schön leuch - tet der Mor - gen - stern, voll
Pronunciation: vi shön lɔıç tet der mor gən shtɛrn fɔl
English: How bright - ly shines the morn - ing star! In

7 Gnad und Wahr - heit von dem Herrn, die sü - sse Wur - zel Jes - se, du
gnat ʊnt var haıt fɔn dem hɛrn di zü sə vʊr tsel yɛs sə du
twi - light sky it gleams a - far; The reign of night is end - ed. Cre -

Sohn	Da - vids	aus	Ja - cobs	Stamm, mein	Kö - nig	und	mein
zon	da vits	aʊs	ya kops	shtam maɪn	kö niç	ʊnt	maɪn
a - tion	stirs	to	hail	the light	Whose	glo - ries	now with

Bräu - ti - gam,	hast	mir	mein	Herz	be - ses - sen,
brɔɪ ti gam	hast	mir	maɪn	hɛrts	bə zɛs sən
ra - diance bright	Stream	forth	in	beau - ty	splen - did.

Lieb - lich,	freund - lich,	schön und	herr - lich	gross und	ehr - lich,
lip lɪç	frɔɪnt lɪç	shön ʊnt	hɛr lɪç	gros ʊnt	ɛɹ lɪç
Both far	and near	All things	liv - ing,	Thanks are	giv - ing,

reich an	Ga - ben,	hoch und	sehr präch - tig	er - ha - ben.
raɪç an	ga bən	hox ʊnt	zɛɹ prɛç tiç	ɛɹ ha bən
Praise out - pour - ing,	Earth and	sky we	are a - dor - ing.

🎵 **LISTENING** CD 22:16

Wie schön leuchtet der Morgenstern
by Philipp Nicolai, arranged by J. S. Bach

Listen to this version of "Wie schön leuchtet der Morgenstern."
It is performed by the King's Consort Orchestra and Choir from
England with the Tolzner Knabenchor, a boys choir from Germany.
Though the words are in German, you can still hear their excellent
vocal sound and articulation.

The King's Consort

CONCEPT
HARMONY
SKILLS
SING: MELISMA

"Estrella brillante" is a song from Mexico, the country just south of the United States. Mexico is a large country full of many different and exciting styles of music, including *mariachi, banda, son jarocho,* and *norteño.* Each region of Mexico has its own style and specific set of instruments to accompany songs.

When you sing this folk song, imagine you are in the town square of a Mexican village at night. Your voice adds to the sounds of laughter, singing, and celebration all around!

VOICE BUILDER: Melisma

Singers often sing more than one note on a single syllable. This is called a **melisma**. Develop your ability to sing melismas with the exercise below. Make sure you sing lightly on the sixteenth notes and use the pure vowel sounds shown here:

Al - le - lu - ia
(ah) (eh) (oo) (ah)

Sing each part in unison and then divide into two parts to perform the harmony.

Al - le - lu - ia!   Al - le - lu - ia!   Al - le - lu - ia!

Find examples of melismas in "Estrella brillante."

MAP
UNITED STATES
MEXICO   BELIZE
GUATEMALA

Estrella bríllante

Shining Star

CD 22:17

Mexican Carol
Arranged by Nancy Grundahl

Brightly

6 *Part I*

Part II

Spanish: 1. Es - tre - lla bri - llan - te,___
Pronunciation: es tre lya bri lyan te
English: 2. Shin - ing star, oh light our way,___

Luz del pe - re - gri - no,___ Es - tre - lla i -
lus ðel pe ɾe gri no es tɾe lya i
Guide us on our path to - day,___ Shine your light so

lu - mi - na___ Hoy es - te ca - mi - no,
lu mi na oi es te ka mi no
all can see,___ Beam your light so bright - ly.___

Es - tre - lla bri - llan - te,___ Luz del pe - re - gri - no,___
es tre lya bri lyan te lus ðel pe ɾe gri no
Shin - ing star, shine from a - bove,_ Light our path to peace and love,___

Es - tre - lla i - lu - mi - na,___ Hoy es - te ca - mi - no.
es tɾe lya i lu mi na oi es te ka mi no
Guide us on the peace - ful way,_ bring - ing love to all, we pray._

More

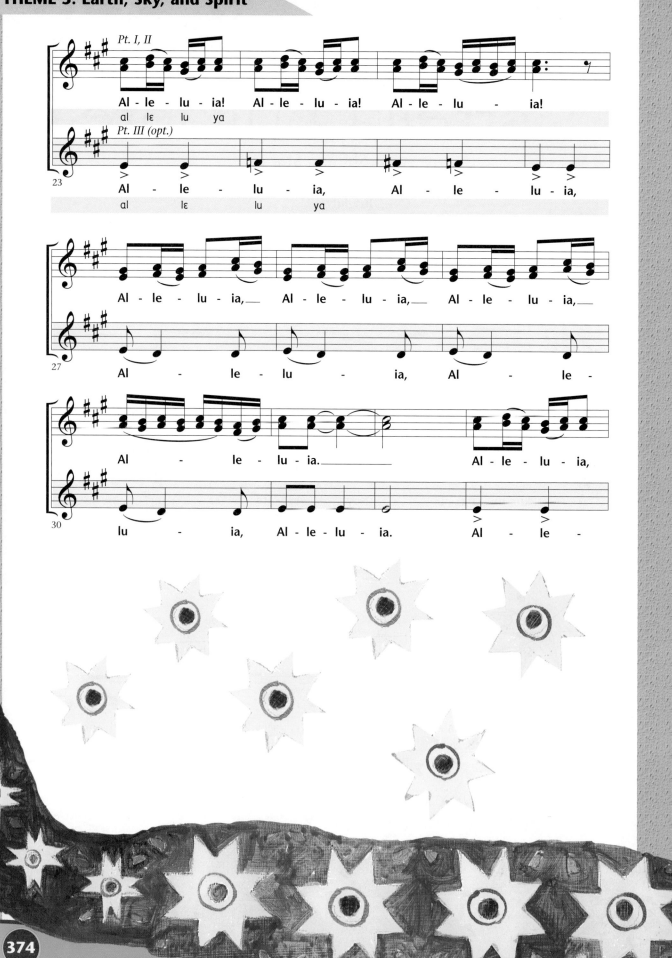

Al - le - lu - ia, Al - le - lu - ia, Al - le - lu - ia,___

lu - ia, Al - le - lu - ia, Al - le -

Al - le - lu - ia,___ Al - le - lu - ia,___ Al - le -

lu - ia, Al - le - lu - ia,

lu - ia.___

Al - le - lu - ia. Al - le - lu - ia.___

Al - le - lu - ia. Al - le - lu - ia.___

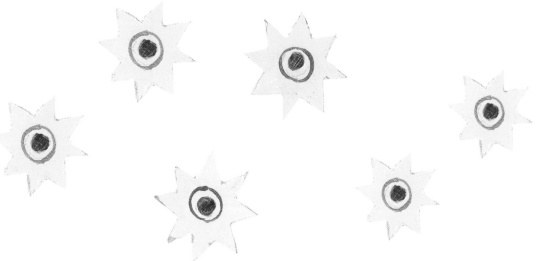

CONCEPT
MELODY

SKILLS
SING

In most cultures around the world, music and dancing go hand in hand. In fact, in many languages the word for music and dance is exactly the same. For many people in northern Thailand, singing and dancing to a song like "Ngam sang duan" can help people forget their troubles for a while.

Imagine you are singing this piece after a long day at work. How would you feel? Would you sing the song differently depending on your mood? Why or why not?

VOICE BUILDER: Legato

A song like "Ngam sang duan" requires a smooth, legato style. Take full breaths with an expanded rib cage and move smoothly from one note to the next without "scooping" or sliding into the note. **Sing** with vertical, round vowels and a relaxed and dropped jaw. Repeat at both higher and lower pitch levels to develop your vocal range.

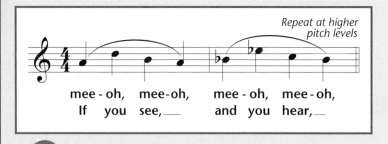

Repeat at higher pitch levels

mee - oh,   mee-oh,   mee - oh,   mee-oh,
If   you   see,____   and you   hear,____

MAP

MYANMAR
LAOS
THAILAND
KAMPUCHEA   VIETNAM

Ngam sang duan

CD 22:23

Shining Moon

Traditional Thai Folk Song
Arranged by Audrey Snyder

Legato, gently rocking

All - Unison
mp

Thai: งาม   แสง   เดื่อน   มา   เยื่อน
Pronunciation: ngam   sæng   du   ən   ma   yu   ən
English: **If   you   see   the moon - beams_**

ส่อง หล้า งาม ใบ หน้า มา สู่ วง รา งาม แสง
song la ngam bai na ma su wong lʌm ngam sæng
shim-mer 'cross the wa - ter as twi - light fades, And you

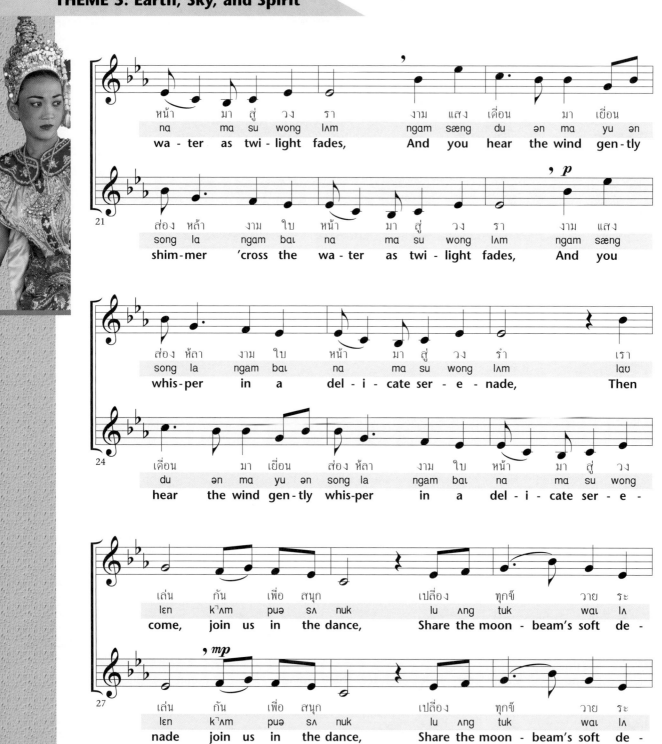

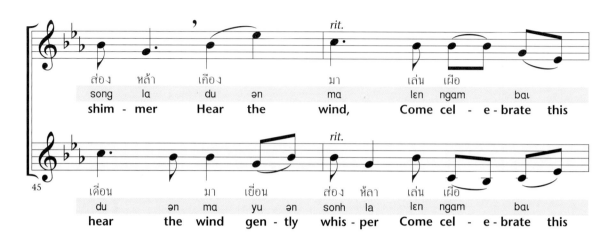

ส่อง หล้า เคือง มา เล่น เผือ
song la du ɔn ma lɛn ngam bɑɪ
shim - mer Hear the wind, Come cel - e - brate this

เดื่อน มา เยื่อน ส่อง ห้ลา เล่น เผือ
du ɔn ma yu ɔn sonh la lɛn ngam bɑɪ
hear the wind gen - tly whis - per Come cel - e - brate this

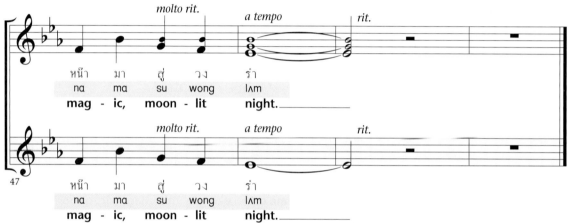

หน้า มา สู่ วง รำ
na ma su wong lʌm
mag - ic, moon - lit night._____

หน้า มา สู่ วง รำ
na ma su wong lʌm
mag - ic, moon - lit night._____

CONCEPT
MELODY

SKILLS
SING

The song "Our World" reminds us that we share our planet with many other living things. People, animals, and plants all have a place on Earth. The words in "Our World" carry an important message. They tell us we need to take special care of our planet so people in the future can enjoy it, too. Once you learn this song, sing it for your friends and family to share its special message.

VOICE BUILDER: Articulation

Just like vowels provide the "sound" of singing, consonants help provide the meaning of the words. Pronouncing consonants clearly is called articulation. **Practice** the following exercise by articulating all the consonants clearly and precisely. Gradually **sing** louder in a *crescendo* as you practice the ascending pattern below.

so₁ do do re re mi mi fa fa so____
I mar - vel at the mir - a - cles I see,____
and trea - sure all the joy they bring to me.____

CD 22:31

Music by Lana Walter
Words by Jane Foster Knox

All - Unison
mf
With feeling

I mar-vel at the mir - a - cles I see,____ and

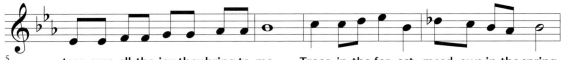

trea-sure all the joy they bring to me.   Trees in the for - est, mead - ows in the spring

More ➡

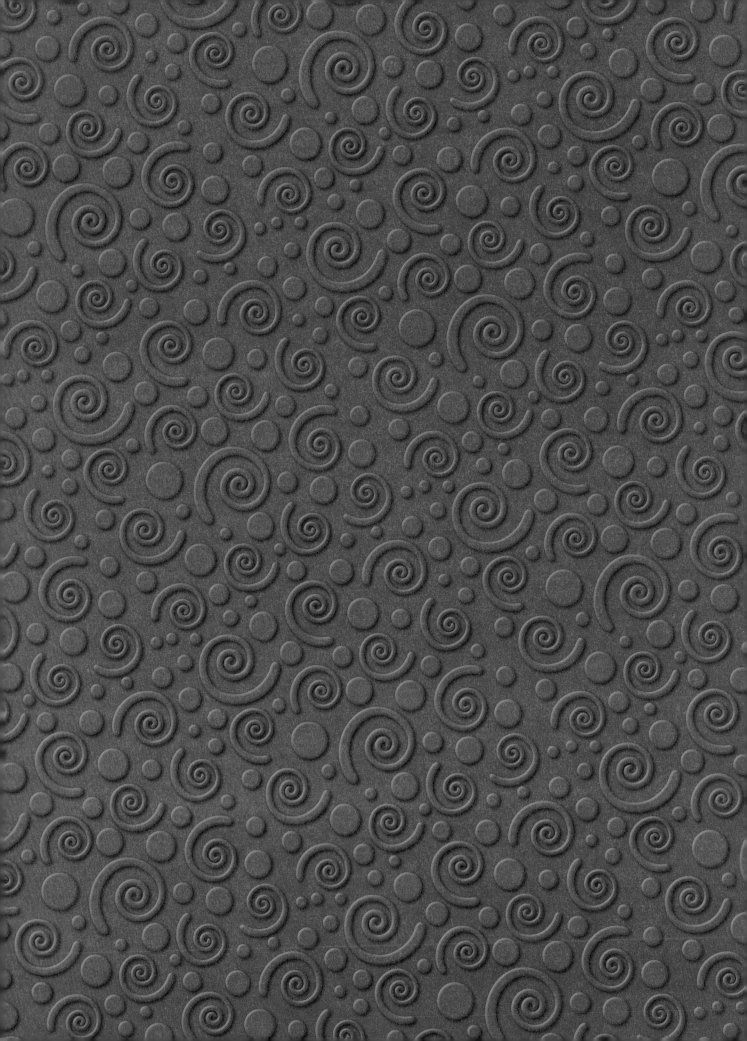

Spotlight on
Celebrations

Spotlight on Celebrations

Spotlight on Celebrations

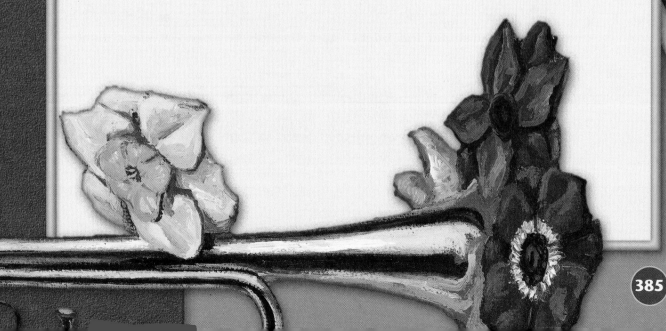

PATRIOTIC

CONCEPT
STYLE

SKILLS
SING, DESCRIBE

Songs of Our Country

During the War of 1812, Francis Scott Key was on board a British warship and was waiting for the outcome of an attack on Fort McHenry in Baltimore. When the smoke finally cleared, Key saw that the flag was still flying above the fort. This sight inspired him to write the poem that would later become the words for "The Star-Spangled Banner."

The Star-Spangled Banner

CD 22:35

Music Attributed to J.S. Smith
Words by Francis Scott Key

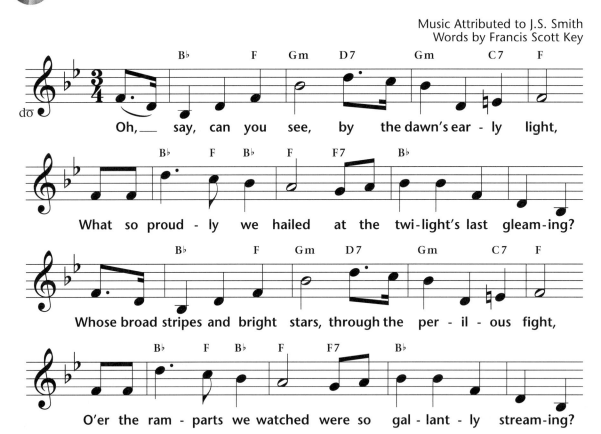

Oh, — say, can you see, by the dawn's ear - ly light,

What so proud - ly we hailed at the twi-light's last gleam-ing?

Whose broad stripes and bright stars, through the per - il - ous fight,

O'er the ram - parts we watched were so gal - lant - ly stream-ing?

Francis Scott Key wrote the words for our national anthem in 1814.

Composite photograph of the 190 year-old Star-Spangled Banner, the flag that inspired the national anthem. Smithsonian's National Museum of American History, ©2002

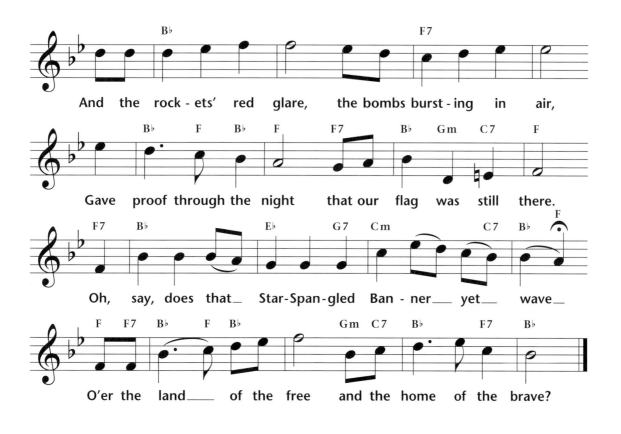

And the rock-ets' red glare, the bombs burst-ing in air,

Gave proof through the night that our flag was still there.

Oh, say, does that_ Star-Span-gled Ban-ner_ yet_ wave_

O'er the land___ of the free and the home of the brave?

CONCEPT
BEAT, METER

SKILLS
SING

On a trip to Pikes Peak, Colorado, in 1893, Katharine Lee Bates was so inspired by the beauty of what she saw that she wrote the poem *America, the Beautiful*.

America, the Beautiful

CD 23:1

Music by Samuel Ward
Words by Katharine Lee Bates

1. O beau - ti - ful for spa - cious skies, For am - ber waves of grain.
2. O beau - ti - ful for he - roes proved In lib - er - at - ing strife,
3. O beau - ti - ful for pa - triot dream That sees be - yond the years,

For pur - ple moun - tain maj - es - ties A - bove the fruit - ed plain.
Who more than self their coun - try loved, And mer - cy more than life.
Thine al - a - bas - ter cit - ies gleam, Un - dim'd by hu - man tears.

A - mer - i - ca! A - mer - i - ca! God shed His grace on thee,

And crown thy good with broth - er - hood, From sea to shin - ing sea.

Heartbeat of Democracy

"Sure, we can," said the man.
And his tone was the bone,
Was the spirit and bone,
With which freedom was sown.
The firm strength of his mood
Was as sleep and as food
To the wavering-willed;
And their spirits were thrilled
To the one effort more
That seemed hopeless before.

There is faith that is fact,
Not a wraith, but an act
That comes up from the earth
With conviction and worth.
It is big and sincere
And holds liberty dear
As its life. Said the man,
"Sure we can. Sure, we can!"
And the air seemed to fill
With the words, "And we will!"

—Virginia Brasier

CONCEPT
FORM
SKILLS
SING, LISTEN

In 1861 after a trip to a Union Army camp, Julia Ward Howe wrote a poem that came to be called the *Battle Hymn of the Republic*.

 LISTENING CD 23:4

Battle Hymn of the Republic Music by William Steffe

This tune is based on the song "John Brown's Body," also from the Civil War period. This version is performed by the Monty Alexander Trio.

Listening Map for Battle Hymn of the Republic

Introduction

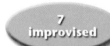
1
Steady beat starts melody

2
melody

7
improvised

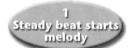
3
improvised

6
NEW key melody

5
improvised

4
improvised more cymbal

Battle Hymn of the Republic

CD 23:5

Music by William Steffe
Words by Julia Ward Howe

Mine eyes have seen the glo-ry of the com-ing of the Lord;

He is tram-pling out the vin-tage where the grapes of wrath are stored;

He has loosed the fate-ful light-ning of his ter-ri-ble swift sword;

His truth is march-ing on.

Refrain

Glo-ry, Glo-ry, Hal-le-lu - jah! Glo-ry, Glo-ry, Hal-le-lu - jah!

Glo - ry, Glo - ry! Glo - ry, Hal-le-lu - jah.

Glo - ry, Glo - ry, Hal-le-lu - jah! His truth is march-ing on!

Glo - ry, Glo - ry! His truth is march-ing on.

CONCEPT
RHYTHM, METER
SKILLS
SING, READ

Each state in the United States is special. Each has unique cities, people, and natural resources. There are many things to learn about each state in this great country of ours! If you could visit any state, which would it be?

Fifty Nifty United States

CD 23:9

Words and Music by Ray Charles

Fif-ty nif-ty U-nit-ed States from thir-teen o-rig-i-nal col-o-nies;

Fif-ty nif-ty stars in the flag that bil-lows so beau-ti-f'ly in__ the breeze.

Each in-di-vid-u-al state con-tri-butes a qual-i-ty that is great.

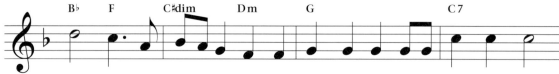

Each in-di-vid-u-al state de-serves a bow, we sa-lute them now.

Fif-ty nif-ty U-ni-ted States from thir-teen o-rig-i-nal col-o-nies,

Shout 'em, scout 'em, Tell all a-bout 'em, One by one till we've

giv-en a day to ev-'ry state in the U. S. A. Al-a-

2nd time as fast as possible

bam-a, A-las-ka, Ar-i-zo-na, Ar-kan-sas, Cal-i-

for-nia, Col-o-ra-do, Con-nect-i-cut; Del-a-ware,

Flor-i-da, Geor-gia, Ha-wai-i, I-da-ho, Il-li-nois, In-di-

an-a; I-o-wa, Kan-sas, Ken-tuck-y, Lou-i-si-

an-a, Maine, Mar-y-land, Mas-sa-chu-setts, Mich-i-gan;

Min-ne-so-ta, Mis-sis-sip-pi, Mis-sou-ri, Mon-

tan-a, Ne-bras-ka, Ne-vad-a; New Hamp-shire,

More

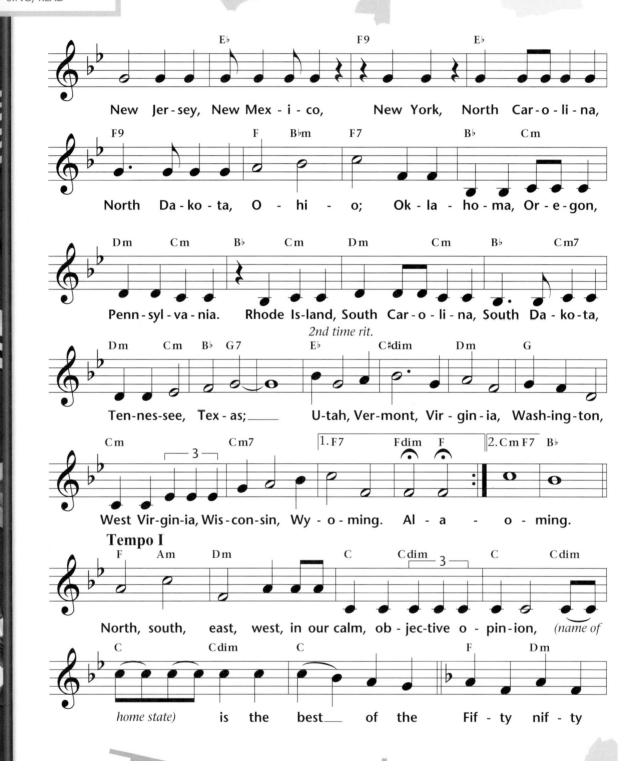

New Jer-sey, New Mex-i-co, New York, North Car-o-li-na,

North Da-ko-ta, O-hi-o; Ok-la-ho-ma, Or-e-gon,

Penn-syl-va-nia. Rhode Is-land, South Car-o-li-na, South Da-ko-ta,

2nd time rit.

Ten-nes-see, Tex-as;___ U-tah, Ver-mont, Vir-gin-ia, Wash-ing-ton,

1. F7 Fdim F 2. Cm F7 B♭

West Vir-gin-ia, Wis-con-sin, Wy-o-ming. Al-a-o-ming.

Tempo I

North, south, east, west, in our calm, ob-jec-tive o-pin-ion, (name of

home state) is the best___ of the Fif-ty nif-ty

394

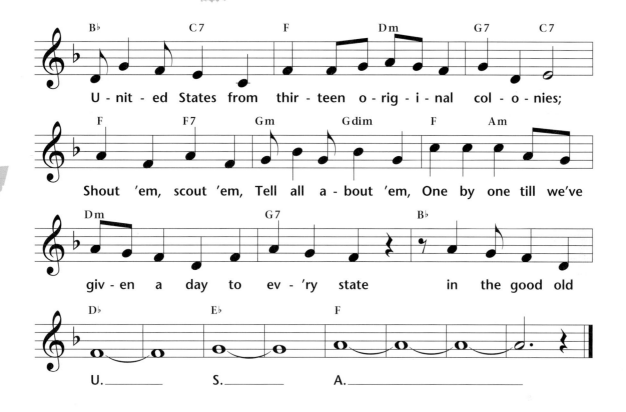

U - nit - ed States from thir - teen o - rig - i - nal col - o - nies;

Shout 'em, scout 'em, Tell all a - bout 'em, One by one till we've

giv - en a day to ev - 'ry state in the good old

U._____ S._____ A._____

LISTENING CD 23:12

The Liberty Bell by John Philip Sousa

"The Liberty Bell" march was written by
John Philip Sousa (1854-1932), America's
"March King," for the occasion of the
Liberty Bell's visit to the World's Columbian
Exhibition in Chicago in 1893.

Hispanic Heritage Month

September 15 to October 15 is National Hispanic Heritage Month. It is celebrated throughout the United States with music and dance. The dance "El jarabe" is a symbol of identity for many Mexicans and Mexican-Americans. It is also known as the Mexican Hat Dance.

Mexican Hat Dance

MAP
UNITED STATES
MEXICO   BELIZE
GUATEMALA

CD 23:13

Mexican Folk Music
Spanish Words and Adaptation by José-Luis Orozco

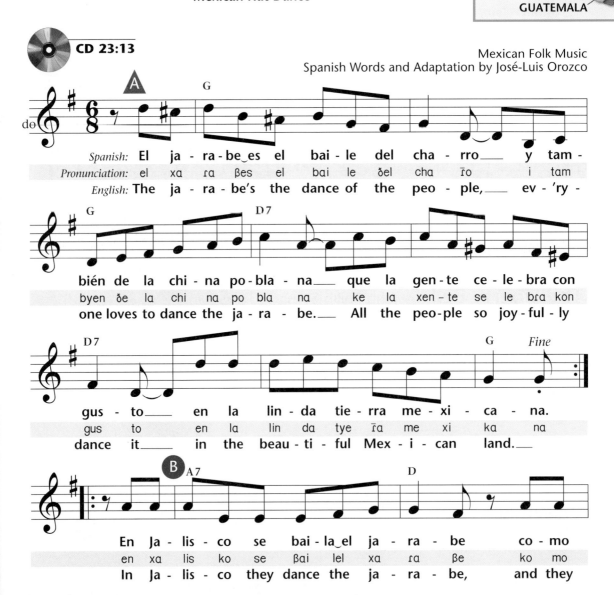

Spanish: El ja - ra - be es el bai - le del cha - rro___ y tam -
Pronunciation: el xa ɾa βes el bai le ðel cha ɾo i tam
English: The ja - ra - be's the dance of the peo - ple,___ ev - 'ry -

bién de la chi - na po - bla - na___ que la gen - te ce - le - bra con
byen ðe la chi na po bla na ke la xen - te se le βɾa kon
one loves to dance the ja - ra - be.___ All the peo - ple so joy - ful - ly

gus - to___ en la lin - da tie - rra me - xi - ca - na.
gus to en la lin da tye ɾa me xi ka na
dance it___ in the beau - ti - ful Mex - i - can land.___

En Ja - lis - co se bai - la el ja - ra - be co - mo
en xa lis ko se βai lel xa ɾa βe ko mo
In Ja - lis - co they dance the ja - ra - be, and they

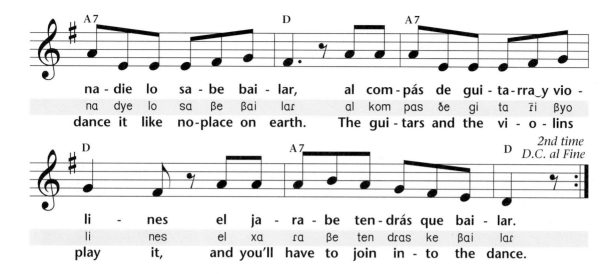

na - die lo sa - be bai - lar, al com - pás de gui - ta - rra_y vio -
na dye lo sa βe βai lar al kom pas ðe gi ta ɾi βyo
dance it like no-place on earth. The gui - tars and the vi - o - lins

2nd time
D.C. al Fine

li - nes el ja - ra - be ten - drás que bai - lar.
li nes el xa ɾa βe ten dɾas ke βai lar
play it, and you'll have to join in - to the dance.

 LISTENING CD 23:17

Son de la negra by R. Fuentes and S. Vargas

This popular Mexican song inspires dance and celebration!

Identify three instruments playing "Son de la negra."

 CD-ROM

Use *World Instruments* CD-ROM to learn more about Mexican instruments.

CONCEPT
RHYTHM
SKILLS
SING, DESCRIBE

Hispanic Americans can trace their roots to the countries of their ancestors, including Puerto Rico, Cuba, Spain, Africa, and the nations of Central and South America. This song, "Santa Marta," is from Colombia.

MAP
PANAMA
ECUADOR
VENEZUELA
COLOMBIA
PERU   BRAZIL

CD 23:18

Words and Music by Francisco Bolaños

Spanish: San-ta Mar-ta, San-ta Mar-ta tie-ne sol, San-ta Mar-ta tie-ne
Pronunciation: san ta mar ta san ta mar ta tye ne sol san ta mar ta tye ne

sol, pe-ro no tie-ne tran-ví-a. San-ta ví-a. Si no
sol pe ro no tye ne tran bi a san ta bi a si no

fue-ra por la zo-na ¡ay, ca-ram-ba! San-ta
fwe ra por la so nai ka ram ba san ta

Mar-ta mo-ri-rí-a ¡ay, ca-ram-ba! Si-no ram-ba!
mar ta mo ri ri ai ka ram ba si no ram ba

Barbacoa para cumpleaños

Carmen Lomas Garza (born 1948) is a Mexican American artist whose painting reflects her cultural traditions. Through her art, she celebrates the good things that she remembers about her childhood growing up in Texas. In the painting *Barbacoa para cumpleaños,* as in many of her works, Garza shows that family is an important part of Hispanic culture.

Describe the family celebration represented in this painting.

AUTUMN: Chusok

CONCEPT
METER

SKILLS
SING

*C*husok is a Korean harvest festival. It is one of the most popular festivals in Korean culture. *Chusok* occurs during the mid-autumn harvest season. Koreans take this time to gather with their families to pay their respects to their ancestors. Korean children wear traditional clothing, and dance, play games, and sing songs.

Ga Eul

Fall

CD 23:22

Music by Dong Eum Ahn
Words by Bok Hyun Choi
English Words by Linda Worsley

D	G	D Bm	G	A A7	

Korean: 대 롱 대 롱 대 추 알 엔 추 석 빛 이 물 들 고 ―
Pronunciation: de roŋ de roŋ de chu al en chu suk bit i mul dəl go
English: Now the date is heav-y with seed, Chu-sok's spir-it draw-ing near.__

D	G	A	D	A	A7	D

토 실 때 실 밤 송 이 엔 가 을 이 익 어 간 다 ―
to sil te sil bam soŋ i en ga əl i ik ʌ gan da
Chest-nut fat and ripe on the tree, mir-rors the rip-en-ing year.__

G	D G	E7	A A7

때 롱 때 롱 방 울 벌 레 들 국 화 꽃 피 우 고 ―
te ruŋ te ruŋ baŋ ul bʊl le dʊl guk hwa gɔk pi u go
"Dae rung, dae rung," crick-et calls out, Field flow-ers bloom in the Fall.__

D	G	A7	D

귀 뚤 귀 뚤 귀 뚜 라 미 노 ― 래 자 랑 한 다 ―
gwi tul gwi tul gwi tu ra mi no re ja raŋ han da
"Gwi tool, gwi tool," Grass-hop-per sings, Fill-ing the air with his call.__

CONCEPT
MELODY
SKILLS
SING

Diwali, also called the Festival of Lights, is celebrated in India and is looked upon as the beginning of the New Year. Homes are decorated with *diyas*—small lamps—to welcome wealth and prosperity. *Diwali* is celebrated for five days. Each day has its own special meaning tied to myths, legends, or beliefs.

Aeyaya balano sakkad

Come, Children

MAP
CHINA
PAKISTAN
NEPAL
INDIA
BANGLADESH

CD 23:26

Words by Smt. Chandra Bhat
Music by M.B. Srinivasan
English Lyrics by John Higgins

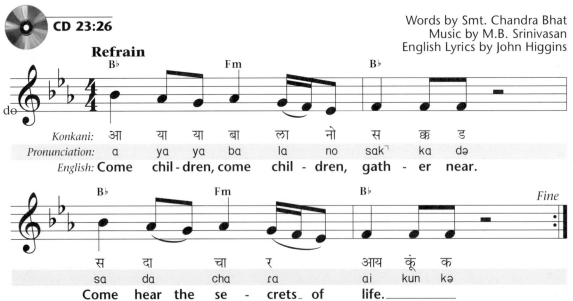

Refrain

Konkani: आ या या बा ला नो स क्क ड
Pronunciation: a ya ya ba la no sak̚ ka də
English: Come chil-dren, come chil-dren, gath-er near.

Fine

स द चा र आय कूं क
sa da cha ɾa ai kun kə
Come hear the se - crets of life.

Verse

सां ग तां तुम कां जी व न नी ति
san ga tā tum kā ji va na ni ti

Child-hood is a gift, it's pass-ing by so fast, we can nev-er ap-pre-ci-ate,

जी व न नी नि सां ग तां तुम कां
ji va na ni ti san ga tā tum kā

some-thing we real-ly should cel-e-brate, child-hood is a gift, it's pass-ing by so

जी व न नी ति स फ ल जां व च्य क
ji va na ni ti sa fa lə jā və cha kə

fast, we can nev-er ap-pre-ci-ate. This is the time when we have the

चो ल री ति स फ ल जां व च्य क
chol chi ɾi ti sa fa lə jā və cha kə

pow-er to learn and grow. This is the time when we all can

D.C. al Fine

चो ल री ति
chol chi ɾi ti

build on the things we know.

 LISTENING CD 23:30

Raga Malika Indian Classical Music

Listen to Ali Akbar Khan playing "Raga Malika." The instruments you hear are *sarod* and *tabla*.

Use *World Instruments* **CD-ROM** to learn more about instruments from India.

403

AUTUMN: Halloween

CONCEPT
MELODY
SKILLS
MOVE

Trick or treating, jack-o-lanterns, goblins, and ghouls—they all mean just one thing. Fall is here, and so is Halloween! Enjoy these frightfully fun songs.

LISTENING CD 24:1

Halloween Montage

Do you recognize this creepy music? It all has to do with the Halloween spirit! See how many songs you recognize.

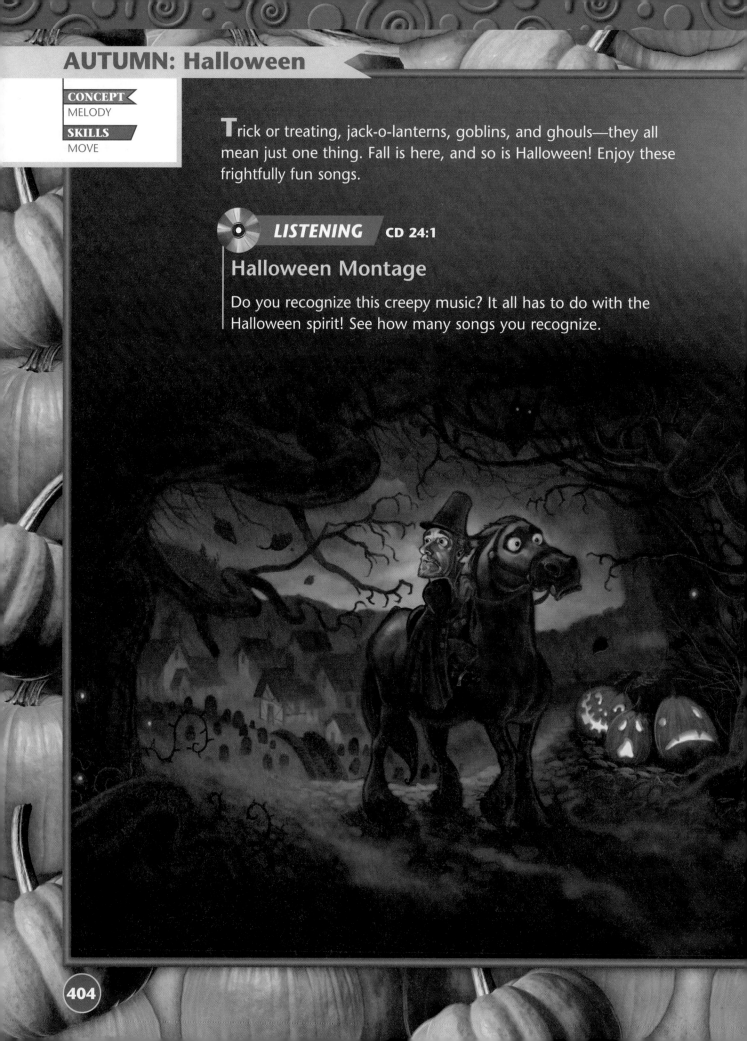

Nottamun Town

CD 24:2

English Folk Song

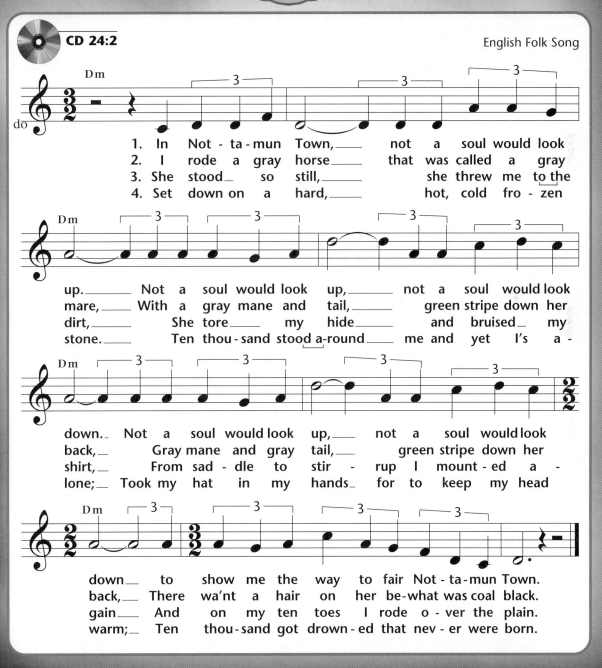

do

Dm

1. In Not - ta - mun Town, _____ not a soul would look
2. I rode a gray horse _____ that was called a gray
3. She stood ___ so still, _____ she threw me to the
4. Set down on a hard, _____ hot, cold fro - zen

Dm

up. _____ Not a soul would look up, _____ not a soul would look
mare, _____ With a gray mane and tail, _____ green stripe down her
dirt, _____ She tore ___ my hide _____ and bruised ___ my
stone. _____ Ten thou - sand stood a - round _____ me and yet I's a -

Dm

down. ___ Not a soul would look up, ___ not a soul would look
back, ___ Gray mane and gray tail, _____ green stripe down her
shirt, ___ From sad - dle to stir - rup I mount - ed a -
lone; ___ Took my hat in my hands ___ for to keep my head

Dm

down ___ to show me the way to fair Not - ta - mun Town.
back, ___ There wa'nt a hair on her be - what was coal black.
gain ___ And on my ten toes I rode o - ver the plain.
warm; ___ Ten thou - sand got drown - ed that nev - er were born.

405

CONCEPT
STYLE, BACKGROUND
SKILLS
SING

The rhythm of this song may set your bones in motion!

CD 24:5

African American Spiritual

A Freely

C   G7   C

E - ze - kiel cried, "Them dry bones!" E - ze - kiel cried, "Them dry bones!"

C   G7   C

E - ze - kiel cried, "Them dry bones, Now hear the Word of the Lord!"

B

The foot bone con - nect - ed to the leg bone.

C#

The leg bone con - nect - ed to the knee bone.

D

The knee bone con - nect - ed to the hip - bone.

D#

The hip - bone con - nect - ed to the back - bone.

The back-bone con-nect-ed to the shoul-der bone.

The shoul-der bone con-nect-ed to the neck bone.

The neck bone con-nect-ed to the jaw-bone.

The jaw-bone con-nect-ed to the head bone.

Now hear the Word of the Lord.

C *fast*

Them bones, them bones gon-na walk a-round. Them

bones, them bones gon-na walk a-round. Them bones, them bones gon-na

walk a-round. Now hear the Word of the Lord.

Seasonal Songs

The beauty of winter can be enchanting! The world around you is a different place when wrapped in a blanket of white. What sights and sounds come to your mind when you think of winter?

Winter Wonderland

CD 24:8

Music by Felix Bernard
Arranged by Marilyn Davidson
Words by Dick Smith

Sleigh bells ring, are you lis-t'nin'? In the lane snow is
way is the blue-bird. Here to stay is a

glis-t'nin'. A beau-ti-ful sight,_ we're hap-py to-night_
new bird. He sings a love song_ as we go a-long_

Walk-in' in a win-ter won-der-land! Gone a-land!

In the mead-ow we can build a snow-man; (And we'll)

Then pre-tend that he is Par-son Brown.

He'll say, "Are you mar - ried?" We'll say, "No, man!___ But

you can do the job when you're in town."___ Lat - er

on we'll con - spire___ as we dream by the fire,___ To

face un - a - fraid___ the plans that we made___

Walk - in' in a win - ter won - der - land.___

CONCEPT
METER
SKILLS
SING

Christmas is a time to open your heart to the spirit of giving. You will be surprised what you can receive in return!

The Season of Hope

CD 24:12

Words and Music by Roger Emerson

1. This is the sea - son of hope;
2. Reach out and try some - thing new;
3. This is the sea - son of hope;

A won - der - ful time of the year.
Start a tra - di - tion, or two.
A won - der - ful time of the year.

Peo - ple are car - ing; giv - ing and shar - ing.
No need to choose; noth - ing to lose.
We can be more! Look what's in store!

3rd time to Coda

This is the sea - son of hope. _____

2. G

hope.

B

B♭   F   D

We put up walls____ from things that are new.

B♭   F   G   C   *D.C. al Coda*

O - pen our hearts;__ is what we must do!____

Coda

C   D   G

This is the sea - son of hope.____

The Sankta Lucia festival started as a Swedish family tradition in which the eldest daughter dresses in white, wearing a crown of candles. At dawn on December 13, she and her sisters and brothers bring coffee and sweets to their parents. There are also Lucia processions in schools, hospitals, and offices.

Saint Lucia was an Italian saint from the early Christian era. Her legend traveled from Italy to Sweden through the song "Santa Lucia," which was later translated into Swedish.

Sankta Lucia

Saint Lucia

CD 24:15

Italian Folk Song

Swedish: Nat - ten går tun - ga fjät runt gård och stu - va.
Pronunciation: nɑ tɛn gɔɾ tʊng a fyɛt ɾʊnt gord ɔk stu va
English: **Night walks with hea - vy steps 'round farm and cot-tage.**

Kring jord, som sol'n för - lät, skug - gor - na ru - va.
kɾɪng yord sɔm soln för lɛt skʊ gor na ɾʊ va
Sha - dows creep 'round the earth, sun - light is hid - ing.

Då i vårt mör - ka hus sti - ger med
do i vort mör ka hüs sti gər mɛd
In - to our dark - ened house en - ters with

tän - da ljus Sank - ta___ Lu - ci - a,
tɛn da yus sank ta lu si a
can - dle light: San - ta___ Lu - ci - a,

1. Sank - ta Lu - ci - a. **2.** Sank - ta Lu - ci - a.
sank ta lu si a sank ta lu si a
San - ta Lu - ci - a. San - ta Lu - ci - a.

CONCEPT
TONALITY
SKILLS
SING

The eight days of Hanukkah are times of rejoicing over a battle won and freedom gained. *Hallel*, or praise, is said during the morning prayer, and grace is said after each meal. Lighting the menorah or *hanukkiah* is part of the Hanukkah celebration. The menorah holds nine candles. Eight candles represent the eight days of Hanukkah and the ninth, the *shamash* (leader or head), is used to light the other candles.

Haneirot Halalu

These Lights

 CD 24:21

Traditional Jewish Song
English Words by MMH

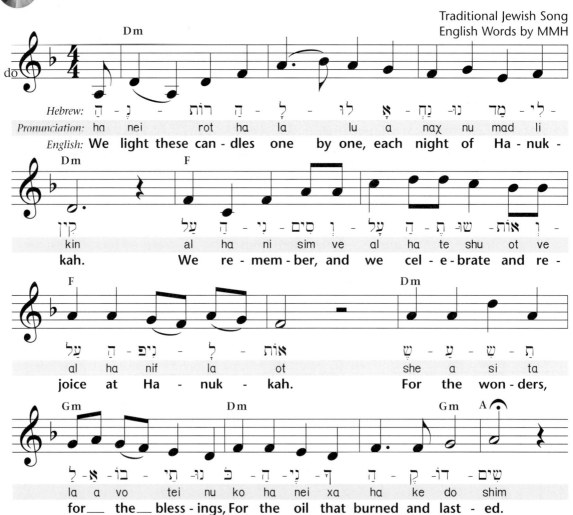

CONCEPT
TONALITY
SKILLS
SING, READ

During Hanukkah friends and family exchange gifts, put up decorations, and light the menorah.

Light One Candle

Words and Music by Peter Yarrow

CD 24:25 **Verse**

1. Light one can-dle for the Mac-ca-bee chil-dren with

thanks that their light did-n't die.

Light one can-dle for the pain they en-dured_ when their

right to ex-ist___ was de-nied.

Light one can-dle for the ter-ri-ble sac-ri-fice

jus-tice and free-dom de-mand.___ But

light one can-dle for the wis-dom to know_ when the

peace - mak - er's time___ is at hand._____

Refrain

Don't let the light___ go out.___ It's last-ed for so___ man-y

years. Don't let the light___ go out.___ Let it

shine through our love and our tears._____

2. Light one candle for the strength that we need
   To never become our own foe.
   Light one candle for those who are suffering
   Pain we learned so long ago.
   Light one candle for all we believe in,
   Let anger not tear us apart.
   And light one candle to bind us together
   With peace as the song in our hearts.
   (To Refrain)

3. What is the memory that's valued so highly
   That we keep it alive in that flame?
   What's the commitment to those who have died
   That we cry out they've not died in vain?
   We have come this far always believing
   That justice will somehow prevail.
   This is the burden, this is the promise.
   And this is why we will not fail.
   (To Refrain)

Holly and ivy are two of the best-known, traditional Christmas plants. In Europe and Asia, these plants were used in winter festivities as a way to make sure that new life and growth would return again in spring.

The Holly and the Ivy

CD 24:28

Old English Carol

1. The hol - ly and the i - vy, when they are both full grown,
2. The hol - ly bears a ber - ry as red as an - y blood,

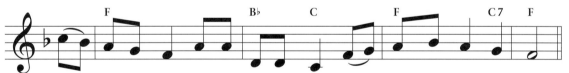

Of__ all the trees that are in the wood, the__ hol - ly bears the crown.
And__ Ma - ry bore sweet__ Je - sus to__ do poor sin - ners good.

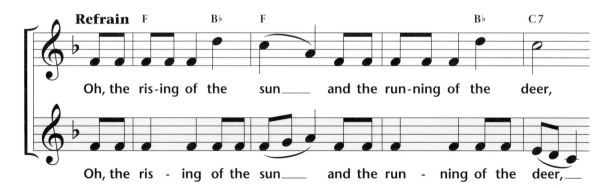

Refrain

Oh, the ris - ing of the sun____ and the run - ning of the deer,

Oh, the ris - ing of the sun____ and the run - ning of the deer,____

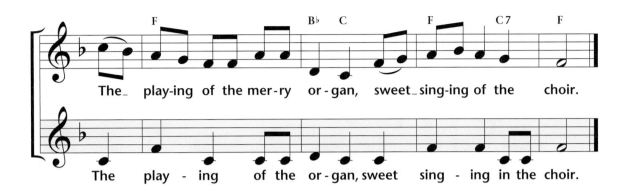

The_ play-ing of the mer-ry or - gan, sweet_ sing-ing of the choir.

The play - ing of the or-gan, sweet sing - ing in the choir.

LISTENING CD 24:32

Hallelujah Chorus from *Messiah*

by George Frideric Handel

The composer George Frideric Handel was born in Germany, but he spent many years in England composing music for the English royalty. He composed many oratorios, which are very long musical compositions in which soloists, a chorus, and an orchestra tell a sacred story.

The "Hallelujah Chorus" is one of Handel's most famous compositions. It is part of his oratorio called the *Messiah*, which is over three hours long.

Listen carefully to the way the different sections of the chorus sing the same melody at different times. This kind of imitation is used in canons, rounds, fugues, and some other kinds of polyphonic music.

CONCEPT
STYLE
SKILLS
SING

Here is a holiday song that is sure to get everyone into the Christmas spirit!

Feliz Navidad

Merry Christmas

CD 25:1

Words and Music by José Feliciano

Spanish: Fe - liz Na - vi - dad. Fe - liz Na - vi -
Pronunciation: fe lis nɑ βi ðɑð fe lis nɑ βi

dad. Fe - liz Na - vi -
ðɑð fe lis nɑ βi

dad, Pros - pe - ro a - ño y fe - li - ci - dad.__
ðɑð pros pe ro a nyo i fe li si ðɑð

I want to wish__ you a Mer - ry Christ - mas

I want to wish__ you a Mer - ry Christ - mas

I want to wish__ you a Mer - ry Christ - mas from the
bot - tom of my heart.__
I want to wish__ you a Mer ry Christ - mas   I want to wish__ you a
Mer – ry Christ - mas   I want to wish__ you a
Mer-ry Christ - mas from the bot-tom of my heart.__

This African American spiritual tells the story of the star in the eastern sky that led the shepherds to the wonder of Christmas morning.

Rise Up, Shepherd, and Follow

CD 25:4

African American Spiritual

Verse
Solo
do

C   F   C

1. There's a star in the East on Christ - mas morn,
2. If you take good heed of the an - gel's words,

Chorus
C   B♭   G

Rise up, shep - herd, and fol - low._____

Solo
C   F   C

It will lead to the place where the babe is born,_____
You'll for - get your flocks, you'll for - get your herds,_____

Chorus
D 7   G 7   C

Rise up, shep - herd, and fol - low._____

This rockin' Christmas tune is a holiday favorite for all ages!

Jingle-Bell Rock

CD 25:5

Words and Music by
Joe Beal and Jim Boothe

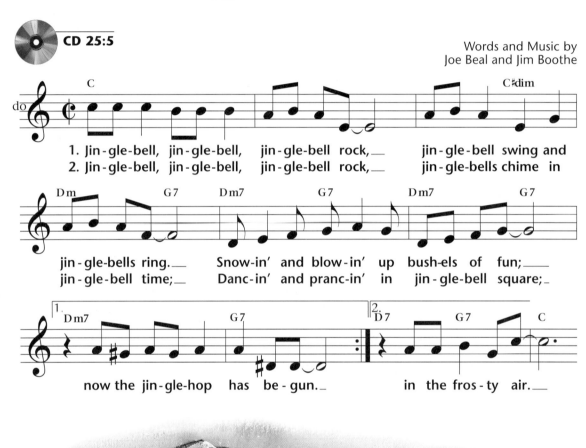

C

1. Jin-gle-bell, jin-gle-bell, jin-gle-bell rock,— jin-gle-bell swing and
2. Jin-gle-bell, jin-gle-bell, jin-gle-bell rock,— jin-gle-bells chime in

C♯dim

Dm   G7   Dm7   G7   Dm7   G7

jin-gle-bells ring.— Snow-in' and blow-in' up bush-els of fun;—
jin-gle-bell time;— Danc-in' and pranc-in' in jin-gle-bell square;—

1. Dm7   G7   2. D7   G7   C

now the jin-gle-hop has be-gun.   in the fros-ty air.—

What a bright_ time,_ it's the right_ time_ to

rock the night a-way._ Jin-gle-bell_ time_ is a

swell time_ to go glid-in' in a one-horse sleigh._

Gid-dy-ap, jin-gle-horse, pick up your feet,_ jin-gle a-round the

clock; Mix and min-gle in a jin-gl-in' beat,_

that's the jin-gle-bell rock. that's the jin-gle-bell,

that's the jin-gle-bell rock.

Kwanzaa is an African American celebration created by Dr. Maulana Karenga in 1966 with focus on traditional African values of family, community, responsibility, self-improvement, and faith. Kwanzaa lasts for seven days from December 26th to January 1st and is based on seven guiding principles, called *nguzo saba* in Swahili, one for each day. *Umoja* is the principle that reminds the African American people of the value of unity among community members.

 LISTENING CD 25:08

Azouke Legba by Vodou Le

This recording was made in New York City, where many Haitian immigrants live. They often gather to play music. The sounds of rattles, sticks, drums, and vocals are reminders of African influence. Listen carefully to the vocal structure.

Identify the vocal structure of the selection "Azouke Legba."

Ujima (collective work and responsibility) is the principle that reminds people who celebrate Kwanzaa of their obligation and responsibility to one another, their communities, and the world.

Ujima

Collective Work and Responsibility

More

CD 25:9

Words and Music by Stan Spottswood

O let us work to-geth - er. O let us help each oth - er.

O let us work to-geth - er. O let us help each oth - er.

U - ji - ma:_ let us work to-geth - er to make_ bet - ter our com-

mun - i - ty.__ We can_ solve,_ solve our_ prob - lems with col-

lec - tive_ work_ and re - spon - si - bil - i - ty. spon - si - bil - i - ty.

C

Rap Solo **mf**

Ec - o - nom - ic op - por - tun - i - ty, not

on - ly to sur - vive, but to thrive; it's a new cen - tur -

y. Don't strive to con-sume, but be a pro-duc - er. Own your own com-pan-

y. Don't make your aim just to get a good job, but

shoot for the moon. If you miss, you'll still be a star,—

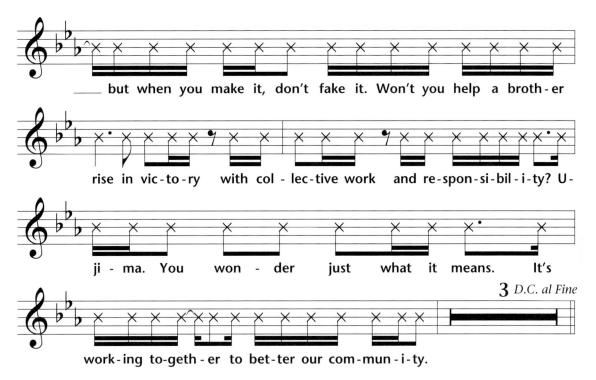

_____ but when you make it, don't fake it. Won't you help a broth-er

rise in vic-to-ry with col - lec-tive work and re-spon-si-bil - i-ty? U-

ji - ma. You won - der just what it means. It's

3 _D.C. al Fine_

work-ing to-geth - er to bet-ter our com-mun - i-ty.

Explain the musical structure of the song "Ujima."

 Art Gallery

Kwanzaa Stamp

The United States Postal Service commissioned Synthia Saint James to create the first Kwanzaa stamp, made available on October 22, 1997. This self-taught artist was born in 1949 in Los Angeles, California. She has received many awards for her children's books and humanitarian activities.

CONCEPT
TONE COLOR
SKILLS
DESCRIBE

Some people have dreams of adventure and exploration. Some people have dreams of freedom and fair treatment for everyone. No matter how great or small, all dreams take commitment and courage to make them come true.

Describe how the song reinforces the idea of having dreams.

Dreamers

CD 25:12

Words and Music by Janet McMahan-Wilson

1. Clara Barton: She com - fort - ed the hurt - ing, _____ she
2. Amelia Earhart: She had a quest to fol - low, _____ and
3. Martin Luther King: He had a dream, a vis - ion, _____ a

cared for those in pain. She gave her - self
blue skies to ex - plore. Her lof - ty dreams
hope for hu - man - kind, to take us to the

to her cause to cre - ate a more hu - mane
soon found wings_ and then she be - gan to soar,
moun - tain - top_ and leave pre - ju - dice be - hind.

ha - ven for the wound - ed; and a ref - uge for the
sail - ing through the hea - vens, she found sol - ace in the
All too soon, he left us, in an in - stant he was

ill. Now all the world re - mem - bers her,
sky. We cel - e - brate the jour - ney of this
gone. His mes - sage still stirs in our hearts, his

and it al - ways will._____
wom - an born to fly._____
mem - o - ry lives on._____

Dream - ers,__ Dream - ers__ are just like me and__ you.

Dream - ers,__ Dream - ers,__ be - lieve in dreams come true. If you

fol - low what you feel, your dreams can be real.

3rd time repeat last line*

Dreamers__ like me and you make dreams come true.

One of the most famous holidays in Brazil is *Carnaval*. It is a five-day festival known for its noisy street parades, lively dancing, colorful costumes, and music filled with strong rhythms. Some groups of dancers and musicians prepare all year long for their carnaval performances. Many people take a holiday from work and school to join in the celebration. Family, friends, and neighbors gather to dance their way through one of the happiest times of the year.

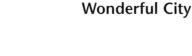

Wonderful City

MAP

BRAZIL

SOUTH AMERICA

CD 25:15

Words and Music by André Filho
Arranged by Elizabeth Souza

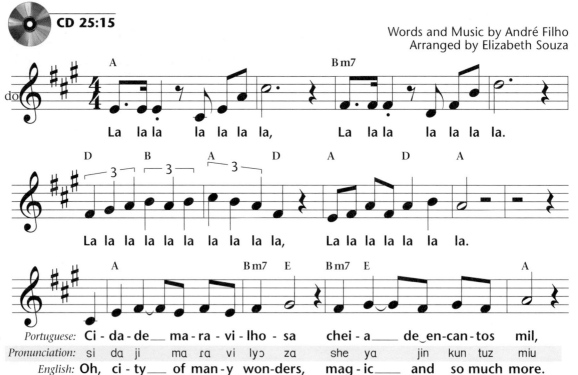

La la la la la la la, La la la la la la la.

La la la la la la la la la la, La la la la la la.

Portuguese: Ci - da - de __ ma - ra - vi - lho - sa chei - a __ de en-can-tos mil,
Pronunciation: si da ji ma ɾa vi lyɔ za she ya jin kun tuz miu
English: **Oh,** ci - ty __ of man - y won-ders, mag-ic __ and so much more.

Ci - da-de___ ma - ra - vi - lho - sa   co - ra - ção do meu Bra - sil.
si   da ji   ma ɾa vi lyɔ za   ko ɾa são du meu bɾa ziu
Oh,   ci - ty___ of man-y won-ders,   soul and beau-ty of Bra - zil.

Ci - da-de___ ma - ra - vi - lho - sa   chei - a___ de en-can - tos   mil,
si   da ji   ma ɾa vi lyɔ za   she ya   jin kun tuz   miu
Oh,   ci - ty___ of man-y won-ders,   mag-ic___ and   so much more.

Ci - da-de___ ma - ra - vi - lho - sa   co - ra - ção do meu Bra - sil.
si   da ji   ma ɾa vi lyɔ za   ko ɾa são du meu bɾa ziu
Oh,   ci - ty___ of man-y won-ders,   soul and beau-ty of Bra - zil.

🔘 **LISTENING**   CD 25:19

Batucada Brasileira Folk Music from Brazil

Every year neighbors gather to create a *batucada*, a percussion piece, for the parade. It is accompanied by movement. Everyone practices hard so that they can win first prize for the best *batucada* of the year!

CONCEPT
STYLE, BACKGROUND

SKILLS
SING

Saint Patrick's Day in America was celebrated for the first time in Boston around 1737. Today it is celebrated in many parts of the world. Parades, shamrocks, and the color green are the order of the day.

MAP
SCOTLAND
NORTHERN IRELAND
ENGLAND
WALES
IRELAND

St. Patrick's Day

CD 25:20

Irish Folk Song

Tho' dark are our sor-rows, to-day we'll for-get them, And

smile thro' our tears like a sun-beam in show'rs; There

nev-er were hearts, if our ru-lers would let them, More

formed to be grate-ful and blest than ours, But

just when the chain has ceased to pain, And hope has un-wreathed it

round with flow'rs, There comes a new link our spir - its to sink. Oh! the

joy that we taste, like the light of the poles is a

flash a - mid dark-ness, too bril - liant to stay; But tho' 'twere the last lit-tle

spark in our souls, we must light it up now on Saint Pa - trick's Day.

Green is a reminder of the richness of the Irish landscape.

Bagpipes are played in Saint Patrick's Day parades.

Laotian New Year

The Laotian New Year takes place in April. It is a time of great celebration and lasts three to seven days. On the last day of the year, houses are cleaned and put in order, expelling any bad spirits that may be hiding in the home. On the first day of the New Year, people go to the temple to pray for good health and prosperity.

 LISTENING CD 25:23

Champa Muang Lao by Uttama Chulamani

This song was composed by Uttama Chulamani while he was studying music in Vietnam. This song became popular among the people of Laos.

Listen to this song about *champa*, the national flower of Laos.

CD-ROM

Use *World Instruments* CD-ROM to learn more about Southeast Asian instruments.

Suk San Wan Pi Mai

New Year's Song

Laotian Song
Collected and Transcribed by Kathy B. Sorensen
English Version by MMH

CD 25:24

CONCEPT
RHYTHM

SKILLS
SING

Concerns are growing about protecting our planet and its resources. Celebrating Earth Day reminds people to look at our planet and think of things we can do to protect it.

CD 25:28

Words and Music by Bill Harley

Verse

There's a lit-tle tree frog liv-ing on the banks of the Am-az-on.
I lie in bed at night and I can feel the sun,

There's a blue whale swim-ming in the cold Arc-tic sea.
Ris-ing ten thou-sand miles a-way.

There's a ze-bra run-ning 'cross the plains of Af-ri-ca.
The wind has blown from half-way 'round the earth, And it

There's a bird out-side my win-dow, I hear it sing-ing to me. It sings
calls me to my win-dow and I hear it say. It says,

"Oo. I hear it sing-ing to me." Yes I do.
"Lis-ten to the song of life." Yes it does.

There are   peo-ple I know, I   see them ev - 'ry - day,_
I stand on the moun - tain top, I   feel__ so__ big,_

in   my town,   while I'm   walk - ing down__my   street.
stand be - neath the stars, you   know I   feel__ so   small.

But   for ev - 'ry friend   that I   know by__   name,_   there's a
Some - where be - tween   this__   earth   and__   sky,__   I__

bil - lion   liv - ing   things   that   I   will   nev - er   meet.}
fin - 'ly   learn_____   that there's   room__   for__   all. }

Refrain

It's a   big big   world,_   some-thing hap-p'ning ev - 'ry min-ute.   It's a

big big   world,_   I'm   more and   more a - ware._   It's   a

big big   world,_   I'm__ just glad I'm in it.   It's a big big world,_   there's

room e - nough   if   ev-'ry-bod-y learns   to   share.

Cinco de Mayo means "fifth of May." Celebrating Cinco de Mayo has become popular in parts of the United States wherever there are people of Mexican heritage. It is a celebration of Mexican culture, food, and music. This celebration originated with the victory of a small Mexican army over the much larger French army at the Battle of Puebla in 1862.

The Sea Snake

MAP
UNITED STATES
MEXICO   BELIZE
GUATEMALA

CD 26:1

Mexican Folk Song
Adapted by José Luis Orozco
English Words by Linda Worsley

Spanish: A la ví - bo - ra, ví - bo - ra de la mar, de la mar, por a-
Pronunciation: a la βi βo ɾa βi βo ɾa ðe la mar ðe la mar poɾ a
English: Oh, the ser-pent, the ser-pent who's from the sea, from the sea, It can

quí pue - den pa - sar. Los de_a - de - lan - te co - rren
ki pwe ðen pa saɾ los ðea ðe lan te ko ɾen
pass on through right here! Those in the front can run quite

mu - cho_y los de_a - trás se que - de - rán, tras, tras, tras, tras.___
mu choi los ðea tras se ke ðe ɾan tras tras tras tras
fast, but those be - hind will be left back, back, back, back, back.___

U - na me - xi - ca - na que fru - ta ven - dí - a, ci -
u na me xi ka na ke fɾu ta βen di a si
Lit - tle Mex - i - ca - na, what fruit is she sell - ing? Some

rue - la, cha - ba - ca - no, me - lón y san - dí - a. Ver -
ɾwe la cha βa ka no me lon i san di a βeɾ
plums and ap - ri - cots, can - ta - lopes, wa - ter - mel - ons. Now,

be - na, ver - be - na, jar - dín de ma - ta - te - na, ver -
βe na βeɾ βe na xaɾ ðin de ma ta te na βeɾ
dance in the gar - den, the gar - den, do not lin - ger, Now

be - na, ver - be - na, jar - dín de ma - ta - te - na.
βe na βeɾ βe na xaɾ ðin de ma ta te na
dance in the gar - den, the gar - den, do not lin - ger.

Cam - pa - ni - ta de_o - ro, dé - ja - me pa - sar con to - dos mis
kam pa ni ta ðeo ɾo ðe xa me pa saɾ kon to ðos mis
Lit - tle gold - en bell, please tell me I can pass, Pass with all my

hi - jos me - nos él de_a - trás, tras, tras, se - rá me - lón, se - rá san -
i xos me nos el ðea tras tras tras se ɾa me lon se ɾa san
chil - dren, all ex - cept the last, last, last! There will be mel - ons, wa - ter -

Repeat 2 times

dí - a, se - rá la vie - ja del o - tro dí - a, dí - a, ¡dí - a!
dya se ɾa la βye xa ðel o tro ði a ði a ði a
mel - ons, but too old in an - oth - er day, an - oth - er day.___

Puerto Rican Day

Puerto Rico is a commonwealth of the United States, and Puerto Ricans are American citizens. Puerto Rican Day is a celebration of Puerto Rican culture and tradition that takes place at various times of the year, wherever there is a sizable Puerto Rican population on the mainland. One of the largest Puerto Rican Day celebrations is held in New York City. Floats, flags, and ethnic food stalls line the streets, and Latin rhythms fill the air as Puerto Ricans celebrate their heritage.

Qué bonita bandera

What a Beautiful Flag

CD 26:5

Puerto Rican Folk Song
English Version by MMH

Spanish: A - zul blan - ca y___ co - lo - ra - da, y'en el
Pronunciation: ɑ sul βlan kɑ i ko lo ɾɑ ðɑ yen el
English: **See our flag of blue,___ white and red.___ In the**

me - dio tie - ne_u-na_es - tre - lla. Bo - ni - ta, se -
me ðio tye neu nɑes tɾe ya bo ni tɑ se
mid - dle, there_ is a star.___ A beau - ti - ful

ñor - es, es la ban - de - ra Puer - to - ri - que - ña. que - ña.
nyoɾ es es la βan de ɾa pweɾ to ɾi ke nya ke nya
ban - ner, my friend, the flag__ of__Puer-to Ri - co. Ri - co.

Refrain

Qué bo - ni - ta ban - de - ra,
ke βo ni ta βan de ɾa
Qué bo - ni - ta ban - de - ra,

Qué bo - ni - ta ban - de - ra, Qué bo - ni - ta ban -
ke βo ni ta βan de ɾa ke βo ni ta βan
Qué bo - ni - ta ban - de - ra, Qué bo - ni - ta ban -

de - ra es la ban - de - ra Puer - to - ri - que - ña.
de ɾa es la βan de ɾa pweɾ to ɾi ke nya
de - ra, the beau - ti - ful flag__ of__ Puer - to Ri - co.

Read the poem "Borinquen" by the Puerto Rican poet Isabel
Freire de Matos.

BORINQUEN

Borinquen es una islita
que parece un caracol,
por encima es una rosa
y por dentro una canción.

Borinquen is a little island,
shaped like a conch shell,
On the outside, a rose,
On the inside, a song.

—Isabel Freire de Matos

Native Americans traditionally believe that all animals, trees, and objects have spirits or power. Songs are offered as prayers to honor the spirits. Songs are often repeated four times to honor north, south, east, and west. In the past, men usually played the drums, but now women often play, too. When honor beats are played, dancers bend low to the ground to honor their ancestors.

LISTENING / CD 26:9

Fancy Dance Song The White Thunder Singers

"Fancy Dance Song" is an intertribal song still performed by Native Americans today at powwows by Native Americans, including those of the Potawatomi nation in northern Indiana and southern Michigan. This singing group took its name from an intertribal gathering drum (used for powwows) called White Thunder.

Listen to "Fancy Dance Song," patting with the steady beat of the drum.

When We Dance, the Spirits Dance

The artist of this work, L. David Eveningthunder, is a member of the Shoshone Tribe. He was born on a reservation in Idaho, but now he lives in Alabama. David was first given pencils for drawing by his uncles, who were all gifted artists. This piece shows a traditional dancer, a fancy dancer, and a mother and her child.

Playing the Recorder

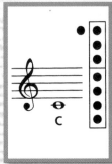

C

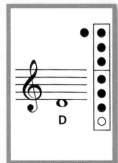

D

E

F

F#

G

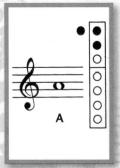

A

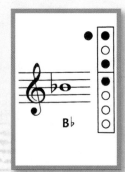

Bb

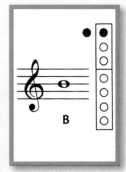

B

C'

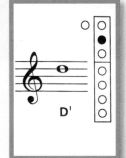

D'

Glossary of Instruments

A

accordion a keyboard instrument that is a kind of portable organ with keys, metal reeds, and a bellows. The bellows forces air past the reeds to produce sound. It is often played while standing and held by straps over the shoulders, **54 CD 28:10**

B

bagpipe a woodwind instrument that is made of a leather bag and pipes. It is played by blowing air through a blowpipe into the bag and then pressing the bag so that the air is forced out through the pipes, **49 CD 28:11**

banjo a string instrument that has a round body, a long neck, and five strings, played by plucking, **23 CD 28:20**

bass drum a very large percussion instrument that gives a deep, booming sound when struck, **17 CD 27:32**

bassoon a low-pitched woodwind instrument with a long wooden body attached to a smaller, curved metal tube with a double reed. It is played by blowing into the reed while covering fingerholes along the body. It is sometimes part of a woodwind quintet, **218 CD 27:15**

C

cello the second-largest instrument in the orchestral string family. It is held between the knees and played by bowing or plucking the strings. It is sometimes part of a string quartet or quintet, **CD 27:6**

clarinet a woodwind instrument that uses a single reed and is played by blowing into the mouthpiece while covering fingerholes along the body. It is sometimes part of a woodwind quintet, **32 CD 27:12**

conga a Latin American hand drum that has a low-pitched sound when struck and is usually played in pairs tuned a fifth apart, **17 CD 28:30**

cymbal a metal, percussion instrument shaped like a plate that is played by hitting one against another or striking it with a stick or mallet to make a clashing sound, **CD 27:37**

D

djembe a West African drum usually made from pottery or wood and played with the hands, **57 CD 28:2**

double bass the largest instrument in the orchestral string family, held upright and played by bowing or plucking the strings, **23 CD 27:7**

flute a long, thin, woodwind instrument that is played by blowing across a hole at one end while covering holes along the body with fingers. It is sometimes part of a woodwind quintet, **49 CD 27:10**

French horn a brass instrument that is played by the buzzing of lips into the mouthpiece while pressing keys with fingers. It is sometimes part of a brass or woodwind quintet, **CD 27:20**

güiro a Latin American percussion instrument that is made from a gourd and has a bumpy surface that is scraped with a stick to make a sound,**17 CD 28:33**

guitar a string instrument with a long neck and usually six strings, played by strumming, plucking, or picking, **21 CD 28:13**

harp one of the oldest and largest instruments of the string family, in which the strings are set in an upright triangle-like frame with a curved top. It is played by plucking or strumming the strings with fingers, **CD 27:8**

Glossary of Instruments 449

K

koto a long, flat, Japanese string instrument that is played by plucking its 13 strings, **149 CD 28:53**

M

mandolin a string instrument that is similar to a small guitar but it has a more elaborately shaped body and 8 metal strings, **23 CD 28:16**

maracas a Latin American percussion instrument that is made from a gourd and is played by shaking, which produces a rattling sound. They are usually played in pairs, **68 CD 28:35**

O

oboe a high-pitched, double-reed woodwind instrument that is played by blowing into the reed while covering fingerholes along the body. It is sometimes part of a woodwind quintet, **218 CD 27:13**

P

piano a keyboard instrument in the percussion family that is played by pressing keys on the keyboard. Its sound is produced by hammers hitting stretched strings, **213 CD 27:41**

piccolo a small woodwind instrument, similar to the flute, but plays higher pitches, **218 CD 27:11**

S

saxophone a woodwind instrument that is played by blowing into the mouthpiece while pushing keys along the body with fingers, **32 CD 27:16**

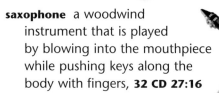

shekere an African percussion instrument that is a hollow gourd covered with a net of beads or seeds, **75 CD 28:8**

slit drum a percussion instrument that is found in Africa, Asia, and Oceania and is formed by hollowing a tree trunk through a slit on one side, **75 CD 28:9**

snare drum a percussion instrument with wires or strings stretched along the bottom. When the top of the drum is struck, the wires vibrate and give the drum a loud, slightly rattly sound, **CD 27:35**

spoons a common household object that is used as a percussion instrument by holding two together and striking them against the body. Musicians sometimes use an instrument created by fastening two spoons together with a wooden handle, **CD 28:23**

taiko drum a barrel-shaped Japanese percussion instrument that is played with sticks, or bachi, **CD 28:51**

tambourine a percussion instrument that is a small, hand-held drum with metal disks attached loosely around the rim. It is played by either shaking or tapping with the hand, **207 CD 27:36**

timpani also known as kettledrums, a set of percussion instruments consisting of two or more large kettle-shaped drums played with mallets, **35 CD 27:26**

trombone a large, low-pitched instrument in the brass family, played by the buzzing of lips into the mouthpiece while moving the slide in or out. It is sometimes part of a brass quintet, **209 CD 27:21**

trumpet the smallest, highest-pitched instrument in the brass family, played by the buzzing of lips into the mouthpiece while pressing keys with fingers. It is often used to play a fanfare to honor important people or to announce an important event, and is sometimes part of a brass quintet, **21 CD 27:18**

Tuba the largest, lowest-pitched instrument in the brass family, played by the buzzing of lips into the mouthpiece while pressing keys with fingers. It is sometimes part of a brass quintet, **CD 27:22**

viola a string instrument midway between the violin and the cello in size, played by being held under the chin and bowing or plucking the strings. It is sometimes part of a string quartet or quintet, **CD 27:5**

violin the smallest of the orchestral string instruments, played by being held under the chin and bowing or plucking the strings. It is sometimes part of a string quartet or quintet, **23 CD 27:4**

xylophone a percussion instrument that is made up of one or two rows of wooden bars of different lengths, played by hitting the bars with mallets, **13 CD 27:30**

Glossary of Terms

$\frac{2}{4}$ **meter** duple meter, **67**

$\frac{3}{4}$ **meter** triple meter, **47**

$\frac{3}{8}$ **meter** a rhythm pattern that has three beats in a measure, with the eighth note receiving one beat, **210**

$\frac{4}{4}$ **meter** a rhythm pattern that has four beats in a measure, with the quarter note receiving one beat, **8**

$\frac{5}{4}$ **meter** a rhythm pattern that has five beats in a measure, with the quarter note receiving one beat, **213**

$\frac{5}{8}$ **meter** a rhythm pattern that has five beats in a measure, with the eighth note receiving one beat, **209**

$\frac{6}{8}$ **meter** a rhythm pattern that has six beats in a measure, with the eighth note receiving one beat, or compound meter with two beats and three eighth notes per beat, **88**

$\frac{7}{8}$ **meter** a rhythm pattern that has seven beats in a measure, with the eighth note receiving one beat, **219**

A

A B form a form of music that has two sections—the A section and the B section, **66**

a cappella without instrumental accompaniment, **144**

A A B A form a four-part form with just two phrases of music—one for each of the A sections and one for the B section, **30**

accent (>) a stress or emphasis on a note by playing louder, **117**

accidental, a sharp (♯), flat (♭), or natural (♮) sign placed before a note, used to alter the note within a measure, **100**

accompaniment a musical background to a melody, **74**

antiphonal sung by two groups by alternating and responding to each other, **62**

arco played with a bow; a way of playing a stringed instrument, **193**

aria a vocal solo typically heard in an opera, **64**

arrangement a different version or adaptation of a musical composition, **86**

articulation 1) the manner in which sounds are performed (for example, smoothly connected or sharply separated), 2) the use of crisp consonants to make the words in a song understandable, **117, 327**

B

ballad a song that tells a story with short simple verses, **146**

ballet a story told through dance and music, **152**

beat a steady silent pulse that underlies most music, **8**

blue notes notes that are lowered or "bent" in the blues, **176**

bluegrass a style of country music, played on stringed instruments, that combines traditional Appalachian music with the blues, **22**

blues a style of music that began in America in the early twentieth century, characterized by flatted notes and a syncopated, often slow jazz rhythm, **174**

blues scale a scale that is similar to the major scale but with the third, fifth, and seventh notes lowered to become blue notes, **176**

breath support control of the amount of air needed to sustain good singing, **314**

C

chamber music music usually played by a small ensemble, **218**

changing meters the alternation between two or more meters in a piece of music, **216**

chord three or more pitches sounded together, **139**

chromatic having a flat, sharp, or natural symbol, **360**

common time (C) $\frac{4}{4}$ meter, **214**

common tone a pitch found in more than one chord, **170**

compound duple meter a rhythm pattern in which two beats in a measure are divided into threes, **96**

compound meter a rhythm pattern in which beats are divided into threes, **88**

contour the shape of a melody, **308**

countermelody a contrasting melody that goes with another melody, **92**

cut time (¢) or $\frac{2}{2}$ a meter signature in which there are two beats in each measure and the half note gets one beat, **143**

diction how clearly words are pronounced, **232, 334**

dotted eighth and sixteenth ( ) the combination of two musical notes that show a sound lasting for one beat, **134**

downbeat the first beat of each measure, **214**

duple meter beats grouped in sets of two, **67**

dynamics the degrees of softness or loudness of sound, **35**

echo a part in music that repeats or copies the part just before it, **62**

eighth rest a silence that last as long as an eighth note, **67**

ensemble a musical group, **49**

expression the communication of feeling or meaning through music, **114**

form the order of phrases or sections in music, **30**

gospel music a style of religious music, started by African Americans, including improvisation and strong feelings, **87**

half step the smallest distance between pitches in most Western music; the distance between a pitch and the next closest pitch on the keyboard, **91**

harmony two or more pitches sounding at the same time, **47**

hora an Israeli circle dance that has a repeated six-beat movement, **55**

improvise to make up music while performing it, **140**

intonation singing in the correct pitch, **340**

inversion the changing or reversing of a chord so that the root is not the bottom of the chord, **172**

irregular meter the organization of beats in sets of 5 or 7, **209**

jazz a type of popular American music created by African Americans, often using syncopation, improvisation, and strong rhythms, **31**

K

key the relationship of a series of pitches to the tonal center, **18**

klezmer a style of music that began with Eastern European Jews, usually played on violin, clarinet, accordion, and drums, **54**

largo a very slow tempo, **106**

legato in a smooth, connected manner, **117**

major scale a diatonic scale with *do* as the tonal center, using pitches *do re mi fa so la ti do*, **91**

mariachi a Mexican street band that often includes trumpets, violins, guitars, a guitarrón, and a vihuela, **66**

melisma a group of notes sung on a single syllable, **372**

minor key a key based on the minor scale, with *la* as the tonal center, **130**

minor scale a diatonic scale with *la* as its tonal center, using pitches *la, ti, do re mi fa so la*, **130**

nationalism a way of writing music that uses folk music melodies and rhythms in large-scale orchestral works, **106**

nongak one of the oldest forms of music and dance that exists in Korea today, typically present at folk celebrations and festivals, **70**

octave a leap of eight steps between two pitches; the distance between two pitches that have the same name, **12**

opera a drama with costumes and scenery, in which all or most of the words are sung, **64**

oral tradition learning through listening rather than by reading, **222**

ornament to decorate a melody, **53**

partner songs separate songs that sound good when sung at the same time, **154**

pentatonic scale a scale of five pitches, usually *do re mi so la*, **12**

percussion ensemble a musical group playing only percussion instruments, **52, 228**

phrase a short segment of music that is one complete thought or idea, **186**

pizzicato played by plucking; a way to play a string instrument, **193**

range the distance from the highest to the lowest pitch that can be sung or played by a performer, **18**

relative major a major key having the same key signature as the minor key three half steps lower, **133**

relative minor a minor key having the same key signature as the major key three half steps higher, **133**

rhythm combinations of longer and shorter sounds and silences, **8**

roll a long sound made by playing very fast notes on one pitch, **107**

root the pitch on which a chord is built, **141**

root position the order in which a chord appears as root, third, fifth, **170**

scat using nonsense syllables, in a style popular with jazz singers, **360**

score written music, often showing all the parts to be performed together, **13**

section a group of related phrases that form a larger unit, **186**

semachi rhythm the most common rhythm used in Korean folk music, **53**

sixteenth note ( ) four notes equal one beat in meters where the quarter note gets one beat, **127**

slur (⌒) a curved line that connects notes of different pitches smoothly, **134**

spiritual an African American folk song, many of which began as religious songs, **11**

staccato in a sharp, separated manner, **117, 332**

string quartet an ensemble made up of two violins, viola, and cello, **228**

style the distinct way that people use the elements of music to express themselves, **22**

Swing a kind of jazz that developed in the 1930s, played by big bands, **31**

suite a musical composition consisting of a succession of short pieces, **192**

symphony a large musical work composed for orchestra, usually consisting of three or four movements, **102**

syncopation a type of rhythm in which stressed sounds occur between beats instead of on beats, **55**

tag extra measures of an ending, **186**

tempo the speed of the beat in a piece of music, **17**

texture the sound created by different pitches, rhythms, and tone colors played or sung together, **26**

theme the main musical idea of a piece of music, **35**

theme and variations a musical form that has a main idea followed by changed versions of the idea, **35**

third an interval from one pitch to a pitch three letters away, counting the top and bottom pitches, **98**

tie (⌣) a symbol that joins two notes of the same pitch into a single sound equal to their total duration, **47**

timbre the special sound of each instrument or voice, **23**

tonal center a pitched resting place in music, the focus or home tone of a scale, **12**

tone a sound thought of in terms of its quality, length, pitch, or loudness, **23**

tone color <see **timbre**>, **23**

transpose to change the key of a piece of music, **61**

triad a chord of three pitches, each one of which is two steps away from the other, **139**

triple meter beats grouped in sets of three, **47**

tutti all parts singing or playing together, **62**

twelve-bar blues a blues chord progression of twelve measures, usually following a set pattern, **174**

unison all performing the same part at the same time, **74, 370**

upbeat the last beat of each measure, **216**

vocables sung syllables that have no specific meaning, **222**

whole step an interval twice the distance of a half step, **91**

Feliz Navidad (Merry Christmas), Music and Lyrics by José Feliciano. Copyright © 1970 J & H Publishing Company (ASCAP). Copyright Renewed. All Rights Administered by Stollman and Stollman o/b/o J & H Publishing Company. International Copyright Secured. All Rights Reserved.

Fifty Nifty United States, Words and Music by Ray Charles. Copyright © 1969 (Renewed 1990) by RONCOM MUSIC CO. International Copyright Secured. All Rights Reserved.

Follow the Drinkin' Gourd, African American Spiritual. Adapted by Paul Campbell. TRO - © Copyright 1951 (Renewed) Folkways Music Publishers, Inc., New York, NY. International Copyright Secured. All Rights Reserved Including Public Performance For Profit. Used by Permission.

Ga Eul (Fall), Words by Bok Hyun Choi. Music by Dong Eum Ahm. Copyright © by SEH KWANG PUBLISHING CO. International Copyright Secured. All Rights Reserved.

Gentle River Runs, A, Words and Music by Andrea Klouse. Copyright © 1993 by HAL LEONARD CORPORATION. International Copyright Secured. All Rights Reserved.

God Bless America®, Words and Music by Irving Berlin. © Copyright 1938, 1939 by Irving Berlin. Copyright Renewed 1965, 1966 by Irving Berlin. Copyright Assigned to the Trustees of the God Bless America Fund. International Copyright Secured. All Rights Reserved. GOD BLESS AMERICA is a registered trademark of the Trustees of the God Bless America Fund.

Good Mornin' Blues, New Words and New Music Arranged by Huddie Ledbetter. Edited with New Additional Material by Alan Lomax. TRO - © Copyright 1959 (Renewed) Folkways Music Publishers, Inc., New York, NY. International Copyright Secured. All Rights Reserved Including Public Performance For Profit. Used by Permission.

Great Big Sea, A, Arranged by LoriAnne Dolloff. Copyright © by Boosey & Hawkes Co., Inc. International Copyright Secured. All Rights Reserved.

Guantanamera, Cuban Folk Song. Arranged by John Higgins. Copyright © 2002 by HAL LEONARD CORPORATION. International Copyright Secured. All Rights Reserved.

Haere Ra (Now Is the Hour), Words and Music by Clement Scott, Maewa Kaithau, and Dorothy Stewart. Copyright © 1928 CHARLES BEGG & CO. LTD. Copyright Renewed and Assigned to SOUTHERN MUSIC PUBLISHING CO., INC. and UNIVERSAL MUSIC CORP. All Rights Reserved. Used by Permission.

Hallelujah, Get on Board, Words and Music based on the Traditional Spirituals "Get On Board, Little Children" and "I'm Gonna Sit at the Welcome Table." Arranged by Rollo Dilworth. Copyright © 2004 by HAL LEONARD CORPORATION. International Copyright Secured. All Rights Reserved.

Hero, Words and Music by Mariah Carey and Walter Afanasieff, Copyright © 1993 RYE SONGS, WB MUSIC CORP. and WALLY-WORLD MUSIC. All Rights for RYE SONGS Controlled and Administered by SONGS OF UNIVERSAL, INC. All Rights for WALLY-WORLD MUSIC Controlled and Administered by WB MUSIC CORP. All Rights Reserved. Used by Permission.

I Am But a Small Voice, by Odina E. Batnag. English Words and Music by Roger Whitaker. Copyright © 1983 by BMG Songs and BMG Music Publishing Ltd. All Rights Administered by BMG Songs. International Copyright Secured. All Rights Reserved.

I Got Rhythm, from GIRL CRAZY. Music and Lyrics by George Gershwin and Ira Gershwin. © 1930 WB MUSIC CORP. (Renewed). All Rights Reserved. Used by Permission.

I Hear America Singing, based on "Walk Together, Children" Traditional Spiritual. Additional Words and Music by Andre J. Thomas. Copyright © 1993 by Heritage Music Press (a division of The Lorenz Corporation). International Copyright Secured. All Rights Reserved.

Iowa Stubborn, From MTI's Broadway Junior Broadway for Kids THE MUSIC MAN Junior. Music and Lyrics by Meredith Willson. Copyright © 1950, 1954, 1957, 1958 by Frank Music Corp. and Rinimer Corporation. Copyright renewed by Frank Music Corp. and Rinimer Corporation. All Rights Reserved. Used by Permission.

Jingle-Bell Rock, Words and Music by Joe Beal and Jim Boothe. Copyright © 1957 by Chappell & Co. Copyright Renewed. International Copyright Secured. All Rights Reserved.

Jó ashílá (Traveling Together) from *We'll Be In Your Mountains,*

We'll Be In Your Songs: A Navajo Woman Sings. Navajo Song. Arranged by Marilyn Help. Copyright © by UNIVERSITY OF NEW MEXICO PRESS. International Copyright Secured. All Rights Reserved.

Joyful, Joyful, from Touchstone Pictures' SISTER ACT 2: BACK IN THE HABIT. Based on "Ode to Joy" from Beethoven's 9th Symphony. Arranged by Mervyn Warren. © 1993 Buena Vista Music Company. All Rights Reserved. Used by Permission.

Just Give Me the Beat, by René Boyer. Used by permission.

Kojo No Tsuki (Moon at the Ruined Castle), Words and Music by Rentaro Taki. English Text and Arrangement by Audrey Snyder. Copyright © 1998 by HAL LEONARD CORPORATION. International Copyright Secured. All Rights Reserved.

La palome se fue (The Dove That Flew Away), Traditional Puerto Rican Folk Song. Arranged by Alejandro Jiménez. Copyright © 1988 Carlos Abril/World Music Press (ASCAP). World Music Press, P.O. Box 2565, Danbury, CT 06813-2565, www.worldmusicpress.com. All Rights Reserved.

La víbora de la Mar (The Sea Snake). Mexican Folk Song. Copyright © by José-Luis Orozco/Arcoiris Records, P.O. Box 461900, Los Angeles, CA 90046. International Copyright Secured. All Rights Reserved.

Light One Candle, Words and Music by Peter Yarrow. © 1982 SILVER DAWN MUSIC. All Rights Controlled and Administered by WB MUSIC CORP. International Copyright Secured. All Rights Reserved.

Like a Mighty Stream, Words and Music by Moses Hogan and John Jacobson. Copyright © 2000 by MUSIC EXPRESS LLC. International Copyright Secured. All Rights Reserved.

Lion Sleeps Tonight, The (Wimoweh) (Mbube), Lyrics and Revised Music by George David Weiss, Hugo Peretti and Luigi Creatore. © 1961 FOLKWAYS MUSIC PUBLISHERS, INC. Renewed 1989 by GEORGE DAVID WEISS, LUIGI CREATORE and JUNE PERETTI. Assigned to ABILENE MUSIC, INC. c/o THE SONGWRITERS GUILD OF AMERICA. All Rights Reserved.

Ngam sang duan (Shining Moon), Traditional Thai Folk Song. Arranged by Audrey Snyder. Copyright © 1996 by HAL LEONARD CORPORATION. International Copyright Secured. All Rights Reserved.

No despiertes a mi niño (Do Not Wake My Little Son), from NEW DIMENSIONS IN MUSIC. Spanish Folk Song. Transcribed by Theo Alcantara. Copyright © 1970 (Renewed) by LITTON EDUCA-TIONAL PUBLISHING, INC. International Copyright Secured. All Rights Reserved.

On the Sunny Side of the Street, Lyrics by Dorothy Fields. Music by Jimmy McHugh. Copyright © 1930 Shapiro, Bernstein & Co., Inc., New York and Cotton Club Publishing for the USA. Copyright Renewed. All Rights for Cotton Club Publishing Controlled and Administered by EMI April Music Inc. International Copyright Secured. All Rights Reserved. Used by Permission.

Our World, Words by Jane Foster Knox. Music by Lana Walter. Copyright © 1985 by Jenson Publications. International Copyright Secured. All Rights Reserved.

Oye como va, Words and Music by Tito Puente. © 1963, 1970 (Renewed 1991, 1998) EMI FULL KEEL MUSIC. All Rights Reserved. International Copyright Secured. Used by Permission.

Path to the Moon, The, Words by Madeline C. Thomas. Music by Eric H. Thiman. Copyright © by Boosey & Hawkes Co., Inc. International Copyright Secured. All Rights Reserved.

Pick-A-Little/Goodnight, Ladies, from MTI's Broadway Junior Broadway for Kids THE MUSIC MAN Junior. Music and Lyrics by Meredith Willson. Copyright © 1950, 1954, 1957, 1958 by Frank Music Corp. and Rinimer Corporation. Copyright renewed by Frank Music Corp. and Rinimer Corporation. All Rights Reserved. Used by Permission.

Power of the Dream, The, Words and Music by Babyface, David Foster and Linda Thompson. Copyright © 1996 Sony/ATV Songs LLC, ECAF Music, One Four Three Music, Warner-Tamerlane Publishing Corp. and Brandon Brody Music. All Rights on behalf of Sony/ATV Songs LLC and ECAF Music Administered by Sony/ATV Music Publishing, 8 Music Square West, Nashville, TN 37203. All Rights on behalf of One Four Three Music Administered by Peermusic Ltd. International Copyright Secured. All Rights Reserved.

Reach, Words and Music by Gloria Estefan and Diane Warren. © 1996 FOREIGN IMPORTED PRODUCTIONS & PUBLISHING, INC.

CREDITS

Illustration Credits: Shannon Abbey: 432, 343, 344. Meg Aubrey: 327, 328, 329, 330, 331. Karen Bates: 100, 101. Pamela Becker: 194, 195, 196, 197, 376, 377, 380. Linda Bleck: 306, 307. Ka Botzis: 178. Bradley Clark: 389. Giovannina Cofalilo: 364, 365. Dick Cole: 354, 355, 356, 357. Mona Diane Conner: 74. David Dean: 206. Parker Fulton: 58, 59, 60. J.D. Gentry: 323. Justin Gerard: 404, 405, 406. Jo Gershman: 340, 341. Gershom Griffith: 156, 157. Susan Guevara: 372, 373, 374, 375. Mizue Ono Hamilton: 349, 350, 351. Amanda Harvey: 332, 333. Seitu Hayden: 113. Nicole in den Bosch: 410, 411. Ross Jones: 318, 319, 381, 382, 383. Tim Jones: 430, 431. Patrick Kelley: 172, 173. Fiona King: 334, 335, 337. Doug Knutson: 189. Katherine Lucas: 234, 235. Tom McKee: 55, 112, 113. Sue Mell: 316, 317. Lyle Miller: 142, 143, 144, 145. Ashley Mims: 368, 369. Yoshi Miyake: 29. Suzanne Mogensen: 148, 149. Robin Moore: 150, 151. Cheryl Kirk Noll: 65. Molly O'Gorman: 310, 311. Rik Olson: 103, 348. David Opie: 314, 315. Frank Ordaz: 127. Anton Petrov: v, 241, Spotlight on Music Reading (2). Cindy Salons Rosenheim: 71. Charlie Shaw: 181. Stephen Snider: 146, 147, 345, 346, 347. Jerry Tirillilli: vii, Spotlight on Concepts (2). Mike Tofanelli: iv, 1, Spotlight on Concepts (2). Winson Trang: 92, 93. Adam Turner: vi, 289, Spotlight on Performance (s). Neecy Twinem: 370. Carolyn Vibbart: 361, 362. Nicole E. Wong: 366, 367, 424, 425.

Photography Credits: all photographs are by Macmillan/McGraw-Hill (MMH) except as noted below.

Allan Landau/MMH: cover. iv-vii: (trombone). 2-3. A-H: (tcr). 38. 68: (tr tcr cr bcr br). 75: (t to b). 82-83. 88: (tr). 122-123. 124. 129: (b). 141: (b). 159. 202-203. 209: (trombone). 211: (cl). 451: (tcl bl). 452: (tl). Shane Morgan/MMH: 164. 169. 180. 199. 207: (b). 211: (b tcl). 214: (c). 218. 318.

iv-vii: (trumpet, silver drum, decorated drum, French horn) Corbis; (others) PhotoDisc/Getty Images. A-H: (tr cl) Comstock Images; (tl br bl tcl br) PhotoDisc/Getty Images; (bcl) Rubberball; (bcr) Stockbyte. A-B: (bkgd) Corel. C: (bkgd) Darrell Gulin/Corbis. E: (bkgd) Corbis; (tr) Henry Diltz/Corbis. G: (br) Corbis; (cl) PhotoDisc/Getty Images; (tl) MetaCreations /Kai Power Photos. G-H: (bkgd) Corbis. 5: (tr) Amy Sancetta/AP Images; (cl) Owaki-Kulla/ Corbis; (bl) Macduff Everton/Corbis; (br) PhotoDisc/Getty Images; (bc) Corel. 6-7: (bkgd) PhotoDisc/Getty Images. 7: (t) Tom Carter/PhotoEdit. 8: PhotoDisc/Getty Images. 9: Chris Polk/AP Images. 10-11: (bkgd) Corbis. 11: (c) Bettmann/Corbis; (br) Robert Brenner/ Corbis. 14-15: (bkgd) Danny Lehman/ Corbis. 15: (r) Thomas Kienzle/AP Images. 16: (cr) Moving Beyond Productions. 16-17: (t) Danny Lehman/Corbis. 18: (bl) Courtesy The Cowper and Newton Museum. 18-19: (t bkgd) Corbis.19: (tr) Corbis. 20-21: (t bkgd). 21: (br) Douglas Mason/AP Images; (tl) Courtesy of David Hooten; (bl) Redferns/Getty Images; (tr) Getty Images. 22: (b) Rob vanNostrand/ PerfectPhoto.CA. 23: (br) Mark Humphrey/AP Images; (tcl) Corbis; (tl tc tcr tr) PhotoDisc/ Getty Images. 24-25: (bkgd) PhotoDisc/Getty Images. 25: (tr) Robert Corwin. 26: (br) Chiindle LLC; (bl) John Running. 26-27: (bkgd) Corel. 27: (br cr) Marilyn "Angel" Wynn/ Nativestock. 28: (t bl) Marilyn "Angel" Wynn/Nativestock. 28-29: (bkgd) Corel. 31: Underwood & Underwood/Corbis. 32: (tr) Bettmann/Corbis. 32 33: (bkgd) PhotoDisc/ Getty Images. 33: (bl) Hans von Nolde/AP Images; (bc) Time Life Pictures/Getty Images; (br) Getty Images. 34-35: (bkgd) Corbis; (t) Randy Faris/Corbis. 35: (br) Tony Freeman/ PhotoEdit. 36: (tr) Bettmann/Corbis. 36-37: (t) Randy Faris/ Corbis. 37: (bkgd) Library of Congress [LC-USZ62-115177]. 41: PhotoDisc/ Getty Images. 42-43: (bkgd) Sandra Baker/ Getty Images; (bc) Bettmann/Corbis. 43: (tr cr) Hulton-Deutsch Collection/Corbis. 44: (tr) Demitrius Balevski/ AP Images; (t) Neal Preston/Corbis; (cl bl) Bettmann/Corbis; (bcl) Hulton-Deutsch Collection/Corbis. 45: (tr) Bettmann/Corbis; (bl) The Granger Collection, NY. 46-47: Will & Deni McIntyre/Getty Images. 48: (br) The Board of Trinity College, Dublin, Ireland/Bridgeman Art Library. 48-49: (bkgd) PhotoDisc/Getty Images. 49: (cr) Kim Garnick/ AP Images; (tr) Michael St. Maur Sheil/ Corbis. 50-51: (bkgd) Chris Lisle/Corbis; (t) Michel Setboun/Corbis. 51: (tl) PhotoDisc/ Getty Images; (c) Robert Seaquist/University of Wisconsin-La Crosse; (b) Jang-Eun, Cho/The National Center for Korean Traditional Performing Arts. 52: (tcr bcr b tr) David P. Ritterling. 52-53: (t) Michel Setboun/Corbis. 53: (br) Kate Mount/Lebrecht Music & Arts Photo Library. 54: Kurt Bjorling/Chicago Klezmer Ensemble. 55: MetaCreations/Kai Power Photos. 56-57: (bkgd) Superstock. 57: (r) Louise Gubb/The Image Works. 60: Lawrence Migdale/PIX. 61: (tr) Lee Snider/ Photo Images/Corbis; (br) PhotoDisc/ Getty Images. 62-63: (t) Corel. 63: (t) Mark Rykoff/ Rykoff Collection/Corbis. 64: (br) Robbie Jack/Corbis; (bkgd) Archivo Iconografico, S.A./ Corbis. 66-67: PhotoDisc/Getty Images. 67: (cr) Jose Fuste Raga/eStock Photo. 68: (bc) North Wind Picture Archives. 68-69: (bkgd) PhotoDisc/Getty Images. 69: (cr) Corbis; (tl) Getty Images. 70: (l) Hideo Haga/HAGA/The Image Works; (b) David P. Ritterling. 70-71: (t): Carl & Ann Purcell/Corbis. 72: (cr) Photo by Todd Cheney, courtesy The School of the Arts and Architecture at UCLA. 72-73: (t) Carl & Ann Purcell/Corbis. 73: (bkgd) Jason Lauré; (a'go'go bells) James Marshall/Corbis; (axatse) PhotoDisc/Getty Images; (atoke, kidi, sogo) Tom Pantages. 75: Lindsay Hebberd/Corbis. 77: Stephen Pryke/The Media Bank/Africa Media Online. 78: Alinari Archives/Corbis. 81: PhotoDisc/Getty Images. 84: Ralph A. Clevenger/Corbis. 85: (tr) Ralph A. Clevenger/ Corbis; (bc) B. Borrell Casals/Frank Lane Picture Agency/Corbis; (br) Joe McDonald/Corbis. 86: (cl) Redferns/Getty Images. 87: (t) PhotoDisc/ Getty Images; (r) Bernard Fau/Corbis. 88-89: PhotoDisc/Getty Images. 90: (tl) Rolf Nussbaumer/Alamy; (b) PhotoDisc/Getty Images. 90-91: (bkgd) Corbis. 91: (br) Ted Spiegel/Corbis; (tr) Getty Images. 92-93: (bkgd) Corbis. 93: (tr) Mark Wagoner; (tl tc) PhotoDisc/Getty Images. 94: (bl) Corbis; (bkgd) City of Westminster Archive Centre, London, UK/Bridgeman Art Library; (b) The Stapleton Collection/Bridgeman Art Library. 94-95: (t) M. Angelo/Corbis. 95: (t) Hulton Archive/Getty Images. 96: (tr cr br) Corbis. 96-97: (t) M. Angelo/Corbis; (bkgd) City of Westminster Archive Centre, London, UK/ Bridgeman Art Library; (b) British Library, London, UK/Bridgeman Art Library. 98: Larry Dale Gordon/Getty Images. 99: John Mitchell/ Alamy. 100: Larry Dale Gordon/Getty Images. 101: Schalkwijk/Art Resource, NY/2005 Banco de México Diego Rivera & Frida Kahlo Museums Trust. Av. Cinco de Mayo No. 2, Col. Centro, Del. Cuauhtémoc 06059, México, D.F. 102: (b) Shawn Baldwin/AP Images; (inset) Dagli Orti/Art Archive/DeA Picture Library. 104: Buena Vista Pictures/courtesy Everett Collection. 104-105: (bkgd) Henry Diltz/Corbis. 106: (bl) Lebrecht Music & Arts Photo Library. 106-107: (bkgd) Hulton Archive/Getty Images. 108: (t) Bettmann/Corbis. 108-109: (bkgd) William Manning/Corbis. 110: (t) Bettmann/ Corbis. 110-111: (t) Elizabeth Simpson/Getty Images; (tc) George Eastman House/Getty Images. 112-113: (t) Elizabeth Simpson/Getty Images. 113: (tcr) State Russian Museum, St. Petersburg, Russia/Bridgeman Art Library. 116: PhotoDisc/Getty Images. 117: (tr) Bob Winsett/ Corbis; (b) Photo by James Campbell, used by permission of the Detroit Symphony Orchestra/ Detroit Symphony Orchestra; (c) UTC. Photo by Rick Owens Photography/University of Tennessee at Chattanooga. 121: (tc) Paul A. Souders/Corbis; (cr) Lebrecht Music & Arts Photo Library. 125: Walt Disney Company/ Courtesy Everett Collection. 126-127 (t, bkgd) MetaCreations/Kai Power Photos. 127: (cr) Bettmann/Corbis. 129: Walter Bibikow/ Photolibrary. 130: (cr) David Findlay Jr. Fine Art, NYC, USA/Bridgeman Art Library. 130-131: (bkgd) Corel. 132-133: (bkgd) MetaCreations/ Kai Power Photos. 133: (tr) New York Historical Society, New York, USA/ Bridgeman Art Library. 134: (bl) Harvey Lloyd/ Getty Images; (l) MetaCreations/Kai Power Photos. 134-135: (bkgd) Chris Hellier/Corbis; (t) Vanni Archive/ Corbis. 135: (r) Jeff Greenberg/The Image Works. 136 137: (t) Vanni Archive/Corbis. 137: (tr) Philadelphia Museum of Art/Corbis; (cr) Private Collection/ Bridgeman Art Library, London; (bkgd) ARPL/ Topham/The Image Works. 138-141: (bkgd) Colin Paterson/Getty Images.144: Paula Burch. 146 147: Corel. 148: (cr) Bettmann/Corbis; (tr) Everett Collection; (tl) PhotoDisc/Getty Images. 149: Dorling Kindersley/Getty Images.150: Paul A. Souders/Corbis. 152: (cr) Nancy R. Schiff/Hulton Archive/Getty Images. 152-153: (c) Bettmann/Corbis. 153: (tr) Jerry Cooke/Corbis. 157: Hulton Archive/Getty Images. 158: MetaCreations/Kai Power Photos. 160: PhotoDisc/Getty Images. 161: Corbis. 162: (b) Lawrence Manning/Corbis. 162-163: (t) AP Images. 163: (cr) Jacques M. Chenet/ Corbis. 165: Redferns/Getty Images. 166: (bl) PhotoDisc/Getty Images. 166-167: Marco Cristofori/SuperStock. 167: (br) Gail Wells-Hess/Corbis; (cr) PhotoDisc/Getty Images. 168-169: Angelo Cavalli/SuperStock. 170: Israel images/Alamy. 174: (cr) Art © Romare Bearden Foundation/Licensed by VAGA, New York, NY/Photo: Smithsonian American Art Museum, Washington, DC/Art Resource, NY; (cl) Hulton Archive/Getty Images. 174-175: (bkgd) Hulton Archive/Getty Images. 176: (br) Hulton Archive/Getty Images. 176-177: (bkgd) Lebrecht Music & Arts Photo Library. 178-179: Kevin Fleming/Corbis. 186: (bl) Corbis; (bkgd) Redferns/Getty Images. 186-187: (t) Corel. 188-189: (t) Corel; (bkgd) Anne Rippy/Getty Images. 191: (br) PhotoDisc/ Getty Images; (tl tc tr) courtesy Sonor Instruments a Division of Hohner, HSS. 192: (tr) Italian School/ Bridgeman Art Library/Getty Images. 192-193: (b) Robbie Jack/Corbis. 193: (tr tcr) G Salter/Lebrecht Music & Arts Photo Library. 194-195: (t) PhotoDisc/Getty Images. 195: (tr) Gallo Images/Corbis. 196-197: PhotoDisc/ Getty Images. 198: courtesy Sonor Instruments a Division of Hohner, HSS. 201: PhotoDisc/ Getty Images. 204: (bl) Patrick Darby/Corbis; (tr) Hulton Archive/Getty Images. 205: Marvy!/ Corbis. 207: (r) © 2011 Estate of Pablo Picasso/Artists Rights Society (ARS), New York. 208: (t) Corel. 208-209: (bkgd) Corel. 209: (trumpet) PhotoDisc/Getty Images. 211: (r) Pete Saloutos/Corbis; (cr) Robert Frerck/Robert Harding World Imagery. 212: (bl) Terry Cryer/ Corbis; (t) Robert Indiana b. 1928, The X-5, 1963, Oil on canvas, 108 x 108 in. (274.32 x 274.32 cm) Five squares, each: 36 x 36 in. Whitney Museum of American Art, New York; purchase 64.9a-e ©Morgan Art Foundation Ltd./Artists Rights Society (ARS), New York. 213: (br) Stew Milne/AP Images; (t) Michael Ochs Archives/Getty Images. 214-215: (bkgd) Jeremy Horner/Corbis; (bc) Bob Krist/Corbis. 216-217: Jeremy Horner/Corbis. 221: (b) Corbis: (t) Roger Viollet/Getty Images. 222: Syracuse Newspapers/The Image Works. 224: Marilyn Help-Hood. 225: Photo by John Running courtesy Canyon Records. 226: courtesy Universal Studios/Zuma Press. 228: (bl) Kayte Deioma Photography; (bc) Odile Noel/Lebrecht Music & Arts Photo Library; (br cr) courtesy U.S. Army. 229: (4) Courtesy of Ludwig Drum Company; (5 6) PhotoDisc/Getty Images; (7) Chris Stock/Lebrecht Music & Arts Photo Library. 231: Corbis Premium RF/Alamy. 232: (br) Jeremy Horner/Corbis; (tr) Artville LLC. 233: Alex Smailes. 234-237: NASA. 238: PhotoDisc/Getty Images. 242: Corbis. 244: Arville LLC. 245: Corbis. 247: Archivo Iconografico, S.A./Corbis. 248: Photolink/Getty Images. 257: L. Hobbs/PhotoLink/Getty Images. 264 268 270: PhotoDisc/Getty Images. 276: (tl) Chris Hellier/Corbis; (bl) ThinkStock/ Index Stock Imagery. 277: Robert Harding Productions/Getty Images. 278 279: PhotoDisc/Getty Images. 280: Michael Newman/PhotoEdit. 281: Hulton-Deutsch Collection/Corbis. 284-285: PhotoDisc/Getty Images. 286: Neal Preston/Corbis. 287: Michael Ochs Archives/Getty Images. 290: (b t) MTI; (cl) Corel. 292: Image Club. 294: (bl br) PhotoDisc/Getty Images; (cl) Corel. 295: (br) MTI; (cr) PhotoDisc/Getty Images. 298: Image Club. 301: (cr) PhotoDisc/Getty Images; (bl) MTI; (bc) Corel. 302: (b) MTI; (bc) Corel. 305: (b) MTI; (bc) Corel; (cr) PhotoDisc/Getty Images. 306: Michael Ochs Archives/Getty Images. 307: MetaCreations/Kai Power Photos. 308: (tr) Comstock Images; (cr cl) PhotoDisc/ Getty Images. 309: (b) Michael Ochs Archives/ Getty Images; (tr) MetaCreations/Kai Power Photos. 311: MetaCreations/Kai Power Photos. 312: (tcr cr) Corbis; (tr) Richard Lord/The Image Works. 313: MetaCreations/Kai Power Photos. 315 317: MetaCreations/Kai Power Photos. 319: Corbis. 320-321: (t) Hulton Archive/Getty Images. 321: (tr) Corbis. 322: Time Life Pictures/Getty Images. 323: Corbis. 324: (tl) Peter Turnley/Corbis; (br) PhotoDisc/Getty Images. 325: Corbis. 326: George Frey/AFP Photo/Getty Images. 327 329 331: Corbis. 333 335 337: PhotoDisc/Getty Images. 338-339: (tc) Hinata Haga/HAGA/The Image Works. 339: (tr) PhotoDisc/Getty Images. 341 343 345 347 349 351 353 354: PhotoDisc/Getty Images. 355: (tr) PhotoDisc/Getty Images; (br) Corel. 356: (bl) PhotoDisc/Getty Images; (tl) Corel. 357 359: PhotoDisc/Getty Images. 360: Anthony Redpath/Corbis. 361: PhotoDisc/Getty Images. 363: (br) Time Life Pictures/Getty Images; (tr) PhotoDisc/Getty Images. 365: PhotoDisc/Getty Images. 366: Nik Wheeler/ Corbis. 367 369: Corel. 371: (b) Jim Four/ Lebrecht Music & Arts Photo Library; (tr) Corel. 373 375: Corel. 376: Paul Almasy/Corbis. 377: (tr) Corel; (br) Earl & Nazima Kowall/Corbis. 378: Kevin R. Morris/Corbis. 379: (r) Jim Zuckerman/Corbis; (tr) Corel. 381 383: Corel. 386: (tl) PhotoDisc/Getty Images. 386-387: (bkgd) PhotoDisc/Getty Images. 387: (tl) North Wind Picture Archives; (tr) Star-Spangled Banner Project, National Museum of American History/Smithsonian Institution. 388: (tr) David Muench/Corbis. 388-389: (flags, bunting, red hat, bow) PhotoDisc/Getty Images; (star, white hat, bell) Image Club. 390: (tl tc tr tr) Corbis. 390-391: (bkgd) PhotoDisc/Getty Images. 392-395: (flags, bunting, red hat, bow) PhotoDisc/ Getty Images; (star, white hat, bell) Image Club. 395 (r) Frances Benjamin Johnston/ Corbis. 397: (cr) Michele/Tom Grimm/Mira; (cl) David Young-Wolff/PhotoEdit; (br) PhotoDisc/Getty Images. 399: (t) 1993 Carmen Lomas Garza/M. Lee Fatherree/Collection of Federal Reserve Bank of Dallas; (bl) PhotoDisc/ Getty Images; (br) Artville LLC. 400: (t b) Michel Setboun/Corbis. 400-401: (bkgd) PhotoDisc/Getty Images. 402: (r) Amit Dave/ Reuters/Corbis; (l b) AFP Photo/Getty Images. 404-407: PhotoDisc/Getty Images. 408: (tl) PhotoDisc/Getty Images. 408-409: (bkgd) Corbis; (tr bl) PhotoDisc/Getty Images. 409: (bc) Comstock Images; (br) PhotoDisc/ Getty Images. 410-411: (bkgd) PhotoDisc/ Getty Images; (bkgd) Image Club. 412: (t b) Chad Ehlers/Alamy. 412-413: (bkgd) PhotoDisc/Getty Images. 414: (tl tr) PhotoDisc/Getty Images. 415-415: (bkgd) PhotoDisc/Getty Images; (bkgd) Image Club. 415: (br) Michael Krasowitz/Getty Images; (bl) Arthur Tilley/Getty Images. 418-419: PhotoDisc/Getty Images. 420: (tr) PhotoDisc/ Getty Images; (tl) MetaCreations/Kai Power Photos. 420-421: (bl) Burke/Triolo/Brand X Pictures; (bkgd) PhotoDisc/Getty Images; (bkgd) Image Club. 421: (br) Mary Kate Denny/PhotoEdit; (tl) MetaCreations/Kai Power Photos. 422-425: PhotoDisc/Getty Images. 426: David Young-Wolff/PhotoEdit. 427: Michael Newman/ PhotoEdit. 428: AFP/Getty Images. 429: U.S. Postal Service (USPS). 430-431: PhotoDisc/ Getty Images. 432-433: (bkgd) PhotoDisc/ Getty Images. 433: (r) Stock Connection/ Alamy; (l) John Maier, Jr./The Image Works. 434: (tl) PhotoDisc/Getty Images. 434-435: (bkgd) Corbis. 435: (br) Chris Pfuhl/AP Images; (bl) Gary Brettnacher/ Getty Images. 436: (cl) Liba Taylor/Corbis; (cr) Bettmann/Corbis. 436-437: (bkgd) PhotoDisc/ Getty Images. 438: (tl tr) Corbis; (tcr) PhotoDisc/Getty Images. 438-439: (bkgd) Corbis. 442: (tcl) Dave Houser/ ImageState; (tl) PhotoDisc/Getty Images; (tr) Suzanne Murphy-Larronde Photography. 442-443: (bkgd) PhotoDisc/Getty Images. 443: (b) PhotoDisc/ Getty Images. 444: (bl) Kevin R. Morris/Corbis; (br) Paul A. Souders/Corbis. 444-445: (bkgd) PhotoDisc/Getty Images. 445: (c) L. David Eveningthunder. 446: Bettmann/ Corbis. 447: PhotoDisc/Getty Images. 448: (br) Jules Frazier/ Getty Images; (tcl tcr): PhotoDisc/ Getty Images. 449: PhotoDisc/Getty Images. 450: (tcl) Corbis; (tr tl tcl) PhotoDisc/Getty Images. 451: (tl) Corbis; (tl tr) PhotoDisc/Getty Images. 452: PhotoDisc/Getty Images.

All attempts have been made to provide complete and correct credits by the time of publications.

Classified Index

Alphabetical Index

Global Voices

Interviews

INDEX OF SONGS AND SPEECH PIECES

466

Pronunciation Key

Simplified International Phonetic Alphabet
VOWELS

ɑ	father	o	obey	æ	cat	ɔ	paw
e	ape	u	moon	ɛ	pet	ʊ	put
i	bee	ʌ	up	ɩ	it	ə	ago

SPECIAL SOUNDS

β	say *b* without touching lips together; *Spanish* nueve, haba
ç	hue; *German* ich
ð	the; *Spanish* todo
ɬ	put tongue in position for *l* and say *sh*
ņ	sound n as individual syllable
ö	form [o] with lips and say [e]; *French* adieu, *German* schön
œ	form [ɔ] with lips and say [ɛ]; *French* coeur, *German* plötzlich
ɾ	flipped r; butter or r native to language
ɼ	rolled r; *Spanish* perro
ɬ	click tongue on the ridge behind teeth; *Zulu* ngcwele
ü	form [u] with lips and say [i]; *French* tu, *German* grün
ü	form [ʊ] with lips and say [ɩ]
x	blow strong current of air with back of tongue up; *German* Bach, *Hebrew* Hanukkah, *Spanish* bajo
ʒ	pleasure
ʹ	glottal stop, as in the exclamation "uh oh!" [ˈʌ ʹo]
~	nasalized vowel, such as *French* bon [bõ]
¬	end consonants *k, p,* and *t* without puff of air, such as sky (no puff of air after *k*), as opposed to kite (puff of air after *k*)

OTHER CONSONANTS PRONOUNCED SIMILAR TO ENGLISH

ch	cheese	ny	onion; *Spanish* niño
dy	adieu	sh	shine
g	go	sk	sky
ng	sing	th	think
nk	think	ts	boats

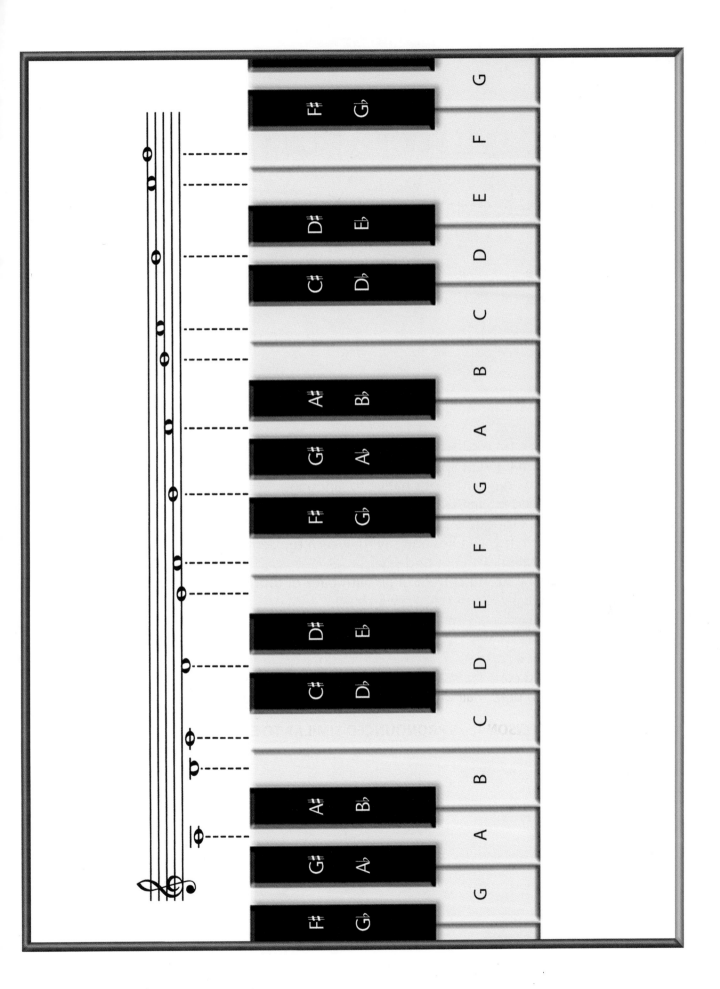